Colonias and Public Policy in Texas and Mexico
Urbanization by Stealth

Colonias and Public Policy in Texas and Mexico

Urbanization by Stealth

Peter M. Ward

University of Texas Press
Austin

HV
4045
.T4
W37
1999

The publication of this book was assisted by a University Cooperative Society Subvention Grant awarded by the University of Texas at Austin.

First edition, 1999

Requests for permission to reproduce material from this work should be sent to Permissions, University of Texas Press, Box 7819, Austin, TX 78713-7819.

∞The paper used in this book meets the minimum requirements of ANSI/NISO Z39.48-1992 (R1997) (Permanence of Paper).

Library of Congress Cataloging-in-Publication Data

Ward, Peter M., 1951–
    Colonias and public policy in Texas and Mexico : urbanization by stealth / Peter M. Ward. — 1st ed.
        p.   cm.
    Includes bibliographical references and index.
    Contents: Introduction to the border region and to the case study cities — Land and housing production in the colonias of Texas and Mexico — Servicing no man's land : ambivalence versus commitment in the Texas-Mexico colonias — Settlements or communities? Social organization and participation in the colonias— Social services to colonias : shifting the focus toward means rather than ends — Conclusion—-Texas colonias and the next policy wave.
    ISBN 0-292-79124-0 (cloth : permanent paper)
    ISBN 0-292-79125-9 (pbk. : permanent paper)
    1. Urban poor—Texas.   2. Slums—Texas.   3. Urban poor—Mexican-American Border Region.   4. Slums—Mexican-American Border Region.   I. Title.
    HV4045.5.T4 W37   1999
    307.3'36416'09721—ddc21   98-25402

For colonia residents in Texas and Mexico, who with or without public-sector support have had to bear the brunt of the social costs of housing themselves.

Recipe

Cecil McDonald's Texas Colonia Creation

Makes 20 or more slices.

1. Preparation: Perform market research. Find a poor community with conservative banks that will not provide mortgage financing for migrants or recent immigrants and which also has a shortage of housing for low-income families.

2. Find a willing attorney to research land development, septic tank, and water supply regulations. In the absence of those regulations, you have a good potential for developing a colonia.

3. Select an area close enough to but at the same time away from the city where building and development activities are not readily noticeable.

4. Negotiate with the landowner, offering to pay double the asking price as long as the sale is owner financed. Offer to pay 10 percent down and the rest in a very short term at a negotiable interest rate; the owner has already made money doubling the price of the land. Do not get any banks involved. The transactions are to be kept secret; you don't want to lose the element of surprise. Fiercely protect the anonymity of the landowner. Sell lots on a Contract for Deed basis.

5. Get a surveyor or engineer to develop the subdivision on paper.

6. Advertise, but not in a nearby city. Ask for a very low down payment, even as low as $25 or as little money as the potential purchaser has in his pocket. Starting next month he will have to produce $125 or $150 until he pays off his debt.

7. By the time local officials realize a colonia is developing, hundreds of lots may be sold and many families may already be living on the site.

8. By the time there is an official local action or state legislation is enacted, the colonia will likely be completely sold.

9. If pressured by the state or county to provide improvements such as water, sewers, or streets, argue lack of funds but continue selling lots in order to finance the improvements. Meanwhile, keep on making money. It may take a year to be subjected to enforcement action, at which time you declare bankruptcy because of the high costs of improvements.

10. Relocate to another city. Communicate with attorneys by mail.

The most important ingredients in this recipe are time, distance, and surprise.

Adapted from Cecil McDonald's recipe for a colonia, dictated to a local health official and reproduced here by permission of Mr. McDonald.

Contents

Illustrations

Figures

Photos

Tables

Abbreviations

AG	Attorney General, State of Texas
BANOBRAS	Banco Nacional de Obras y Servicios Públicos
BECC	Border Environmental Cooperation Commission
BIP	Border Industrialization Program
BNHUOPSA	Banco Nacional Hipotecario Urbano de Obras Públicas
BNOSPSA	Banco Nacional de Obras y Servicios
CCN	Certificate of Convenience and Necessity
CDBG	Community Development Block Grant
CFE	Comisión Federal de Electricidad
CfHUD	Center for Housing and Urban Development (at Texas A&M)
CNC	Confederación Nacional Campesina
CNOP	Confederación Nacional de Organizaciones Populares
COLEF	Colegio de la Frontera Norte
COPLADE	Comité de Planeación para el Desarrollo Estatol
COPLADEMUN	Comité de Planeación para el Desarrollo Municipal
CoRett	Comisión para la Regularización de la Tenencia de la Tierra
DGHP	Dirección General de Habitación Popular (in the Depto. del Distrito Federal)
DIF	Desarrollo Integral de la Familia
DTPA	Deceptive Trade Practices Act
EAP	Economically Active Population
EDAP	Economically Distressed Areas Program

EPA	Environmental Protection Agency
EPISO	El Paso Interreligious Sponsoring Organization
ESL	English as a Second Language
ETJ	Extra Territorial Jurisdiction
FEMAP	Federación Mexicana de Asociaciones Privadas de Salud y Desarrollo Comunitario
FHP	Fondo de Habitación Popular
FmHA	Farmers' Home Administration (now RECDA)
FOGA	Fondo de Garantía de Vivienda
FONHAPO	Fondo Nacional de Habitación Popular
FOVI	Fondo de Vivienda
FOVIMI	Fondo de Vivienda Militar
FOVISSSTE	Fondo de Vivienda del Instituto de Seguridad y Servicios Sociales de los Trabajadores al Servicio del Estado
GATT	General Agreement on Tariffs and Trade
GBWG	Governor's Border Working Group
GDP	Gross Domestic Product
GED	General Equivalency Diploma
HB	House Bill
HUD	U.S. Department of Housing and Urban Development
IMSS	Instituto Mexicano de Seguro Social
INDECO	Instituto Nacional de Desarrollo de la Comunidad
INEA	Instituto Nacional de Educación para Adultos
INEGI	Instituto Nacional de Estadística Geográfica e Informática
INFONAVIT	Instituto Nacional de Fondo de Vivienda para los Trabajadores
ISSSTE	Instituto de Seguridad y Servicios Sociales de los Trabajadores al Servicio del Estado
JTPA	Job Training Partnership Act
LGAH	Ley General de Asentamientos Humanos (The General Law of Human Settlements)
LVWDA	Lower Valley Water District Authority
MALDEF	Mexican-American Legal Defense Fund
MSA	Metropolitan Statistical Area
MSRs	Model Subdivision Regulations
MUD	Municipal Utility District

NAD Bank   North American Development Bank
NAFTA   North American Free Trade Agreement
NGO   Nongovernmental Organization
OAG   Office of the Attorney General
PAN   Partido Acción Nacional
PARM   Partido Auténtico de la Revolución Mexicana
PINAH   Partners for Improved Nutrition in Health
PRD   Partido de la Revolución Democrática
PRI   Partido Revolucionario Institucional
PRONAF   Programa Nacional Fronterizo
PRONASOL   Programa Nacional de Solidaridad (The
                National Solidarity Program of Mexico)
PROGRESA   Programa de Educación, Salud y Alimentación
PRP   Policy Research Project (LBJ School of Public
                Affairs, UT-Austin)
PSB   Public Services Board
RECDA   Rural Economic and Community Develop-
                ment Agency (formerly FmHA)
SAHOP   Secretaría de Asentamientos Humanos y Obras
                Públicas
SB   Senate Bill
SEDESOL   Secretaría de Desarrollo Social
SEDUE   Secretaría de Desarrollo Urbano y Ecología
SIDZs   Social Interest Development Zones
SPSS   Statistical Package for the Social Sciences
SS   Secretaría de Salud
TCDP   Texas Community Development Program
TDHCA   Texas Department of Housing and Community
                Affairs
TEA   Texas Education Agency
Texas A&M   Texas Agricultural and Mechanical University
TNRCC   Texas Natural Resources Conservation
                Commission
TRLA   Texas Rural Legal Aid
TWDB   Texas Water Development Board
UNCHS   United Nations Center for Human Settlements
UT-Austin   University of Texas at Austin
WHO   World Health Organization
WIC   Women, Infants, and Children program
WSC   Water Supply Companies

Acknowledgments

This study derives from a yearlong Policy Research Project (PRP) at the LBJ School of Public Affairs at UT-Austin, under the codirectorship of UT professor Dr. Peter Ward and (then) Texas A&M professor Dr. Duncan Earle during the academic year 1994–1995. Thus, much of the initial data collection and preliminary writing of draft reports were undertaken by the following graduate students who participated in that PRP. Laura Powell and Alex Batres are warmly thanked for editing that first draft of the PRP report. Further research and fieldwork were conducted by the author between 1995 and 1997, and the book was completed during a semester Faculty Research Assignment leave in Spring 1997, and during the summer thanks to funding support received from the LBJ School's PRI (Policy Research Institute). PRI support in 1998 is also acknowledged for cartographic and photographic costs in preparation of this volume. I wish also to acknowledge the research assistance of Jeremiah Carew during Summer 1998, and his preparation of several of the maps.

The PRP students were Martin Acevedo, Samuel Archer, Alejandra Batres, Mary Catherine Burns, Norris Cochran, Lara Coger-López, Ellie Fowler, Scott Gessner, Peter Hajmasy, Jason Leuck, Yolanda Logan, Thomas Luschei, Jennifer Oetzel, Heather Pierson, Laura Powell, Robin Redford, Patricia Rodríguez, Jennifer Steele, Amanda Timm, Marialaura Valencia, David Vázquez, Thomas Vincent, Matthew Watson, Jennifer Webster, and Alice Zimmerman.

I should like to warmly acknowledge the detailed reading and constructive comments provided by border experts Drs. Richard Bath (UTEP) and Larry Herzog (San Diego State University). I am also indebted to Teresa May, Executive Editor at UT Press, for her support in getting this book published in such a timely fashion in preparation for the Spring 1999 Texas legislative session. During 1998 it was a great pleasure and honor to have the opportunity to discuss the contents of this volume with a number of senior lawmakers, public officials, and their staffs. Naturally, I alone remain responsible for the views expressed in this book and for any factual errors that it may contain.

Finally, in the various iterations of manuscript preparation the full and unstinting support of my LBJ School faculty assistant Debbie Warden is, as always, warmly appreciated.

Colonias and Public Policy in Texas and Mexico
Urbanization by Stealth

Introduction

Perspectives on Texas Colonias
and the Project Methodology

This book is about the phenomenon of *colonias* in Texas and in northern Mexican border states.[1] While the focus is upon the Texas-Mexico border, the findings will bear scrutiny in all of the border states, given that throughout the border region colonias are important low-income housing areas, the principal characteristics of which are cheaply acquired land, inadequate infrastructure, and self-help dwelling construction. But despite the enormous social costs associated with living and raising a family under these conditions, colonias are home for a large number of people—indeed, in Mexico, for the majority of the population in many cities. Fortunately, the physical conditions in colonias improve over time. They are, in the words of one author, "Slums of hope" (Lloyd 1979), such that between fifteen and twenty years after their establishment they have often become integrated working-class districts with paved roads, services installed, and consolidated dwellings, many with two stories. They are, then, both a problem and a solution—at least if one takes a long-term perspective (Mangin 1967).

Although different in certain respects from their Mexican counterparts, Texas colonias are fundamentally the same phenomenon. While colonias exist throughout Texas, by far their largest concentration is in the border region with Mexico, where more than 1,400 such settlements house approximately 350,000 people (OAG 1996; see also LBJ 1997, 2:TWDB data). Certain border counties have particularly large concentrations: El Paso County has 157 colonias with almost 73,000 people; Maverick County has 44 colonias housing some 14,000; and Webb has 43, housing 8,000 (see Table 1, and Davies

Table 1. Distribution of Colonias and Colonia Populations by Border Counties in Texas

County	EDAP No. Colonias	EDAP Population	Non-EDAP No. Colonias	Non-EDAP Population	Total No. Colonias	Total Population
Bee			4	1,269	4	1,269
Brooks			7	612	7	612
Cameron	55	24,262	57	14,577	112	38,839
Coryell	14	2,481			14	2,481
Dimmit	3	2,362	3	1,777	6	4,139
Duval			1	100	1	100
Edwards			1	1,321	1	1,321
El Paso	100	46,374	57	26,380	157	72,754
Frio			3	730	3	730
Hidalgo	583	80,782	285	43,228	868	124,010
Hudspeth	1	887	2	131	3	1,018
Jeff Davis			1	200	1	200
Jim Hogg			3	130	3	130
Jim Wells			16	5,576	16	5,576
Kinney	1	81	1	250	2	331
La Salle			6	505	6	505
Maverick	10	7,998	34	5,971	44	13,969
Newton			6	7,960	6	7,960
Pecos			5	1,450	5	1,450
Presidio	1	59	6	697	7	756
Red River			11	886	11	886
Reeves			2	540	2	540
Sabine			5	6,975	5	6,975
San Patricio	13	9,430	6	1,406	19	10,836
Starr	29	7,378	99	26,466	128	33,844
Terrell	1	1,000			1	1,000
Uvalde	8	2,136	1	110	9	2,246
Val Verde	2	1,450	9	2,017	11	3,467
Webb	18	12,335	25	4,018	43	16,353
Willacy	2	2,728	6	814	8	3,542
Zapata	2	2,242	5	1,492	7	3,734
Zavala	2	4,404	12	1,632	14	6,036
Total					1,524	367,609

1995, 47). The heaviest concentration falls in the Lower Rio Grande counties of Starr (128 colonias with 34,000 people), Hidalgo (860 with 124,000), and Cameron (119 with 39,000).

Generally the characteristics of Texas colonias are fairly uniform (see Chapter 3, Table 13 for further details). Invariably they are low-density peri-urban settlements located within or beyond the Extra Territorial Jurisdiction (ETJ) of cities, lacking in basic services such as running water, drainage, street lighting, and paving. Some do not even have electricity. People must purchase water and store it in 55-gallon drums or in larger tanks. Alternatively they sink shallow wells and draw water from what are increasingly likely to be contaminated groundwater sources, given that households have to make do with pit latrines and cesspools instead of proper sewage disposal systems or septic fields. Given the appalling environmental conditions, diseases are endemic, and the rates of shigellosis and hepatitis A are more than twice the U.S. rate. Eighty percent of colonia residents have incomes at or below the poverty level. Their homes are a mixture of trailers and self-built constructions, with the long-term goal of achieving a fully consolidated brick-built dwelling. With exploitation by land developers, the modal purchase price of lots is between $1,000 and $2,000 (but often rising to $10,000). These lots were bought under a Contract for Deed mechanism which, until recently, allowed land to be subdivided and sold without services under terms which were poorly understood by purchasers, and allowed for immediate and total forfeiture if one or more monthly payments were missed. Colonia population is almost uniformly Hispanic. On average between 65 and 80 percent of adults are U.S. citizens (OAG 1993). An estimated one-third of colonia residents do not speak English. Nevertheless, despite the common stereotype, that colonias are a refuge and a reception point for undocumented aliens, in fact they are primarily poor neighborhoods of U.S. citizens (even if a large proportion of adults and family heads may have originated in Mexico). These conditions are the principal reasons for the public outrage that began to emerge in the late 1980s at these "Third World" settlements in the world's richest nation. Until that time they had been neglected and ignored, sometimes referred to as *harijan* (outcaste) settlements without any legal or juridical status (Davies and Holz 1992). However, notwithstanding the rising concern about colonias in Texas, especially at the state government level, the prospects for successful upgrading and urban integration of the

Texas colonias—unlike their Mexican counterparts—remain bleak, and a primary aim of this book is to discover why.

The inspiration for this study and for the two-semester LBJ School Policy Research Project from which it derives began with a Governor's Task Force meeting on the colonias held in Austin in 1992. That task force brought together a mixed-constituency group of academics, public officials, nongovernment organization representatives, and religious and other leaders from all over the state. Although my PRP codirector Duncan Earle had been actively engaged in the colonias through his duties at the Center for Housing and Urban Development (CfHUD) at Texas A&M University, my own experience was exclusively in Mexico and in "Third World" colonias. As one who then knew very little about Texas colonias, but had studied and advised Mexican governments over twenty years on the parallel and much more widespread phenomenon of illegal urban growth and so-called irregular settlements (also called colonias), I was immediately surprised to discover that Texas appeared to be seeking to "reinvent the wheel" in its response to the existence and expansion of its colonia problem. Many researchers and public officials—invariably in good faith—were seeking to understand the underlying causes and nature of colonia growth. They were asking how public policy might respond to colonia land developers. How to effectively address land title ambiguities and insecurities. How to provide essential services of water, power, public transport, and social service infrastructure to low-income and low-density populations. How to engage with these settlement populations and with the community development organizations that had evolved within them.

These were all very pertinent policy questions, but no one seemed to be asking what we might learn from Mexico about these processes and about the appropriate public policy response. After all, in many Mexican cities over one-half of the built-up area began as colonias, and these settlements represent the *only* affordable low-income housing option for over 60 percent of the population (Ward 1982a; Connolly 1982; Regalado 1995; Villarreal and Castañeda 1986). Moreover, Mexican national, state, and local governments have over twenty years' experience of policies in response to these same questions, and, notwithstanding the nation's relative poverty and level of underdevelopment, federal and local governments have been successful in gradually integrating such areas into the physical fabric of the city. Indeed, at the risk of appearing to trivialize an extremely urgent and pressing social problem, it seemed to me that the only thing that Texas had learned from Mexico in this respect was what to call the phenomenon—colonias.

Therefore, this Policy Research Project (PRP) was conceived with the express purpose to analyze the colonia phenomenon on *both* sides of the border. My assumption was not that the colonias in Texas and Mexico were the same, but that they would benefit from being analyzed comparatively, and that they form part of a common logic of economic development and labor power reproduction.[2] I also began with the assumption that Texas could *learn* from some of the tried and tested policy approaches in Mexico, and that policymakers and community officials on both sides of the border would benefit from a cross-border dialogue regarding their respective housing and community development experiences. In part, at least, this dialogue was fostered by an end-of-project conference organized by the LBJ School and the Mexican Center at UT-Austin, which brought together academics, policymakers, and colonia residents and activists from both sides of the border.[3]

Indeed, as the chapters in this volume and presentations at the conference show, there are fundamental differences between the nature of colonias and colonia development in Texas and Mexico. Briefly, Texas colonias are different in the following important respects. First, unlike their Mexican counterparts, the land development process has usually been legal (through Contract for Deed). This means that there is rarely recourse to tenurial "regularization" in Texas (i.e., the legalization of so-called "clouded" land titles), whereas in Mexico this has emerged as one of the single most important policy arenas. Second, Texas settlements are much smaller both physically and in terms of their population. Moreover, they usually comprise considerably larger lots, which creates low population densities and makes public intervention much more expensive in unit-cost terms; smaller absolute population numbers and low voter registration also make them less imperative in political (voter-electoral) terms. Third, Texas colonias are different insofar as they possess little or no sense of community; formal and informal community organization structures are weak or nonexistent, especially during the process of settlement development. Fourth, there are major differences in the jurisdictional coverage they are accorded, and in the nature of public-sector (city) responsibilities and responsiveness. In Texas, colonias are invariably located in an administrative no man's land falling beyond the city's limits or in the discretionary ETJ, where there is neither the incentive nor the statutory requirement for the city to respond. In Mexico, there is no such jurisdictional ambiguity since the city and municipality (county-equivalent) authorities are one and the same. Here the only problem is when colonias extend across more than one municipality, making coordination necessary between two or more municipal authorities. Finally, arising from the previous point, Texas colonias are subject to more multiplex interventions from public- and private-sector organizations at various levels, often acting independently of one another—to a much greater extent even than in their Mexican counterparts, where this has also been a common feature, especially in the past (Ward 1986).

Moreover, Texas does not appear to have an integrated housing policy, but rather a series of segmented lines of action often reporting to different levels of government. The colonias housing "problem" is conceived more as an issue of environmental and health care concern, rather than a housing issue per se, as it is in Mexico. Thus, public-sector responses are construed in terms of task forces and strike forces which view the problem in partial and temporary terms as a dysfunctional aberration, and not as an integrated problem of housing and regional economic underdevelopment.

The Policy Research Project was undertaken at the Lyndon B. Johnson School of Public Affairs at UT-Austin over a two-semester period in 1994–1995. It was codirected by the author on behalf of the LBJ School, and by Dr. Duncan Earle on behalf of the Center for Housing and Urban Development (CfHUD) at Texas A&M University.[4] Through its support from the Texas Legislature, CfHUD had taken the lead in developing research and supportive actions in the colonias of Texas. Given the LBJ School's expertise in public policy, and its strength in contemporary Mexican and border research, this PRP was commissioned. It was funded by CfHUD, and I am grateful to its director, Mr. Kermit Black, for his belief that Texas might have something to learn from Mexico about how to approach the colonias problem, and for his willingness to set aside academic and institutional rivalries in order to bring our collective expertise to bear on what is, perhaps, the single most pressing problem facing the State of Texas at this time, albeit one that is spatially limited.

Changing Approaches to Colonias in Mexico since the 1970s

Before proceeding to outline the research project and methodology I should, perhaps, pause and review the way in which the understanding of and approaches to colonias or irregular settlements have developed in Mexico during the past two to three decades. Several important shifts in housing policy may be identified. During the 1960s Mexican governments followed the orthodoxy of formal housing projects, stereotyping colonias as a "cancer," and as marginal and dysfunctional aberrations arising from rapid urbanization. Policies at that time were principally those of eviction, limited-scale formal housing projects, and laissez faire (which amounted to neglect given the magnitude of the problem).

However, from the mid-1970s onward colonias began to be viewed more positively in Mexico, and policy sought to embrace self-help by proposing small-scale interventions that would legalize illegal land titles, provide essential services, support community organizations and initiatives, etc. (Turner 1976; Ward 1982a). New forms of small credit were generated, and a series of agencies emerged with specific responsibility for housing-sector policies (Gilbert and Ward 1985). The 1980s saw a streamlining of those agencies and greater integration of their efforts supported by national housing policy legislation (Ward 1990, 1993). Many of the federal initiatives began to be applied more widely by state and local government (Villarreal and Castañeda 1986). Increasingly, too, there has been a focus upon rental and non-owner housing and policy interventions (Gilbert and Varley 1991).

During the 1990s, World Bank orthodoxy in the form of the New Urban Management Policy has found a strong echo in Mexico, seeking, as it does, to incorporate colonias into the fiscal and regulatory basis of the city, and to stimulate whatever urban productivity, as it is called, that may be derived from such areas—both as source of income for cities, and for residents through the equity and production activities that lot holding and occupancy may offer (Doebele 1994; Jones and Ward 1994; UNCHS 1996).

In Texas, however, there continues to be a tendency to view colonias as a temporary problem of dysfunctional urbanization and as a refuge settlement for cross-border immigrant populations (Davies and

Holz 1992). Their role as legitimate working-class communities and their contribution to economic and industrial development in the border region have been neither sufficiently recognized nor emphasized (Earle 1995; Peña 1997). Leadership exercised by state government has been limited, while local governments are unwilling and/or ill prepared to respond to colonia needs. In short, there is an urgent need to give greater consideration to the way in which we, in Texas, approach the colonias phenomenon, and to think more aggressively and imaginatively about how we can intervene more effectively. I believe that important lessons may be learned from Mexico in this respect.

A Note on Methodology

When one analyzes colonias one does so through a particular "optic"—often implicitly, without understanding that the particular lens that is used colors and defines the way of viewing and responding to the problem at hand (see Jones and Ward 1994; Tipple and Willis 1991). There are two broad paradigms that are widely used today. First, a neoclassical economics approach, which tends to disaggregate different housing markets and their operationalization in terms of supply/demand, location, and the extent to which the market responds smoothly. Public policies here seek to make the market operate more efficiently. Second, the political economy focus, which looks at actors, interest groups, and the alignment and interactions of those interests in articulation of capital accumulation. It focuses more upon the ways in which housing is produced and articulated with a wide range of interests by state policy (or nonpolicy). In this case policies tend to depend more heavily upon state intervention and activism. Both approaches are valid, but the important point is to recognize the relationship that will be invoked between the methodology adopted and policy approaches.

Traditionally, in Texas, the former approach has been adopted. However, following the research of an increasingly large number of analysts worldwide (see Gilbert and Ward 1985; Mathéy 1992), and the approach most usually adopted in Mexico, it was decided to use a political economy paradigm for this study. In so doing, it was anticipated that we would be able to gain insights about the *production* of the built (colonia) environment, disaggregating the economic and political interests that are involved with the creation and dynamics of colonia development processes. The hypothesis was that these are not housing areas which arise by default through labor market dysfunctionality, but are part and parcel of an ongoing process of development and low-cost labor market creation. Clearly, within that overall process, default policy actions and inaction, market blockages, human agency, migration, institutional rivalries, and so on, all play a part. But the nub of the argument is that colonias are actively *produced and articulated*, rather than being a residual outcome of rapid urbanization—hence the title of the originating LBJ School Policy Research Project, *Housing Production, Social and Physical Infrastructure, and Public Policy in the Colonias of the Border Region of Texas and Mexico.*

THE STUDY METHODOLOGY AND TIMELINE

Under Ward and Earle's direction much of the fieldwork was conducted by twenty-four graduate students, almost all of whom came from UT-Austin: from the LBJ School, from the Institute of Latin American Studies (ILAS), and from the Department of Community and Regional Planning.[5] The class comprised one three-hour seminar meeting each week, with frequent additional subgroup meetings to elaborate research agendas, data analysis, and preparation of documents for presentation and discussion. As well as being featured in this book, some of the group's findings were also presented in four separate papers at the May 1995 housing conference (see endnote 3).

Data collection and analysis were undertaken according to a common methodology applied in six paired border cities: Ciudad Juárez and El Paso, Nuevo Laredo and Laredo, and Matamoros and Brownsville. The first ten weeks involved preparation, during which the group focused upon reviewing the literature about self-help and low-income housing issues in general, and about the border context specifically. This resulted in the creation of the first of several of what we called base documents, which offered a diagnosis of the geography, economy, demography, and culture of the border region for the state of Texas on the U.S. side, and on the Mexican side, principally the states of Chihuahua and Tamaulipas. Some of these materials have been incorporated into Chapter 1 of this volume. In addition, extensive analysis and archival research of the housing problem and its sectoral manifestations were undertaken, as well as of the statutory arrangements for Texas and for the two Mexican border states, and of the six cities themselves.

In short, the methodology sought to identify how colonias are produced on both sides of the border. Specifically, it addressed the following areas: (1) the actors involved, and the processes of land and housing development; (2) the physical and social infrastructure providers, their responsibilities, actions, and impacts; (3) the wider political-administrative environment which shapes public and private responses and state-community interaction and liaison; and (4) the social and economic organizations of the populations themselves, selecting in each city two or three colonias for detailed survey and analysis. Several visits were made to each city by members of the research group, starting in November 1994 with a small number of the group making preliminary surveys of the city and reconnoitering possible case study colonias. The following January the full team (usually four students in each city) conducted the first round of fieldwork. This comprised semistructured (in-depth) interviews with private developers, public-sector officials, nongovernment organizations, community leaders and residents, service providers, politicians, and so on, in order to explore firsthand the processes and research questions identified above.

The spring semester 1995 was directed toward analyzing the materials in comparative perspective. Throughout the project groups were required to look *across the border* rather than *up and down the border*. The aim was to ensure that we did not fall into the trap of looking at the housing situation solely in Texas or in Mexico, and to develop instead a genuine cross-border perspective. Thus, while members of the group had a particular city case study to track, they also belonged to sectoral subgroups (land and housing, physical infrastructure, social and community organization), each being responsible for intensifying further the literature review for Mexico and Texas. A common research agenda for each of these systematic areas of study was developed in a cross-border context, and then applied to each city during fieldwork.

In order to sustain comparisons, further base documents were elaborated according to agreed frameworks for each city, so that by mid-March 1995 we had detailed annotated directories of the colonias phenomenon as well as for public- and private-sector responses for each city. The remainder of the semester involved group members moving back into their sectoral groups, each working with materials relating to all six case study cities, identifying the nature of housing processes and public policy initiatives in the Mexico-Texas border region. These analyses formed the basis of paper presentations at the May 1995 conference, and ultimately after many iterations, for the principal chapters of this book manuscript.

In parallel with this main research thrust during the spring was a subsidiary study which focused upon the Texas A&M–sponsored community centers, of which two were up and running (Cameron Park and El Cenizo) and a third (in Sparks, El Paso) was about to be inaugurated. At the request of the project sponsors the aim here was to offer an independent evaluation of the impact upon colonia populations that service providers were having through those centers. This involved further surveys by a small subgroup: the first being a sample of households interviewed in the settlements, while the second was a postal survey of the service providers themselves. This research also forms part of this volume (Chapter 5), as well as an earlier stand-alone internal report prepared for CfHUD.

Draft PRP chapter reports were edited by two members of the group during the summer of 1995, and these formed the basis for the author's elaboration and extension for this volume, most of which was undertaken during 1997. Each of the following chapters deals with one of the systematic aspects that had become the focus of our research agenda, and in most I provide a series of specific recommendations for action and for learning about the different elements of housing and community "production." In addition, I have prepared in Chapter 6 a brief synthesis of the broad conclusions and proposals for future policy actions, aimed specifically at the next two legislative sessions (1999 and 2001).

This study is unique insofar as it seeks to make a genuinely cross-border analysis of colonias. Although there are several excellent texts on border urban environments, I know of only one other study that seeks to look systematically at the intimate *interconnections* between border twin cities, and that is Staudt's (1998) volume, which examines informal activities in El Paso and Ciudad Juárez, and which also discusses comparatively issues of colonia formation, street trading, governance, and state-society relations within two adjacent polities. Moreover, we still know all too little about the connections across borders—formal and informal—and even less about what might be termed the "spillover" effects of one side upon the other. Such spillover effects are more than economic and demographic; they occur in

a variety of dimensions of daily life such as housing searches, land purchase, investments, health care, popular culture and language, and so
on. And yet we seem to hold back from analyzing their two-way osmosis, preferring instead to look up and down the border, rather than
analytically across it. While as academics we deny the significance of
the boundary, arguing for a more regional approach, we still seem very
fixed on one side or the other, with certain significant exceptions, such
as trade and immigration flows.

While this book seeks to break with that mold, it does so in a way
that continues to maintain an eye focused particularly upon policy recommendations and concerns for Texas and for local counties and cities
along the border. This was because my principal concern was to improve the policy responsiveness in Texas, and because most of the lessons to be learned come from Mexico to Texas rather than the other
way around. For that reason the primary conclusions drawn in this
study look *along* the border, as well as back toward the political center—toward the state legislature and state housing agencies.

By looking at colonias in three Texas city locations, and by doing
so in a cross-border context, I have been privileged to have the opportunity to be able to stand back and see the broader picture, rather than
getting too drawn into the minutiae of case studies, or becoming too
bogged down in the local institutional dynamics. While I firmly appreciate the need for a nuanced understanding both of the processes
and of the policy-making constraints operative in particular locations,
it also became quickly apparent that one of the principal barriers to
effective action was the "balkanization" of public-sector responses,
and the strong resistances born of turf and administrative rivalries between agencies, and sometimes between counties and cities. I hope
that the comparative perspective adopted here has helped to free me,
analytically at least, from such considerations and that this will have
contributed to policy insights that may have general relevance.

One

Introduction to the Border Region and to the Case Study Cities

The border between the United States and Mexico extends for nearly 2,000 miles, or 3,200 kilometers. On the U.S. side, Texas shares the largest stretch of that border, with 868 miles between El Paso and Brownsville, the Rio Grande–Río Bravo marking the boundary between the two countries (Figure 1) for the whole of that extension. The Texas-Mexico border zone spans the four Mexican states of Chihuahua, Coahuila, Nuevo León, and Tamaulipas, comprising twenty-five Mexican municipalities and fifteen Texas counties that abut the international border. Two other states form part of the U.S.-Mexican border on the Mexican side (Sonora and Baja California), while on the U.S. side, in addition to Texas, are New Mexico, Arizona, and California. Inclusion of the latter state in any border analysis significantly distorts the borderland profile given its enormous population, high GDP and relative incomes, and yet small common frontier. Nor is San Diego, with a metropolitan population of 2.85 million, truly a border city. For these reasons most border profiles exclude both California and San Diego from their reckoning and depiction of the general trend.

Table 2 contains data portraying the respective counties and municipalities that are the focus of this analysis. As may be observed, these areas are characterized by higher than average overall growth rates, especially on the Mexican side, where population doubles every twenty years. Health facilities are also lacking, especially in Mexico with its low ratio of paramedical staff (nurses, etc.) to doctors. In Texas schooling levels are low relative to the statewide average, but they are significantly higher than their Mexican counterparts.[1] Servicing levels are poorer on the Mexican side, although, as we shall observe later,

Table 2. Selected Data for the Case Study Counties and Municipalities

	Texas			Mexico		
	El Paso County	Webb County	Cameron County	Ciudad Juárez	Nuevo Laredo	Matamoros
Total area in km²	2,623	8,694	2,346	4,854	1,666	3,352
% overall annual growth rate	2.1	3.7	3.5	4.4	3.5	3.5
Nurses/1,000 population	5.2	4.1	5.5	1.8	0.8	0.9
Doctors/1,000 population	1.0	0.9	1.0	1.3	0.6	0.7
Hospital beds/1,000 population	4.4	3.8	3.8	1:0	1.8	1.5
Total yrs. schooling for adults over 25	10.8	9.5	9.5	6.3	6.2	6.0
% population with drinking water supply	97.0	97.6	95.0	87.8	89.2	79.8
Water consumption in liters per capita/day	702	758	615	396	648	216
Population with drainage (%)	91.7	91.2	78.5	66.9	76.2	75.2
Population with a fosa séptica (%)	7.6	6.3	19.9	6.6	4.0	15.6
Wastewater treatment plant?	yes	yes	yes	no	yes	no

Source: Suárez y Toriello and Chávez 1996. Data extracted from various tables. Note that definitions of "drainage" and "drinking water supply" may mean different things in different contexts and are probably not strictly comparable.

colonias are underprivileged on both sides, and particularly so in Texas. Indeed, all of these data mask the severe deprivation of colonias relative to the rest of the county, with the greatest disparities being observed in Texas (OAG 1993).

This book looks at three pairs of sister cities along the border (from west to east): El Paso/Ciudad Juárez, Laredo/Nuevo Laredo, and Brownsville/Matamoros. On the Mexican side, Ciudad Juárez lies in the state of Chihuahua, and both Nuevo Laredo and Matamoros are in Tamaulipas. Each city is located within a single municipal authority, the size of which varies from 1,874 square miles for Ciudad Juárez to 647 for Nuevo Laredo (1,294 for Matamoros). All three cities from the Texas side are county seats—El Paso in El Paso County (1,013 square miles), Laredo in Webb County (3,347 square miles), and Brownsville in Cameron County (906 square miles). The large differences in the size and population of these municipalities and counties make statistical comparisons sometimes difficult and misleading. Nevertheless, these cities on both sides of the border are linked not only by their geographic proximity, but also by demographic and economic similarities (Tables 2 and 7). The primary aim of this chapter is to present demographic and economic statistics for the border region as a whole, as well as specific data for the six cities studied (and for some of the survey settlements).

Border Region

DEMOGRAPHY

As a whole, the entire border region is sparsely populated, with an average of only about 40 residents per square mile (Davies 1995). However, this figure is misleading because the majority of people live in the urban areas of the fourteen pairs of sister cities that span the U.S.-Mexican border. On the U.S. side, 72 percent of the border population lives in the fourteen U.S. sister cities (*Colonia Profile* 1994, 18). In recent decades, the border region has experienced high population growth rates. On the Mexican side, the total border states' population has grown from 1,400,872 in 1900 to 13,246,991 in 1990. On the U.S. side, in the border states (*including* California), population has increased from 4.85 million to almost 52 million during the same time period (Lorey 1990, 103). Tables 3 and 4 show the growth of the cities studied from 1940 to 1990. Toward the end of 1995 it is estimated that almost 8 million people lived in the border counties and municipalities (*excluding* San Diego County), with the slightly larger proportion on the Mexican side (Suárez y Toriello and Chávez 1996). In Ciudad Juárez and Matamoros in Mexico, and in Laredo, Texas, the rate of growth seems still to be increasing, while in the other three cities the rate of population increase slowed between 1980 and 1990 (Table 4). While Ciudad Juárez' natural growth rate has also declined (to 1.9 percent per annum), it continues to experience high rates of in-

Table 3. Population Growth of Border Cities

City, State	1940	1960	1970	1980	1990
Ciudad Juárez, Chih.	48,881	262,119	407,370	544,496	789,522
El Paso, Tex.	96,810	276,687	425,259	452,259	515,342
Nuevo Laredo, Tams.	28,872	92,327	148,867	201,690	218,413
Laredo, Tex.	39,274	60,678	69,024	91,449	122,899
Matamoros, Tams.	15,699	92,627	137,749	188,703	266,055
Brownsville, Tex.	22,083	48,040	52,522	84,997	98,962

Source: Lorey 1990.

Table 4. Percentage of Population Growth

City, State	1970–1980 (%)	1980–1990 (%)
Ciudad Juárez, Chih.	34	45
El Paso, Tex.	32	21
Nuevo Laredo, Tams.	35	8
Laredo, Tex.	32	34
Matamoros, Tams.	37	61
Brownsville, Tex.	62	16

Source: Lorey 1990.

migration, making it still one of the fastest-growing cities with an es-timated current population of more than 1 million (Suárez y Toriello and Chávez 1996). In all the cities studied, the population continues increasing at a faster rate than the national rates for the United States and Mexico.

In 1990, on the U.S. side of the border, 41 percent of the popula-tion was of Hispanic origin. By the year 2010, it is expected that more than half of the U.S. border population will be Hispanic (*Colonia Pro-file* 1994, 30). Overall the region has a relatively young population,

Table 5. Median Age of Border Residents

City	Total (in years)	Non-Hispanic (in years)	Hispanic (in years)
Ciudad Juárez	18.8		
El Paso	25	29.4	22.4
Nuevo Laredo	18.5		
Laredo	23.6	30.9	22.9
Matamoros	18.7		
Brownsville	25	40.8	21.7

Source: Ham-Chande and Weeks 1992, 16–17.

although the median age of Mexican border city residents is 18.6 (versus 17.6 for Mexico as a whole). The median age of the non-Hispanic population in the United States is 30.6. Table 5 shows the median ages in the six specific border cities.

The Mexican border region has a more educated work force than the interior of Mexico. Expanding public education has led to increased educational attainment among younger age groups, and this trend is expected to continue. There is some variation between the major Mexican border cities, but in general education statistics are more similar along the border than across the border (Ham-Chande and Weeks 1992, 92). In Texas, while high school completion and educational attainment rates are much higher than in Mexico, they are also much lower than the U.S. average. For the Texas border, one out of three adults has less than a ninth-grade education, and almost 50 percent of adults do not have high school diplomas (Table 6).[2] Factors contributing to low levels of education in Texas include the need for adolescents to work to earn income for their families and a low property tax funding base for schools (*Texas Governor's Office Border Report* 1993).

Women are closing the traditional gender gap in educational attainment on the U.S. side of the border. It is difficult to judge women's progress in education in Mexico because the census does not offer information on education by gender. However, a survey of four Mexican border cities shows that as women's education levels rise, their participation in the labor force grows, and at the top levels of education, participation by men and women in the labor force is nearly equal

Table 6. Percentage of Population Having Completed High School, 1980

City	18–25 Years Old (%)	25 Years or Over (%)	Hispanic* Origin 25 Years or Over (%)
Ciudad Juárez	17.9	10.1	
El Paso	69.9	59.9	40.8
Nuevo Laredo	22.3	11	
Laredo	56.2	41.5	37.7
Matamoros	20.4	10.9	
Brownsville	54.5	43.8	29.8

Source: Ham-Chande and Weeks 1992, 70–72.
* "Hispanic" here includes immigrants from Central America, South America, and the Caribbean, as well as Mexico.

(Ham-Chande and Weeks 1992, 201). Moreover, the *maquila* industries in Mexico have a strong tradition of employing female labor, such that female labor participation rates are much higher than average (Sklair 1993).

URBANIZATION

The first stage of urbanization along the border began in the mid-nineteenth century with modest industrialization which took place mainly on the U.S. side. In the late nineteenth century, under the presidential administration of Porfirio Díaz, Mexico constructed a national railroad that tied the northern states to the nation's center and facilitated commercial ties with the United States. The Mexican border region continued to grow following the Mexican Revolution in 1910, due to land reallocations and the influence of national leaders from northern states.

A second stage of urbanization began in the 1940s, and since that time the focus has shifted firmly to the Mexican side. Rapid urbanization in Mexico was partly the result of deliberate development policies by the Mexican government, such as the Programa Nacional Fronterizo (PRONAF), and the Border Industrialization Program (BIP) begun in the 1960s. Growth on the U.S. side was largely market-led, but it was also influenced by federal incentives such as subsidies of infrastructure projects and economic development.

Since the 1980s the border has entered its third and most accelerated stage of urbanization and growth. Of the fifteen largest cities in Mexico today, eight are located in border states and three lie on the border itself. While the cities on the U.S. side do not hold such paramountcy, on both sides of the border urbanization is happening at some of the fastest rates in the world. The border region attracts both people and economic growth, making the cities studied increasingly more important as urban centers (Herzog 1990; Suárez y Toriello and Chávez 1996).

Immigration and migration are crucial in understanding these growth rates on both sides of the border. Since the Bracero Agreements (1942–1964), the demand for migrant workers has facilitated the establishment of networks of kinship and communities which transcend border boundaries. The Bracero Program established a tradition of labor migration from the interior of Mexico to the north, and this did not end with the termination of the program in 1964 (Langewiesche 1993). Both sides of the border have, therefore, long attracted those from rural Mexico seeking employment and better opportunities.

Increased urbanization and high population growth rates have created problematic housing conditions on both sides of the border. Along the Texas side in 1990, 20 percent of the households lived in crowded conditions, compared to 8 percent in the state and 4 percent in the United States as a whole. In addition, the 1990 census shows that on average 3.44 persons lived in each household on the border, while for the state and the United States the figures were 2.73 and 2.63, respectively (*Texas Governor's Office Border Report* 1993). While comparable figures from the Mexican side are not available, the housing situation on the Mexican border is also characterized by high densities and by a lack of formal-sector housing supply, but with the important difference that these are not out of line with the national norm for other rapidly urbanizing areas of the country.

THE BORDER ECONOMY

There is a sharp upward economic gradient from south to north in Mexico. At the southern border in the city of Tapachula, Chiapas, for example, the average family income is around US$50 per month, whereas in Piedras Negras, Coahuila, on the U.S.-Mexico border it is 2.5 times higher; and crossing over into Maverick County, Texas, albeit one of the poorest counties in the United States, the average family income is 24 times that of Tapachula, and almost 7 times that of Piedras Negras (Suárez y Toriello and Chávez 1996, 13). On the Texas side of the border, all of the counties report that from 35 percent to 45 percent of residents have incomes which are below the national poverty level, and as many as 75 percent of residents in certain colonias live below the poverty level. In comparison, the statewide average poverty level is 18 percent. In the Texas border region one out of two children under the age of eighteen lives in poverty, compared to one out of five in the United States. Almost 40 percent of colonia residents work for the minimum wage or less (OAG 1996). For the border counties, 23 percent of residents are migrant/seasonal workers or their dependents (*Texas Governor's Office Border Report* 1993). Comparable estimates do not exist for Mexico of the percentage of the population living under the U.S. definition of poverty. However, some estimates place the proportion of northeastern-region Mexicans living in poverty conditions as high as 51 percent (Betts and Slottje 1994, 33).

The high income differential between the Mexican and Texas border regions serves as a magnet for northward migration. Median incomes in the U.S. border cities are generally three to four times higher than in Mexican border cities. For example, although somewhat dated, a comparison in 1980 showed the median annual income for Ciudad Juárez was $2,696 versus $8,470 in El Paso (Ham-Chande and Weeks 1992, 34).[3] The minimum wage in the United States was approximately eight times higher than in Mexico in 1988 (after the erosion of minimum wages during the austerity period of the 1980s). This narrowed to five times prior to the crisis in 1994–1995, with the statutory minimum wage in border states of northern Mexico standing at around $30 per week compared with the minimum of $160 in the United States. However, many Mexican formal-sector workers earn around twice the statutory minimum and receive additional benefits such as health services from the IMSS, and many low-income families also receive coupons for basic foodstuffs and for cooking fuels (Ham-Chande and Weeks 1992, 86). Even so, the important points to recognize are the sharp differential in wages on either side of the border,

Table 7. Median Annual Income per Capita in Mexico and Texas Border Counties, 1984 (in U.S. dollars)

City or County	Average Income*	% of Texas Avg.*	% of U.S. Avg.
Ciudad Juárez	$2,696	21.4	21.1
El Paso County	$8,745 (9,150)	69.5 (71)	68.4
Nuevo Laredo	$2,544	20.2	19.9
Webb County	$6,030 (6,771)	47.9 (52)	47.2
Matamoros	$2,669	21.2	20.9
Cameron County	$6,769 (7,125)	53.8 (55)	53.0

Source: Ham-Chande and Weeks 1992, 81–84; Lorey 1990.
*Figures in parenthesis are for 1992–1993, taken from Suárez y Toriello and Chávez 1996.

and that while income is generally higher in the northern Mexican border area than in Mexico as a whole, wages on the Texas side are far lower than in the rest of Texas, and in the United States generally. In 1990, per capita income on the border was 50 percent below the average for the nation. At that time, the annual per capita income for the Texas border was $7,697 compared to $12,904 for all of Texas and $14,420 for the United States (*Texas Governor's Office Border Report* 1993). Table 7 presents the median annual incomes of the areas studied. The differentials between Texas and Mexican cities are striking and remain so in the 1990s. Only 24 percent of families in Hidalgo County colonias have total incomes over $27,000 compared with almost 40 percent in the county, while 42 percent have incomes below $12,500 (OAG 1993, 9).

Unemployment rates are relatively high on the U.S. side of the border. According to a 1989 study by the U.S. Department of Labor, the highest three unemployment rates for U.S. metropolitan areas were for Texas border cities: McAllen-Edinburg-Mission, Laredo, and Brownsville-Harlingen. El Paso was also listed in the top ten (Ham-Chande and Weeks 1992, 15). Male unemployment rates in border counties with colonias ran at 14 percent in 1990 compared with 6.7 percent in the state overall (LBJ 1997, 1:53). On the Mexican side open unemployment rates are very low (1–3 percent for Ciudad Juárez, for example), although this partly reflects the way in which unemployment is classified in Mexico, and would be considerably higher were underemployment or "disguised" employment taken fully into account (Staudt 1998, 39). While types and levels of employment have increased on the Mexican side of the border, there is still a shortage of semiskilled workers, technicians, and executives.

Maquiladoras have become one of the bigger draws for employment along the Mexican side of the border, and services also employ a larger part of the economically active population (EAP) than in the interior of the country. Over 560,000 border states residents were employed by the *maquiladoras* in 1994 (Suárez y Toriello and Chávez 1996, 61). In the three case study towns on the Mexican border, there were over 200,000 *maquila* workers, of whom an estimated 162,000 were in Ciudad Juárez alone. In the Mexican border region, women also play a much more important role in the labor force than in the interior of Mexico. This is partly due to their employment by *maquiladoras*, even though men have become an increasing percentage of *maquiladora* employees in recent years. Between 1975 and 1988, the proportion of women operatives in *maquiladoras* decreased from 78.3 percent to 64.2 percent (Sklair 1993, 167). Another economic trend on the U.S. side of the border, particularly in the Lower Rio Grande Valley, has been a pronounced shift from agricultural to service-oriented employment. Between 1940 and 1980, participation in professional and related services in the Valley grew from 6.5 percent to 18.6 percent of the EAP, while agriculture decreased from 42.4 percent to 8.7 percent (Briody 1986, 260). By 1992, wholesale and retail trade accounted for 27 percent of the employment in the Texas border region, while the government provided 24 percent of employment. Services provided 19 percent of the employment, and manufacturing 14 percent (*Texas Governor's Office Border Report* 1993). Table 8 shows the percentage breakdown of the industrial and manufactured products of border industry for both Mexico and the United States.

Finally, another major cross-border discrepancy is in the total budget exercised by city authorities. For example, the San Diego city budget is sixty-one times that of Tijuana; the El Paso budget is nine times higher than Ciudad Juárez'; while Brownsville's is ten times that of its counterpart in Matamoros (Suárez y Toriello and Chávez 1996). On the Mexican side much of these budgets is spent on administration, and on both sides federal and locally generated revenues are important if major public works are to be undertaken. But these discrepancies emphasize the need for Mexican border cities

Table 8. Products of Mexican and U.S. Border Industries

Products	Mexico 1991 (%)	United States 1989 (%)
Electronic/electric materials and supplies	34	23
Metal industries	6	16
Petroleum, plastics, chemicals	6	20
Transportation equipment	13	13
Clothing and other textiles	2	1
Food and agricultural	5	8
Electronic/electric equipment/apparatus	9	4
Services	6	2
Medical supplies	5	—
Other manufactured products	14	13

Source: Colonia Profile 1994, 23.

to "do more with less" than their U.S. counterparts (Rodríguez and Ward 1992; Rodríguez 1995).

COLONIA DISTRIBUTION IN TEXAS

The broad distribution of colonias in Texas is displayed in Figure 1. As one may observe, the heaviest concentrations in terms of numbers are in the Lower Valley Area counties of Starr, Hidalgo, and Cameron, with 128, 868, and 112 colonias, respectively (see Table 1). In population terms this adds up to 34,000, 124,000, and 39,000 for each county, respectively. Other important counties are El Paso with 157 colonias containing almost 73,000 people, Maverick with 44 colonias (14,000 population), and Webb with an estimated 22,726 in its 43 colonias.[4] Taken together, the three Texas-side survey cities and their respective counties (El Paso, Webb, and Cameron) make up some 21 percent of the total number of colonias and 33 percent of the estimated total population, and this rises to 77 percent of all Texas colonias and 68 percent of the population if one includes Hidalgo County, which is adjacent to Brownsville. The large number of colonias (1,500) relative to the population (350,000) defines another important characteristic, namely that individual settlements are rather small. The average population per colonia in Texas is only 230 people.

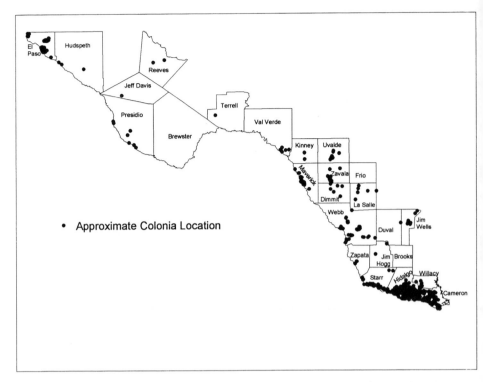

Figure 1. Distribution of the 1,332 Texas colonias within 110 miles of the Rio Grande. Adapted from Texas Water Development Board 1995.

Mexican colonias invariably will contain between five and ten times that number, and sometimes several thousand inhabitants.

The Cities

El Paso

El Paso lies on the westernmost corner of the Texas border and is the county seat of El Paso County.[5] Its surroundings can be characterized most generally as a desert environment edged by the Rio Grande flowing southeast from Colorado and New Mexico toward the Gulf of Mexico. The Franklin Mountains, which are part of the southern Rocky Mountains, provide the northern backdrop for the city. A large military base, Fort Bliss, is located at the north end of the city. Much of the land can be described as low-density residential. Heavy industrial and commercial land uses are generally found along the Interstate 10 corridor, which runs east-west through the city. Upper- to middle-class neighborhoods are generally located in the western and northeastern parts of the city, while low-income residents live in south El Paso, east of the city, and in the lower valley area of El Paso. The city has been limited in its expansion by the border with New Mexico to the west, the Franklin Mountains to the north, and Mexico to the south. As a result, urban expansion has taken place largely to the southeast and east along I-10.

Demography El Paso has followed the general border trend of rapid population growth. In 1990 the population of the city was 515,342, showing an increase of 21 percent over the 1980 population.[6] It is projected that between 1986 and 2025, the area's population will almost double (Texas Department of Commerce 1989b, 3–4). The population density for El Paso County is 3.5 people per acre, and the household density is 3.5 per unit.

In 1990, the ethnic composition of the city and the county was 63 percent Hispanic, 28.2 percent Anglo, and 4 percent African-American. It is estimated that by the year 2000, three-fourths of the population in the county will be of Hispanic origin (*Colonia Profile* 1994, 30). The 1990 census shows that the native population of the city of El Paso was 394,910 and the foreign-born was 120,432 (i.e., 23.4 percent). Thirty-five percent of persons over eighteen living in colonias are estimated to lack U.S. citizenship (OAG 1993, 12). The majority of the immigrants are Hispanic and come from Mexico: 66 percent of the population in 1990 was of Mexican descent. Very few colonia residents do not have at least one parent or grandparent of Mexican origin and "Households are frequently a complex mosaic of migrant parents and birthright citizen-children" (Staudt 1998, 46). However, individuals surveyed in the *Colonia Profile* also indicated a wide variety of ethnic origins other than Mexican. Most of these individuals registered in the 1990 census were highly mobile residentially, having moved into their current dwelling units between 1985 and 1988, while some 11 percent of the foreign-born population had entered the United States between 1980 and 1990.

The education figures for El Paso County show that educational attainment is better than along the border as a whole. Nevertheless,

less than 60 percent of the persons age twenty-five and over have a high school diploma, and about 25 percent have less than a ninth-grade education, rising to 43 percent in colonias (*Texas Governor's Office Border Report* 1993; OAG 1993, 12; see also Table 6).

The Economy   The median family income for El Paso is $24,174 and the median household income is $23,383. In 1990, the per capita income was estimated to be $9,603, and 25 percent of the population had incomes below the poverty line. (In Texas 18 percent of the population lived below the poverty level.) Table 9 gives the breakdown of income levels for the city. In terms of the economically active population, there are 370,702 persons over the age of sixteen in the city of El Paso, but only 61.2 percent of these are active in the labor force. In terms of gender participation rates, 73 percent of males participate in the labor force compared with 51 percent of females. The overall unemployment rate is 10.3 percent, split 9.9 percent for males and 10.7 percent for females. Paralleling population growth, between 1986 and 1988 the labor force grew by 8.4 percent (Texas Department of Commerce 1989b, 6).

Because El Paso is a major population center located at the midpoint of the entire U.S.-Mexican border, federal, state, county, and city government form a large component of the employment and economic base. The military base at Fort Bliss is another major industry associated with the government. In the private sector, the manufacture of durable goods associated with the booming *maquiladora* industry, as well as nondurable goods, make up a significant part

Table 9. Median Household Income, El Paso, 1990

Income	Households (%)
Less than $15,000	32.1
$15,000–24,999	21.1
$25,000–34,999	16.4
$35,000–49,999	14.8
$50,000–74,999	10.6
Above $75,000	5.0

Source: United States Census 1990.

of the economy. Both wholesale and retail trade are important. Occupations are scattered fairly evenly across seven categories: administrative support occupations; professional specialty occupations; sales occupations; service occupations; executive, administrative, and managerial occupations; precision production, craft, and repair occupations; and machine operators, assemblers, and inspectors. In 1988, most of the jobs in El Paso came in the form of educational services, apparel and other finished products, health services, and eating and drinking establishments. At that time the major money-making activity was retailing, followed by manufacturing and wholesale trade (U.S. Census 1990; Texas Department of Commerce 1989b, 12–13).

El Paso Colonias and the Study Settlements As Figure 2 clearly indicates, the built-up areas of El Paso and Ciudad Juárez are contiguous. They grew up at the narrow break forged by the Rio Grande through a range of mountains: the Franklin Mountains on the El Paso side and the Juárez Mountains on the Mexican side. Highway 10 runs through this narrow pass and enters New Mexico some ten miles to the north of the downtown area. The city of El Paso is located in a county of the same name, and its ETJ extends some five miles beyond the formal city limits shown in Figure 2. Most of the built-up area of El Paso is incorporated within the city, with the exception of a small area to the north, the towns of Vinton and Antony, and a larger area to the south embracing Socorro and San Elizario to Clint. This southeastern area of the city is largely agricultural, and much of the recent thrust of city development is along and on land either side of Highway 10. In addition, there is some limited expansion to the northeast along the margins of Biggs army base, and more importantly directly east out along the extension to Montana Road (U.S. 62-180).

With the exception of the agricultural land to the south of the city, much of this land is arid semidesert. Colonia development has taken place outside of the city limits: to the north in the Upper Valley along the Strehan Road; to the south in the Lower Valley; and to the east, north, and south of U.S. 62 in Krag and Montana Vista. This latter area, while outside the city, is just inside the ETJ.

The Survey Settlements Two colonias were selected for intensive study in El Paso. First, Southwest Montana Vista, which actually comprises some eight designated colonias within the Homestead Municipal Utility District south of U.S. 62 (see Figure 2).[7] These colonias began to be settled around 1982 with quarter-acre lots, and have an

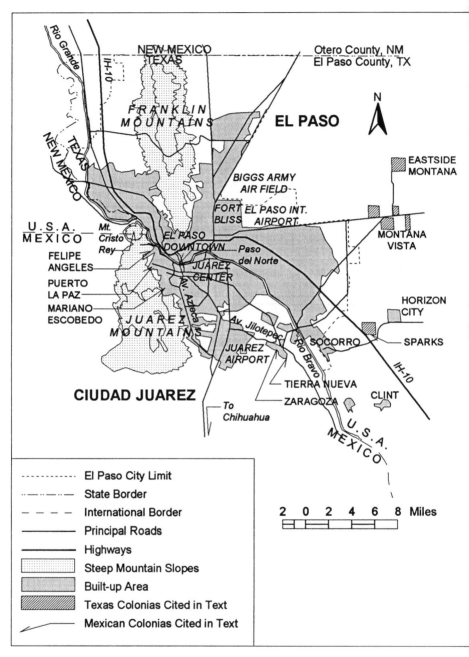

Figure 2. Built-up area of Ciudad Juárez and El Paso showing city boundaries and the survey colonias.

estimated total population of just over 5,029 in some 1,117 house-holds. In contrast to those north of the road, they are among the better developed and better off of all the colonias studied (LBJ 1997, 2:62). Compared with many other areas analyzed in this study, a relatively low proportion (33 percent) of households was classified as being be-low the poverty line, and the median household income in Montana Vista was estimated at the last census at almost $21,000 (cf. the city median of $23,383). Moreover, integration within the Homestead Utility District meant that these colonias were able to make some progress in generating local utility services. Because water has been extended to the settlements since 1992, they have continued to im-prove apace. All homes have a metered water supply; but none has a central wastewater service. A number of lots along the principal feeder road have gas hookups, while others have large propane tanks filled periodically by the propane tanker lorry. The principal roads are paved, as are a number of side streets. Very recently the colonias have begun to have garbage collection service (EP Disposal). Many of the dwellings are substantial and relatively new trailer homes; but many others are "consolidated" homes (Photo 1). According to one source two-thirds of all lots are occupied (LBJ 1997, 2:62), although site vis-its in 1997 suggest considerably less. Sales continue to be promoted—legally now that services have been installed.

In sharp contrast to Montana Vista, the colonias on the other side

1. View across Colonia Montana Vista (El Paso County) showing mixture of paved and unpaved roads, trailer home with propane gas tank, and adjacent homes in the process of consolidation.

2. *Eastside Montana (El Paso County) colonias are low density, with lower levels of home consolidation and very few services. This photo shows a typical small trailer home and its water storage tank alongside.*

of Route 62 are more typical of Texas colonias. These colonias are far less developed, with propane gas tanks, unpaved roads (with the exception of the main feeder roads), and no piped water supply (but large water tanks served by tanker lorry). Dwellings have electricity and are mostly trailer homes, with only a few homes showing any significant extensions and self-help consolidation (Photo 2). Population density is very sparse, with only a small proportion of lots occupied.

The second colonia selected was Sparks, located in the south just off I-10 and below the relatively affluent suburb of Horizon City (Figure 2). Sparks began in the early 1960s and, although somewhat larger than many colonias, is otherwise fairly typical of Texas colonias, with a median household income of just over $13,000 and 60 percent of its 600 households deemed to be below the poverty line.[8] Compared with Montana Vista, generally there is a much lower level of house consolidation (Photo 3). Homes are a mixture of trailers and semi-consolidated dwellings, and most homes use electricity for power and cooking (two streets fortuitously have gas lines and are hooked in). A piped water supply has recently been provided by the Lower Valley Water District Authority (LVWDA), but there is no drainage. The arroyo in the middle of the colonia continues to be designated as unsuitable for habitation and outlawed for service provision (Photo 4).

3. Sparks colonia (El Paso County). Trailers, shacks, homes, and vacant lots.

4. Sparks colonia development in arroyo floodplain.

During heavy rains it is susceptible to inundation with sewage effluent from Horizon City.

Approximately one-third of the lots are occupied. Having languished without services and been largely ignored for so long, Sparks has now begun to show significant signs of improvement since our survey was undertaken in 1995. Although it would be premature to suggest that its future looks bright, the installation of water and the growing interest of the city in developing the southern corridor that abuts the colonia do raise some optimism for its future development and consolidation. But, as we shall observe in this book, it still has a long way to go.

CIUDAD JUÁREZ

The municipality of Ciudad Juárez[9] is the Mexican sister city of El Paso, and the two cities are separated by the Río Bravo. Like West Texas, the area around Ciudad Juárez in Chihuahua is extremely arid, with summers that are especially hot and dry. Juárez is bordered by the Sierra Madre mountains to the west, where colonias dot the mountainside. The city is expanding to the southeast also, where the city hopes to channel future growth and to relocate those currently living in high-risk areas in the western mountains. Thirty-seven percent of the inhabitants of the Mexican border region live in Juárez alone (*Texas Governor's Office Border Report* 1993).

Demography   Ciudad Juárez has experienced tremendous population growth, increasing from 424,135 people in 1970 to 798,499 in 1990 (an increase of 86 percent over a twenty-year period), and to over an estimated 1 million today. Ciudad Juárez officials estimate that currently over forty families move to the city every day. Juárez experienced its fastest growth rate of 7.7 percent in the 1950s, after which the growth rate dropped to a low of 2.8 percent in the 1970s. However, in recent years the rate has once again increased to over 4 percent per year, largely due to sustained in-migration. The number of inhabitants per individual dwelling unit (household density) has decreased over the last twenty years from 5.5 in 1970 to 4.9 in 1980, and marginally again to 4.5 in 1990, although this remains relatively high. There are currently about 47 persons per hectare, and through settlement densification programs local planning officials expect to increase that figure to 87 by the year 2015.

According to the *XI Censo General de Población*, of the 28.6 percent of city residents who were born outside the state of Chihuahua: 34 percent were born in Durango, 20 percent in Coahuila, 16 percent in Zacatecas, and 30.4 percent came from other states. Government statistics also reveal that in 1990 only 3.5 percent of the residents of Juárez were illiterate compared to the 6.1 percent average in the state as a whole. Of the population over fifteen years of age, 48 percent had an education beyond primary school compared to 43 percent in the state as a whole.

The Economy   The majority of the residents who are working (some 38.4 percent of the total city population) of Ciudad Juárez earn the equivalent of one to two Mexican minimum salaries.[10] Compared to the rest of the state, there are more residents of Juárez who earn two to five minimum salaries than in the state as a whole.

The total economically active population for 1990 numbered 289,554. Of the 275,607 males over the age of twelve, 73 percent were active in the labor force, and of those only 2.4 percent were defined as being unemployed. Of the 287,513 women who were over the age of twelve, 31 percent were active in the labor force, and of those almost 2 percent were unemployed. As a whole, women make up 33 percent of the work force (Ham-Chande and Weeks 1992, 201). In 54.4 percent of the housing units there were two or three employed persons, and in 42.9 percent of the housing units only one person was employed. This is quite a high household participation rate by Mexican and international standards (Chant 1996).

The main sectors of employment for Juárez are the secondary sector, at 49.3 percent, and the tertiary sector, with 45 percent. Manufacturing employs 32 percent of the EAP in Ciudad Juárez (Ham-Chande and Weeks 1992, 76). Of the Mexican cities along the Texas border, Ciudad Juárez has the largest number of *maquiladoras*—some 309 plants in 1994 with almost 154,000 employees (Suárez y Toriello and Chávez 1996, 61–62), increasing since to 360 plants with 162,000 workers in 1997.

Ciudad Juárez Colonias and the Study Settlements   Until the late 1960s city development in Juárez was split: the poor moved westward into newly founded colonias such as Paso del Norte, Colonia Popular, and Josefa Ortiz de Domínguez, leaving behind the cramped central working-class tenement just west of the downtown itself (Barrio

Alto); while the middle classes moved to suburbs to the southeast. A few years later the Bermúdez family began to develop the industrial parks—also in the southeast—abutting the border itself. Thus the social divide was created and intensified during the 1970s. However, the low-income colonias (mostly invasions) were now reaching up into the mountains, where the broken and steep topography made public transportation access extremely difficult and the prospects for subsequent service provision limited. Colonia growth, therefore, also shifted southward along the main thoroughfare to Chihuahua (west of the Pan American Highway), and along another link road which skirts the mountains (Avenida Aztecas). Most of these developments occurred on private land, often promoted by the landowners, who sold lots without services. The younger colonias which formed in the middle 1970s and 1980s run up into the hillsides off Avenida Aztecas. During the same period, there was also heavy in-filling in what had been low-density colonia subdivisions between the airport and Avenida Jilotepec, which runs southwest toward the (then) distant pueblo of Zaragoza (see Figure 2). The last ten years have seen further development of (middle-class) residential estates in the southeast. In addition, with the slowdown of new colonia formation beginning in the late 1970s, there have been in-filling and densification of low-income settlement (colonias as well as large government [INFONAVIT] housing projects) all along the two southern axes, and south of the Jilotepec link to Zaragoza. Today this former agricultural village is a bustling small town surrounded by colonias, but it remains a good forty-minute bus ride from the downtown and main *maquila* sites. Unlike most Mexican cities, the primary industrial and employment locations are diametrically across town from the colonias, and the dislocation makes for longer and more difficult commutes than is usual for a large proportion of the work force. The 1980s were a period of intense public-sector housing production, especially by INFONAVIT, which built 63 percent of its 20,000 new homes during that decade. Between 1990 and 1992 INFONAVIT and the State Housing Institute each added almost 3,000 units (Ruf 1995). However, with the city almost doubling in population during the decade, the addition of a further 15,500 housing units for the working poor was nowhere near sufficient, meeting only an estimated one-third of the effective demand of those people earning between 1 and 2.5 minimum wages.[11]

The old *fundo legal* (the area designated for settlement) has long since been superseded, but this "city" versus county definition does not exist in Mexico, where the municipality (county equivalent) and city are run by the same authority, which is the Ayuntamiento.[12] In Ciudad Juárez all of the built-up area is contained well within the limits of the municipality. This has important repercussions for policy development, as I will argue in later chapters.

The Survey Settlements Four colonias were examined in detail during fieldwork. They contrast in many respects with their counterparts in Texas, but two characteristics stand out especially. First, it is very rare these days to see unoccupied lots. In Mexico lots are occupied fairly swiftly in the first years after establishment, and this leads to much higher densities and much more contiguous street frontages. A second difference is the large number of small business establishments that serve colonia populations. Stores, materials yards, and repair workshops abound, particularly along the principal access roads. By contrast, in Texas colonias intrasettlement business establishments are almost nonexistent—maybe at most a bakery or an occasional corner store.

Colonia Felipe Angeles is one of the oldest in the city, beginning around 1970. An estimated five thousand families live in the colonia, and despite its age it has suffered by virtue of its location in the western steep hillside sector of the city, which the authorities have been highly ambivalent about servicing. There are two reasons for this attitude: the added costs of servicing in the broken terrain, and the desire to discourage further settlement up into the western hills. Although legalization of land titles is now proceeding and services have finally been installed, the colonia's physical development has been stunted (certainly compared with more recently developed counterparts to the south). While dwellings are largely in the process of consolidation, and there is a sense of dynamic upgrading, much of this is relatively recent (Photos 5 and 6). Ordinarily the level of physical development in Felipe Angeles would correspond to a settlement some ten or fifteen years younger than it actually is. Water has recently been installed to each dwelling; the principal streets are paved, side streets are not, and the municipio has recently installed street lighting.

Until the recent spate of development in Felipe Angeles, it had long since been overtaken by the second colonia selected, Colonia Puerto la Paz, which is much smaller (two hundred families) and began to be occupied in the early 1980s. Topographically its location is less adverse, and this has meant that it has been more rapidly hooked into

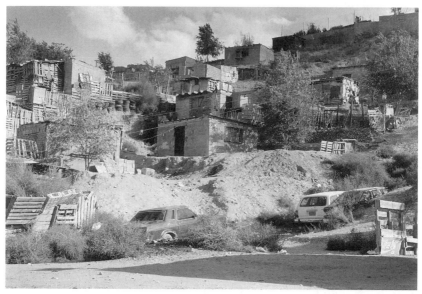

5. Part of Ciudad Juárez western colonia frontier. Very recently erected unserviced shacks using recycled materials (pallets), and incipient dwellings built on terraces cut into the hillside.

6. View westward toward Colonia Felipe Angeles (in distance) across moderate-density consolidating colonias. Note the mixed paved and unpaved streets.

the extensions of infrastructure by city authorities. Somewhat farther south, Mariano Escobedo is a sizable settlement of over four hundred families and is the most consolidated of the three, with all services now installed (including drainage); many streets are paved and the colonia has a school. It began in the mid-1970s and was settled progressively over several years. Residents appear to have been especially active in mutual aid projects to improve the colonia and helped construct the bathrooms for the school and contributed their labor to pave the road to the school.

Finally, Tierra Nueva is interesting because it did not begin illegally with a squatter invasion of lands as did the other three, but is a sponsored municipal site-and-service scheme begun in 1993–1994. The land was acquired in part from expropriation of an *ejido* and is in part on private land donated by the powerful local Bermúdez family. Some twelve hundred families are estimated to be beneficiaries, and lots are 160 m² (somewhat smaller than the usual modal sizes, which are 200 m² to 300 m²). Lots have basic services installed, and residents are expected to build a core unit of main room, kitchen, and bathroom. Further extensions come later. Families are screened before occupancy and must aim to build their home (to one of several modular designs) within three months. The lot costs the equivalent of $1,200 to purchase, recovered over four years at very low interest. Similarly, families receive a construction materials credit of about the same amount, which is paid back over thirty months. Once all debts are cleared the owner receives full title, and while the dwelling may be sublet (rented), the lot cannot be sold until a further five years have elapsed (although this will probably be difficult to enforce and will almost certainly lead to subsequent tenure irregularities). The logic is to avoid the land and materials subsidy being appropriated by the beneficiary and sold on as a speculation. The aim originally was to promote Tierra Nueva as a resettlement project for those living on the western hillsides, but the overall demand, and opposition from people who did not want to move, have made this impossible. The municipality, therefore, has acted pragmatically.

Laredo

Laredo is the county seat and the only fully serviced city of Webb County, which is also the sixth-largest county in Texas in terms of square miles. Much of the county is rural, but the land is generally infertile and dry. The total acreage of Laredo in 1994 was 52,385 acres, of which 14,375 acres were used for residential purposes; 19,451 acres remained vacant. The city is located on the Rio Grande and is a major port of entry to the United States, connecting I-35 with the Pan American Highway, which stretches into Central and South America.

Demography   According to a joint master plan for the sister cities of Laredo and Nuevo Laredo, the population of the Texas city for 1994 was estimated to be 149,398. The city has experienced high rates of population growth between 1980 and 1990, when the population grew by 45 percent. It is expected that between 1986 and 2025, the metropolitan area of Laredo will grow by 160 percent, and it is considered the second-fastest-growing city in the United States (Texas Department of Commerce 1989a, 5). Estimates of the Hispanic portion of the total population are as high as 95 percent in parts of Webb County (*Colonia Profile* 1994, 30). The average age of Laredo residents was twenty-six in 1994. Over 36 percent of the population is under eighteen years of age (*Texas Governor's Office Border Report* 1993).

The young population and high population growth rate have had a serious effect on Laredo's schools. One of the main school districts serving the area reported a 75 percent increase between the enrollment in 1990 and that expected in 1995. Even so, in 1990, for adults over twenty-five years of age in Webb County, 37.2 percent had less than a ninth-grade education and only 48 percent had high school diplomas. For people of this age group across Texas, those holding high school diplomas average 72 percent (*Texas Governor's Office Border Report* 1993).

The Economy   More than a third of the population in Laredo (37 percent) live below the poverty level (the state average is 18 percent). The per capita personal income in 1990 was $6,981, compared to the Texas average of $12,904, and the median family income was $19,910. Of employable adults in Laredo, 58 percent are active in the labor force. Unemployment is high, at 11.6 percent, compared with the state average of 7.1 percent. Seventy percent of males participate in the labor force, while only 47 percent of women are active. Between 1986 and 1988, the labor force grew by 9 percent compared to the state average of 2.2 percent (Texas Department of Commerce 1989a, 40).

The service industry plays an important role in the Laredo economy, employing 35 percent of the EAP. For example, in 1987 educational services, health services, and eating and drinking establishments employed the greatest number of people. The major money-making industry in the area is retail trade, which has increased in importance over the last ten years. Mining and wholesale trade follow in importance. The importance of the *maquiladora* industry in the economy is also growing, followed by oil and gas, and agribusiness. Over 3,000 Laredo residents are estimated to work in the *maquiladoras* in Nuevo Laredo, and thirty of the fifty *maquiladoras* on the Mexican side have office, distribution, or manufacturing facilities in Laredo. The primary employers in Laredo are the school districts, Mercy Hospital of Laredo, and the City of Laredo (Ham-Chande and Weeks 1992, 81; Texas Department of Commerce 1989a, 16, 19).

Colonias in Laredo and the Study Settlements As I have observed, Laredo has experienced rapid growth in the past decade and a half. The city runs north-south alongside the Rio Grande, wrapping itself around the sharp bend in the river in which the downtown core of its Mexican neighbor nestles (Figure 3). Despite Laredo's smaller size, the land allocated to commercial and industrial use in the city is much more extensive than in Nuevo Laredo, a large proportion comprising warehousing and light industry stretching north on either side of Highway 35. The commercial-industrial area of both cities is the major freight and trucking break point between the United States and Mexico (increasingly across the new Solidarity Bridge to the west), and major areas of land use within each city are assigned to trucking and freight storage.

Residential densities in Laredo are approximately half those of Nuevo Laredo. Colonia formation has occurred in three principal areas (see Figure 3). First, there are a number of colonias straddling Highway 359, running eastward. Some of these are within the city's ETJ, but by 1995 none of them had received street lighting, water, or sewage, although most now have electricity. The second cluster of colonias is located in the south off Highway 83 and includes Río Bravo and El Cenizo. Until very recently both were well beyond Laredo's ETJ. Similarly, in the north along the Mines Road is a third cluster of colonias, most of which are relatively small—Ranchos Penitas West being the largest with an estimated 914 inhabitants, none of whom are served by public water supply (LBJ 1997, 2:127).

The Survey Settlements The first colonia selected for more detailed study actually comprises a cluster of colonias on Highway 359,

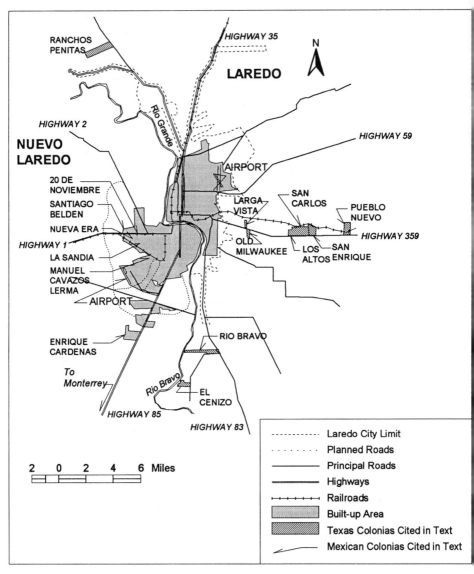

RANCHOS
PENITAS

HIGHWAY 35

N

LAREDO

Rio Grande

HIGHWAY 2

NUEVO
LAREDO

HIGHWAY 59

AIRPORT

20 DE
NOVIEMBRE

SANTIAGO
BELDEN

NUEVA ERA

HIGHWAY 1

LA SANDIA

MANUEL
CAVAZOS

LERMA

AIRPORT

LARGA
VISTA

SAN
CARLOS

PUEBLO
NUEVO

OLD
MILWAUKEE

LOS
ALTOS

SAN
ENRIQUE

HIGHWAY 359

ENRIQUE
CARDENAS

RIO BRAVO

To
Monterrey

Rio Bravo

EL
CENIZO

HIGHWAY 85

HIGHWAY 83

2   0   2   4   6   Miles

- - - - - - - - -   Laredo City Limit
· · · · · · · ·   Planned Roads
─────────   Principal Roads
═════════   Highways
+−+−+−+−+   Railroads
▓▓▓▓▓   Built-up Area
▨▨▨▨▨   Texas Colonias Cited in Text
╱────   Mexican Colonias Cited in Text

Figure 3. Built-up area of Nuevo Laredo and Laredo showing city boundaries and the survey colonias.

and here I will discuss several of them.[13] They range from the extremely well-consolidated and provided-for colonia of Larga Vista, which is far and away the closest to the city (less than two miles from the boundary) and has benefited from full service integration in the past two years, to the frontier colonia of Pueblo Nuevo, a further eight miles east, which has virtually no services to speak of except electricity. Larga Vista is relatively small, comprising two streets and 129 lots, 90 of which are occupied. It has water, wastewater, fire hydrants, gas lines, good-quality street paving, garbage collection, and a community center. Lot size is relatively small, measuring approximately one-tenth of an acre (60 × 80 feet frontage and depth measurements). By contrast, Old Milwaukee colonia, a half-mile farther east on the opposite side of the road, is a single street with small side cul-de-sacs running off one side, and has 53 dwellings on 40 lots (LBJ 1997, 2 : 127). Apart from the higher lot densities, it may be considered much more typical of colonias than Larga Vista, having no services except for electricity. Water is stored in tanks, and residents who use gas have propane tanks of different sizes. The street is unpaved, and the colonia is adjacent to a very large flea market which opens weekends. The entrance is the future location for a Webb County Self-Help Center, and it seems likely that this small colonia will receive county and city support to enhance its upgrading in the not too distant future.

The same cannot be said, however, for the remaining colonias along Highway 359. Their greater distance from the city, large areas, and low densities make them poor prospects for public-sector-led development. To the extent that they receive services, these are likely to come from private companies (indeed, telephone and cable companies have already laid lines into these areas and were in the process of doing so in Pueblo Nuevo when I visited the colonia in December 1997). According to Texas Water Development Board data (LBJ 1997, 2 : 127) the first in this cluster—Los Altos colonia—has 100 lots, of which 75 percent are occupied. It is difficult to tell where Los Altos ends and Tanquecitos begins, but together they comprise approximately 200 lots, of which approximately one-half are occupied (although my survey suggests a considerably lower rate of occupancy). It may be that some land within these colonias is not yet formally platted, and therefore does not appear in the lot count. Los Altos is a designated site for a Webb County Self-Help Center. Water in these colonias is stored in variously sized tanks, with most using large oil drum–size plastic containers (see Photos 7 and 30). A few lots have

7. *San Enrique colonia (Webb County [Laredo]). Two-story wood frame building. Note elevated black water tanks at side and rear of dwelling, and the low density.*

street lamps on adjacent posts (or even internal to the lot), and these are provided on private contract to that householder. Both San Enrique and San Carlos colonias have rudimentary arches or *portones* advertising their existence. As is the case for all of these colonias, neither has water, which must be purchased from water trucks, or brought in by householders themselves using trailers rigged for the purpose (see Photo 31). Although there is no bus service, school buses do fetch and carry children from the colonias, busing them across the United Independent School District.

As one moves farther east, lot sizes increase substantially. In San Carlos the modal lot size is a half-acre, but many plots are considerably larger, measuring an acre or more in size (1 acre = 43,560 square feet). Given such large lots, there is some evidence of internal subdivision, probably between kin-related households, but even so, individual plots remain relatively large. Finally, Pueblo Nuevo lies some four miles farther east, with fenced, rough grazing ranchland between it and the other colonias. A colonia served by a broad main (unpaved) thoroughfare, its side-road feeders appear to be out of proportion with the main street. Once again, the roughly 300 lots are generally very large, and of these less than one-quarter are occupied. This colonia gets its water from a well which cost the settlement residents some $36,000 to set up, the funds coming from a lawsuit against Texas developer, Cecil McDonald, who has been particularly influential in Webb County, as I shall describe in Chapter 2. In the mid-1990s the city and the county were awarded a joint $1 million grant to bring services to these colonias.

Moving some sixteen miles to the south of Laredo along Highway 83, one reaches a junction which leads to two settlements which were also created by Cecil McDonald—Río Bravo and El Cenizo. While only the latter was selected for detailed survey, Río Bravo also merits attention in this book since, although its formation and development trajectory is almost identical to that of El Cenizo, it has fared considerably better. Both are very large by Texas colonia standards, especially considering their remoteness in relation to Laredo. Río Bravo has some 1,300 lots across its three sections, of which just under three-quarters are occupied, while only 60 percent of El Cenizo's 920 lots are occupied (LBJ 1997, 2 : 128 [EDAP data]). All dwellings are now served by a public water supply, and approximately half in El Cenizo have central wastewater service (ibid.). Both colonias are far from being built through; and while they are fully platted, many lots remain unoccupied and are held by absentee lot owners. Average lot size is quite large, ranging from one-quarter to three-quarters of an acre. All lots have water onto the lot; streets are paved and many plot owners have installed "public" street lighting on the electricity posts outside their homes. Both colonias opted to incorporate themselves as separate cities. In Río Bravo there is a regular garbage collection service in trash receptacles provided by the City of Río Bravo (Photo 8). The level of dwelling improvement and consolidation is considerably higher in Río Bravo than in El Cenizo (cf. Photos 8 and 9). Located in a one-hundred-year floodplain, the two colonias were very fortunate to escape widespread flooding from Tropical Storm Charley in August 1998.

El Cenizo is located some four miles down the road from Río Bravo. Like Río Bravo, it enjoys the service of a private bus company (El Aguilar), which is contracted to the county and runs a service to Laredo some four or five times daily. However, while the access road into the colonia is paved (concrete), the majority of the other streets are unpaved (Photo 9). Water has also been installed, and ostensibly servicing levels are the same as described for Río Bravo, but the "City of El Cenizo" is obviously less successful than its neighbor, for there

8. Río Bravo colonia (Webb County [Laredo]), showing homes along street, concrete paving, and "Río Bravo City" trash bins.

9. El Cenizo (Webb County [Laredo]). Low-density semiconsolidated dwellings, unpaved streets.

is no regular trash collection, and the garbage truck and fire engine lie defunct outside of city hall (cf. Photos 39 and 40). The colonia has a community center (see Chapter 5), and although it was one of the first to be inaugurated in 1994, it, too, looks a little the worse for wear, and there has recently been a change in staffing of the center, suggesting a lower level of resident confidence in colonia/city officials.

NUEVO LAREDO

Nuevo Laredo is the sister city of Laredo across the Rio Grande–Río Bravo. The city is the largest in the state of Tamaulipas, and while its population has grown relatively modestly in the past twenty years (from 200,000 to almost 250,000), it remains considerably larger than Laredo. Like its twin city it is expected to add a further 100,000 population over the twenty-year period 1990–2010. It serves as one of the most important cities for trade between the United States and Mexico, and like its neighbor has developed as an important trucking and railhead freight break point. In addition, of course, it has important *maquila* production functions, though this is less important than in Ciudad Juárez. The municipality of Nuevo Laredo covers about 1,665.5 km², or up to 2 percent of the state of Tamaulipas. The area is characterized as having the driest and most extreme temperatures in the state, and the terrain is flat. Nuevo Laredo has never been an important agricultural region, partly because of its climate, and in 1980 agriculture employed only 5 percent of the active labor force (Alarcón Cantú 1993; Secretaría de Gobernación 1988).

Demography The 1990 census estimated that Nuevo Laredo had a population of 217,912 people, compared to 203,286 in 1980. This increase of 7 percent over the ten-year period was lower than had been projected, but still high.[14] Estimated population figures for Nuevo Laredo in 1994 showed a total of 227,887 people for the city. While the growth rate from 1980 to 1990 was not as high as that of its sister city, Nuevo Laredo continues to have high rates of population increase. The city is densely populated, with 122 residents per square kilometer, compared to the state average of 28 residents per square kilometer (Gobierno del Estado de Tamaulipas 1991, 7). The average household size in Nuevo Laredo was 4.5 inhabitants in 1994, while the average age of the population in Nuevo Laredo was twenty-six. Immigrants to Nuevo Laredo account for 10.6 percent of intrastate migrants in

Tamaulipas (Gobierno del Estado de Tamaulipas 1991, 8). Officials of the city estimate that 25–30 percent of the residents of colonias in Nuevo Laredo are originally from southern Mexico and Central America.

The Economy The economy of Nuevo Laredo is strongly tied to interaction with the United States through import-export, tourism, and *maquiladoras*. In 1980, 32 percent of the city's population was active in the labor force (Secretaría de Gobernación 1988), and women made up 24 percent of the work force. According to Instituto Nacional de Estadística Geográfica, e Informática (INEGI) figures in 1986, 91 percent of the males over the age of twelve were economically active, while only 45 percent of the females of the same age participated in the labor force (Ham-Chande and Weeks 1992, 201–205).

Of note in Nuevo Laredo is the importance that the tertiary sector has played in employing the EAP. In 1980, almost two-thirds of the EAP worked in the tertiary sector, compared to the state average of 54.3 percent (Alarcón Cantú 1993, 5). More specifically, in 1990 31 percent of the EAP worked in services, up from 21 percent in 1980. Manufacturing has also recently increased in importance due to the *maquiladoras*. In 1980, only 12.5 percent of the EAP worked in manufacturing, but by 1990, the proportion had increased to 25.2 percent (Lorey 1990, 83). The *maquiladoras* did not always make such a large contribution to the economy of Nuevo Laredo, especially during the period 1975–1986. However, since that time the expansion of the *maquila* factories has taken off. Between 1987 and 1989 the number of people employed by *maquiladoras* in the municipality increased from 6,777 to 16,218 (Alarcón Cantú 1993, 7). In 1995 there were over fifty *maquiladoras* providing employment to Nuevo Laredo residents.

Colonias in the Built-up Area and the Study Settlements As Figure 3 shows, Nuevo Laredo nestles within the bend of the Río Bravo and extends southwest out along Highway 85 to the industrial giant of Monterrey, located some two hundred miles to the south in Nuevo León. (The latter state also enjoys a small segment of border with Texas just west of Nuevo Laredo, which is where the Solidarity Bridge was built.) Another highway extends west to the important industrial center of Monclova in the state of Coahuila. A third spoke radiating out of the city leads northward, linking the trucking parks with the new Solidarity Bridge. Bounding the city is the loop of the airport highway, which extends as the Luis Donaldo Colosio Boulevard on the east side of Highway 85 (Figure 3).

Despite its larger population, the built-up area of Nuevo Laredo is much smaller and more compact than that of Laredo. Until twenty years ago it comprised mostly the core area in the bend of the river, but as industrialization occurred it grew westward, and then south and northwest along the aforementioned exit routes, spawning the new colonias. Most recently, both freight terminal parking and colonias have begun to spill beyond the loop. Colonias to the south are low density, while those on the west side have become high density residential as a result of small lot sizes and on-lot densification. Some of these freight terminal sites are enormous, particularly those located alongside the airport boulevard.

The Survey Settlements Most of the settlements selected for further study were located in the western section of the city, but before describing them it is worth mentioning the rather different nature of the colonias in the south along the highway to Monterrey. These colonias were developed on private land by developers. Colonia Enrique Cárdenas (named for an earlier governor) was begun some twenty years ago by a company of illegal developers called Fraccionamientos América. Lots are relatively small, 200–300 m² (30 × 60 to 45 × 60 feet). Both main streets are paved (concrete), while linking side streets are not, but just have the curbs delineated. The colonia has electricity, street lighting, and water (metered). Neighboring colonias (Colonia Regina and Colonia Treviño) were developed as *granjas* (market garden lots) on private land. These have much larger lots of a half-acre or a full acre, so that densities are much lower. Many lots are used as trucking parks, usually associated with small firms. Services include electricity and "austere" (low) levels of street lighting, and the streets are unpaved. Regina has no water, although this is currently being installed under the municipality's "Hand-in-Hand" (Mano con Mano) program at a cost of around US$100,000. Colonia Treviño already has water. In all cases, levels of dwelling consolidation are mixed, but most homes are brick-built.

The west-side colonias I've analyzed are mostly former *ejidal* (community) lands that have been illegally sold off by the *ejidatarios*, who ostensibly had only use rights on the land (see Chapter 2). The area called Voluntad y Trabajo actually comprises three sections, each of which has adopted a separate name and identity (making for some level of confusion over identification). Thus, the first colonia selected,

Veinte de Noviembre, is in fact Voluntad y Trabajo I, and it developed
around 1987 through an invasion of *ejidal* land to which the *ejidatarios*
turned a blind eye. Lots are 10 × 20 meters, and the main streets are
paved and lit; water is installed in each lot, and a wastewater service
has been installed. Yet despite active intervention from the municipality the levels of dwelling improvement are lower than might nor-
mally be expected for a colonia which began ten years ago: although
many homes are brick-built, others are shacks and provisional dwellings (Photo 10). A second colonia studied, La Sandia, developed from
the *ejido* of the same name and forms part of what is also known as
Voluntad y Trabajo II. Also begun some ten years ago, it is very similar
in appearance to Veinte de Noviembre.

Colonia Nueva Era is more recent, having begun in 1990 or
thereabouts as a somewhat controversial and conflictive invasion of
ejidal land founded by a local leader, Jesús González Bastién, with the
support of a minor political party (the PARM), generally loyal to
the governing party, the PRI. After González Bastién was jailed the
colonia began to support the PRI authorities more directly, but has
been plagued by new invasions and extensions for more recent arrivals.
However, in the main part of the colonia the municipality is actively
intervening to install drainage (water is already provided to each lot).

*10. Veinte de Noviembre, Nuevo Laredo, is more than ten years old and has substantial
services, including some paved streets (as here), but many dwellings here are still built of
provisional materials.*

11. Nueva Era, Nuevo Laredo. A seven-year-old colonia that is beginning to receive government attention and intervention. Note street lighting and sidewalk edgings.

There is no street paving, nor will there be any until the infrastructure is complete. Electricity is provided by concrete (rather than wooden) posts. Consolidation is underway, although an adjacent colonia and Nueva Era offshoots that are less than three years old mostly contain shacks (Photo 11). The total population of Nueva Era is estimated to be around 12,000, living in almost 2,500 homes. A similar development is taking place on the other side of the loop, this time promoted by a major opposition party, the Partido de la Revolución Democrática (PRD), and named for a local PRDista, Santiago M. Belden. The PRD has a site office at the entrance of the colonia, but as yet the settlement has no services except partial electricity (Photo 12).

Colonia Cavazos Lerma also has close ties with a political party, this time the governing PRI, but the PRI was not formally involved in its formation, which began in 1992 with the low-cost purchase of lots from individual *ejidatarios*, who sold off parcels of 5 hectares each divided into 200 m² lots at a cost (then) of around US$100. The sale was promoted by two leaders affiliated with the ACOT (Asociación de Campesinos y Obreros de Tamaulipas). Legalization of titles is now underway at a further cost of just over US$100. The colonia began

12. Colonia Santiago Belden (Nuevo Laredo), a two-year-old squatter invasion promoted by the PRD, whose office (seen here) stands at the entry to the two-street incipient colonia.

when Manuel Cavazos Lerma was still PRI candidate for the governorship, which, fortuitously for the colonia's development, he won. The colonia has received strong PRI municipal government support and has electricity, water, drainage (about to be connected once the primary collector has been completed), and curbing on the main street (Photo 13). According to data provided by the university (COLEF), the colonia has some 3,400 residents.

BROWNSVILLE

Brownsville is the county seat of Cameron County and is one of the main population centers in the Lower Rio Grande Valley area, which is made up of Texas' four southernmost counties. This is also one of the poorest regions in the United States, and the Lower Rio Grande Valley was cited in the 1990 census as having one of the highest levels of unemployment and poverty in the nation, along with some of the lowest education levels.

The city and surrounding area comprise a low-lying floodplain, with many floodways and old oxbow lakes. Roads tend to be raised slightly and have ditches running alongside them which drain what is a

13. Colonia Manuel Cavazos Lerma (Nuevo Laredo). Five-year-old consolidating settlement. "Austere" street lighting, unpaved main street.

rich farmland. Despite having a total population less than one-third that of its Mexican neighbor of Matamoros, the built-up area is considerably larger, although the city boundary is carefully gerrymandered to leave the principal colonia areas outside (Figure 4). Cameron County has traditionally been Democratic, and notwithstanding Brownsville's reticence to recognize colonias within its ETJ, the county has generally sought to take a more proactive and well-intentioned approach toward colonia populations, albeit often a problematic one (as will be described in greater detail in Chapter 2).[15] There are three international bridges, one in Cameron County, the other two in Brownsville itself. Immediately to the west of the city lies Hidalgo County, and the city forms part of the Brownsville-Harlingen Metropolitan Area.

Demography   The census estimated that there were 98,887 people living in the city of Brownsville in 1990, 85 percent of whom were born in Texas, while 11 percent were recorded as having moved to the United States between 1980 and 1990. The projected population growth rate for the Brownsville-Harlingen Metropolitan Area between 1986 and 2025 is 151.4 percent (Texas Department of Commerce 1989a, 5). In 1990, 82 percent of the population in Cameron County was of Hispanic origin, with projections increasing that proportion to

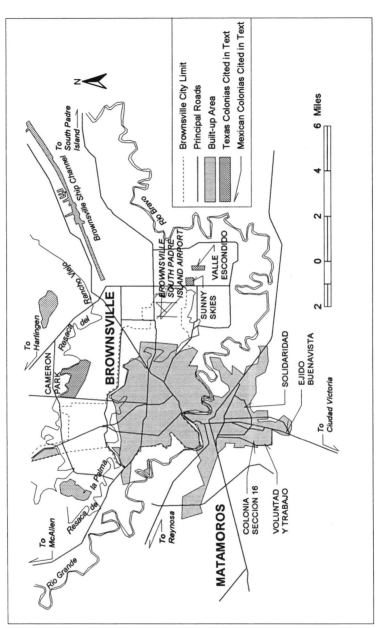

Figure 4. Built-up area of Matamoros and Brownsville showing city boundaries and the survey colonias.

86.3 percent by the year 2000 (*Colonia Profile* 1994, 30). Some 95 percent of the colonia populations are Hispanic (OAG 1993, 12).

In terms of education, Brownsville statistics are similar to those of the Texas border in general. In Cameron County, 50 percent of persons twenty-five and over do not have a high school diploma, and less than 60 percent have received a ninth-grade education (*Texas Governor's Border Report* 1993).

The Economy The 1990 census estimated that 44 percent of Brownsville residents were living below the poverty line. In 1990, of the 67,256 persons over sixteen years of age, 56 percent were active in the labor force, and of those, 15.2 percent were unemployed. Males made up 55 percent of the labor force, and females 45 percent. This exhibits a slight change from the 1980 census, in which 58 percent of the labor force was male, and a more dramatic departure from the 1970 census, when 64.7 percent of the work force was male. In 1990, the median income for males was $16,540 and for females, $12,470. The average median household income was $15,895, and the average median family income was $16,889.

In 1990, 22 percent of the labor force worked in the retail trade industry, followed by 16 percent in educational services and 14 percent in the manufacture of durable and nondurable goods. In the 1980 census, service industries, such as education, professions, and repair services, provided 29 percent of the jobs in Brownsville, while the retail industry employed 19 percent of the labor force. In 1988, manufacturing was the largest money maker, followed closely by retail trade (Texas Department of Commerce 1989a, 18).

Between 1969 and 1979 an industrial boom occurred and a number of corporations relocated to the Brownsville area. According to the Brownsville Chamber of Commerce, the following manufacturers provide the majority of the area's employment outside of the retail and service sectors: Levi Strauss, Hagar Apparel, Breed Automotive, Norton Company, Ft. Brown Manufacturing, and Anfel's Ship Building and Repair.

Colonias in the Built-up Area and the Study Settlements
Cameron County offers a classic example of "rural" colonia development tied to a (primarily) agrarian past. Small rural colonias dot Cameron County southeast of the Brownsville airport like buckshot (see Figure 4). Invariably very small, they often contain some 20–30 lots

along dirt roads dividing cornfields. One may be excused for viewing colonias on the east side of Brownsville as being a rural rather than an urban phenomenon. Small and surrounded by fields, only their poorly serviced nature suggests that they are marginal settlements whose economic raison d'être originates in low-wage urban services. Interspersed with these rural colonias are small clusters of commuter homes, for this area is barely six or seven miles from downtown Brownsville.

The Survey Settlements   Cameron Park is exceptional both in its notoriety and size. One of Texas' best-known colonias, it has some 1,624 lots and 1,100 dwelling units, although the TWDB lists it as having 750 families occupying the same number of lots (LBJ 1997, 2:49). (This discrepancy may be explained by the fact that the Model Subdivision Rules with which TWDB must work do not recognize "shared" or subdivided lots for rent, of which there are a considerable number. Some 40 percent of households are estimated to be either renting or sharing their lots with another family.) Thus, although less than half of the colonia lots are formally "occupied," in actual fact the number of vacant lots is considerably less, and site visits in 1997 estimated that the number of vacant lots was on the order of 20–25 percent. These are held by absentee owners, since all of the lots have been platted.

The settlement comprises 400 acres, and, when it was first developed in 1961, it was truly rural, abutting the Rancho Viejo floodway on its northern side. This was the earliest part of the community to develop, followed by sections to the south and then to the east abutting the Paredes Line Road (and the boundary of the city). Lots are modest in size, and many of the street blocks have 40 houses per block (resembling quite closely their Mexican counterparts). The majority of the streets are unpaved, and constructed with hard-core caliche to make them passable to vehicles. Late in 1997 there was considerable activity to upgrade the streets and deepen the drains that run alongside all of the streets, and to provide concrete water pipes under each access point to individual lots (Photo 14). Flooding is a major concern in Cameron Park, surrounded as it is on three sides by drainage canals/ floodwater channels. Many dwellings are raised on small brick stilts in accordance with the code requirement. Probably because of the need to raise them above the ground, most houses are wooden structures (Photo 15), rather than consolidated brick-built and two-story.

14. *Cameron Park (Cameron County [Brownsville]). First section of the colonia now receiving drainage under lot access and hard core for street pending.*

15. *Cameron Park (Cameron County [Brownsville]). Raised wood dwelling showing propane gas tanks and water faucet on side.*

16. Cameron Park (Cameron County [Brownsville]). Consolidated dwellings and trash box at front.

Most residents also adhere to local building codes in terms of set-backs from the road and clearance of property lines. The colonia has electricity and water, and in the earliest section drainage is being installed. There is a regular garbage collection service, and trash is placed in raised wooden boxes outside the home (Photo 16). As is often the case, there is no street lighting, a problem that is aggravated in the colonia by the fact that no less than three electricity companies run power and hookups to different streets (see Chapter 3). The colonia was selected for one of the first Texas A&M community centers, located close to one of its main entrances, and unlike its El Cenizo counterpart, the Cameron County facility looks well kept and active.

Colonia Valle Escondido is rather more typical of the small colonias which abound southwest of the Brownsville airport. It began in 1985 and comprises four (unpaved but improved) streets off a paved feeder road from FM 1419. There are 56 lots, of which I estimate two-thirds are occupied. Lots are modest in size (90' × 160'), and the colonia has water and electricity. Lots were sold off by the developer at a cost of $8,500, while water installation cost $1,500 and individual septic fields $2,000. Most of the homes are consolidating; a few remain rather dilapidated (Photo 17). The colonia has a major problem with flooding, and was actually built over what used to be a lagoon. This has prompted periodic interventions from the state and the Red Cross to help residents.

17. Valle Escondido (Cameron County [Brownsville]). Typical scene from small rural colonias showing low-density patterns and vacant lots (foreground).

Sunny Skies was another study settlement, and the details of its land development are described in Chapter 2. It, too, is very small, consisting of two streets and a small rear extension on the corner of Dockberry Road and Road 511. It is a subdivision of 40 acres, with quarter- and half-acre lots for the most part developed in 1988. While it was poorly serviced only two years ago, it has improved dramatically recently. The two streets are paved, all services are installed, and gas meters indicate that several households have accessed the gas line that runs along 511 (Photo 18).

MATAMOROS

Matamoros is on the northeastern edge of Mexico, also in the state of Tamaulipas. Topographically, the region conforms to a lowland drainage flat, sloping toward the Río Bravo and the Gulf of Mexico. Its most notable geographical feature is the river. The climate is warm; freezes in winters are rare, and summers are extremely hot. Irrigation from several nearby rivers allows for cultivation of the area's fertile land. The size of the municipality is 3,352 km², making up 4.19 percent of the state's land area.

Matamoros' land-use patterns have been shaped by its early existence as a walled city. The walls originally bridged the bow in the river

18. Large lot with trailer in Sunny Skies (Cameron County [Brownsville]). Note the gas supply meter at front.

in which the city lies, and essentially confined growth to within the walled area. The nucleus of the old city is therefore now surrounded by a comparatively young urban area. Until the 1940s the bulk of the economic activity of the city occurred within the walls. After that time, the area surrounding the city opened up to agricultural development, especially of cotton. In the 1960s, the *maquiladora* plants, mainly in the northwestern part of the built-up area, began to revitalize the city, and today there are over a hundred *maquiladoras* in Matamoros.

Demography   Matamoros has grown in population from 137,749 residents in 1970 to 188,703 in 1980, and finally, to 303,293 in 1990 (a rate of growth between 1980 and 1990 of 41 percent). In 1990, 24 percent (71,591) of the residents of Matamoros came from outside of the municipality. Of those who migrated from within Mexico, the largest number (20,592) came from San Luis Potosí and 10,162 came from Veracruz. Within the state of Tamaulipas, 40.5 percent of all the migrants move to Matamoros (Gobierno del Estado de Tamaulipas 1991, 8).

   Matamoros is densely populated. In 1970, the population density was 55.3 people per square kilometer; by 1987, the density had increased to 72.4 people per square kilometer. The total area of the city is 3,944 km², or 394,400 hectares (Merla Rodríguez 1987). In 1970 there were 5.4 occupants per household. This figure declined over the next twenty years, to an estimated 4.0 occupants per household in 1980, and 4.5 occupants per household in 1990. The average number of rooms per dwelling unit has increased over time, resulting in decreasing household density (number of persons per room). In 1970, the majority of households (65.5 percent) lived in houses of one or two rooms, and the average household had 2.3 rooms. In 1990, the greatest proportion of households, 62.6 percent, lived in houses of two to four rooms, while the average household had 2.6 rooms. The average household density in 1970 was 2.3 persons per room, while this had declined in 1990 to 1.7 persons per room, a decrease of 26 percent.

In 1980 only 11 percent of the population over twenty-five years of age had finished high school. However, education levels among younger residents of the city indicate that educational access is expanding, as 20.4 percent of the adults currently between the ages of eighteen and twenty-four have completed high school (Ham-Chande and Weeks 1992, 72).

The Economy In 1990, the rate of male participation in the labor force was 70 percent, and for women the rate of participation was 31.2 percent. In 1990, the majority (66.2 percent) of the economically active population in Matamoros earned between 1 and 3 minimum salaries. However, men made up a disproportionately large share of workers earning 3 to 5 minimum salaries and 5 to 10 minimum salaries, while women were a greater percentage of the workers earning only 1 to 2 minimum salaries. The median income in the city increased 29 percent between 1980 and 1990, when the median was 1.27 minimum salaries (Nolasco Armas and Acevedo Conde 1989, 273). Matamoros wage levels are similar to those of other border cities in Tamaulipas and Chihuahua, but lower than those of cities farther west, such as Tijuana and Ensenada. In 1980, the median annual income in Matamoros was $2,669 in U.S. dollars (Ham-Chande and Weeks 1992, 82), and there is little reason to expect that it is much higher than that today.

Manufacturing now employs the majority of the economically active population in Matamoros, and its importance has grown in the last two decades. In 1990, 38 percent of the EAP worked in manufacturing, compared to only 14.5 percent in 1970. In 1990, services employed the second-largest percentage of the EAP. Since 1970, primary

Table 10. Percentage of Economically Active Population
per Sector in Matamoros

Sector	1970	1980	1990
Primary activities	26.9	11	7.3
Petroleum industry	0.1	—	—
Mining	0.3	0.1*	0.1*
Manufacturing	14.5	17.7	37.9
Construction	5.8	6.7	8
Utilities	0.3	0.2	0.6
Commerce	13.6	12	12.9
Transportation	3.5	4	4.1
Services	25.5	17.6	23.1
Government	3.7	—	3.1
Unclassified	5.9	30.8	2.9

Source: Lorey 1990.
* Includes petroleum industry.

activities (agriculture, fishing, forestry, etc.) have decreased in importance, employing only 7.3 percent of the EAP in 1990. Table 10 provides further information about the breakdown of EAP by sector of employment.

In terms of percentage contribution to the city's GDP, trade, restaurants, and hotels made up the largest proportion (26 percent) of GDP in 1980, with services (18 percent) coming in second. More recent data from 1989 show that 37 percent of the GDP for the city came from the value added of *maquiladora* products, and 34.7 percent of the economy consisted of border transactions. Among the Mexican border cities, Matamoros has the third-largest number of hectares of land designated for agriculture such as temporal plants, corn, cotton, fruit, okra, and plants for export to the United States. The city also has the third-largest economic sector based on animals and their products, primarily cattle, pigs, and fish. As of 1988, 85.7 percent of the manufacturing EAP was in the *maquiladora* industries, and 72.4 percent of those workers were women. By 1989, there were 53 major industrial establishments and 76 *maquiladoras* in the city, which employed 38,517 people. By 1992, the number of *maquiladoras* had increased to 97 (Alarcón Cantú 1993, 21; Nolasco Armas and Acevedo

19. Colonia Sección 16 (Matamoros). Consolidated buildings, paved streets, full services, and "austere" lighting on one side of street only.

Conde 1989, 273; *Colonia Profile* 1994, 22). Overall, women make up 36 percent of the total work force (Ham-Chande and Weeks 1992, 201).

Matamoros and the Study Settlements   As noted above, Matamoros displays two distinctive features: a densely populated urban area, the oldest part of which presses hard up against the inside bend of the Río Bravo where it intrudes north into Texas. A second feature is the very rapid population increase experienced since 1980, which has led to the sprawling development of colonias to the east, south, and west. So extensive and rapid was the expansion of these colonias that Matamoros' principal arterial roads are poorly developed and integrated. Although several major thoroughfares are depicted in Figure 4, these leave much to be desired, often petering out into unpaved routes, and failing to provide adequate east-west linkage, particularly south of the Ayuntamiento–Manuel Cavazos loop. Nowhere else in the six cities is arterial development so poorly articulated (not even Ciudad Juárez). The principal exit route is to the south to the state capital of Ciudad Victoria. Another major exit leads northwest to the border city of Reynosa.

The *maquila* expansion has developed in both the eastern and west-

20. *Colonia Voluntad y Trabajo (Matamoros), showing consolidated dwelling on lot with propane tank and water heater. Note also the water tank on roof.*

21. *Colonia Solidaridad (Matamoros), showing incipient/early consolidating dwellings; low service levels and unpaved streets.*

ern parts of the city, and has attracted substantial colonia development on adjacent properties. To the south there are also numerous trucking and haulage parks, although not on the same scale as was observed in Nuevo Laredo. Given that the region is an extensive floodplain, the water table is close to the surface, making the unpaved roads a quag-mire after any significant rains. Unlike the other Mexican border cities analyzed, Matamoros is surrounded by highly fertile and intensively farmed agricultural land, much of which was designated as *ejidos* under Mexico's Agrarian Reform Program. As a result, most of the colonias that have developed in Matamoros are on land that was originally *ejidal*. Today unserviced vacant lots are freely available on *ejidos* in many peripheral areas of the city at a cost of NP$5,000 (new pesos) or thereabouts (around US$700).

The Survey Settlements Colonia Sección 16 is located on the western margin of the southern expansion (Figure 4), and when it began in the 1970s it was surrounded by intensively farmed agricultural land. The land was purchased by the Mexican Workers' Confederation (CTM), and 200 m² lots were sold off by the union to its worker affiliates. The colonia boasts a small plaza with a bandstand dedicated to the CTM's leader of fifty years Fidel Velázquez, who died in 1997 at the age of 97, while still head of the union. Given its ordered origins and close CTM ties to the national PRI leadership, the colonia is well developed, having electricity, water, drainage, and street paving throughout, although the surface is often badly deteriorated. Residents attribute this largely to the recent intervention of the telephone company to lay new cables. There are an estimated 2,800 plots in the colonia, and most homes are well consolidated (Photo 19).

Adjacent to Sección 16 is the second colonia studied, Voluntad y Trabajo, whose origins are the more familiar sale by *ejidatarios* to would-be residents in 1986. Its 1,500 lots have recently had water installed, although drainage is still lacking (Photo 20). Few of the streets are paved, although most main thoroughfares have been improved by a caliche hard core. Dwelling consolidation is mixed, as one would expect for a colonia approximately ten years old.

Colonia Solidaridad is on the east side of the southern extension (Figure 4) in a wide arc of land partially bounded by a loop that is still to be paved in many parts. This area has seen a rapid growth of colonias whose names ("Solidaridad," "Carlos Salinas de Gortari") depict their recent phase of development (i.e., 1989–1994). Other colonia names reflect the agrarian and *ejidal* nature of the land's origins ("Emiliano Zapata," "Ejido Buenavista," etc.). Solidaridad began with an invasion of *ejidal* land and subsequent regularization by CoRett. The colonia has electricity, and since our original survey in 1995 water spigots have been installed on each lot. Toilets are pit privies, and there is no street paving, although some streets have sidewalk edges laid and consist of a caliche hard core. Dwellings are rudimentary for the most part, being a mixture of shacks and one- or two-room brick dwellings (Photo 21). There are even more recently developed colonias surrounding Solidaridad (e.g., Ampliación Solidaridad), in which services are almost nonexistent. Despite their relatively recent origins, these settlements are quite densely populated, with a large number of 200 m² (approximately 30' × 60') lots, almost all of which are occupied.

Conclusion

In conclusion, the six cities in our study are similar in terms of general trends such as high growth rates, low educational attainment, high poverty levels, and important roles for the manufacturing and services sectors in their economies. However, one important difference between the two sides of the border stands out. In Mexico, many of the demographic and economic indicators are better along the border than in the country as a whole, while the opposite is true on the Texas border. Thus, the border region offers increased economic opportunities, acting as a magnet for many in southern Mexico and Central America who are looking for economic improvement. It is also important to note that often the sister cities have more in common with each other than with other interior cities in their own country. Despite the legal and geographical boundaries separating the two countries, the border cities are highly interconnected. The *maquiladora* and retail industries are only two examples of the economic links that transcend the international boundary. In addition to the flow of goods, there is a constant movement of people between the cities on either side of the Rio Grande–Río Bravo. The economic and demographic realities of the border give rise to the unique housing and infrastructure conditions in the region, and the ties between the three pairs of cities must be used as starting points for understanding how to deal with these conditions.

Two

Land and Housing Production in the Colonias of Texas and Mexico

Self-Help Housing and Urbanization

When it comes to land and housing production leading to colonia formation in the United States, there is relatively little written, at least until recently. In contrast, the literature about land and low-income housing production in Mexico and elsewhere is very extensive, and it provides considerable insight about the processes which have led to the development of colonias throughout the border region. My argument is that they respond to a common logic, albeit the weights (extent) and nature (levels of poverty) may differ.

Rapid urbanization began in many developing countries in the 1940s and 1950s, drawing in labor from provincial areas, rural and urban, in order to man the factories created by governments eager to adopt the import substituting industrialization philosophy then being promoted by the United Nations Economic Commission for Latin America (ECLA/CEPAL). From the 1950s through the 1970s major cities in Mexico and elsewhere were almost doubling in size every decade as a result of the influx of migrants, and later as a combination of in-migration and the high birth rates generated by what had become a young adult population at the beginning of its family building cycle (Ward 1998b). With birth rates over 3 percent in Mexico, and migration adding a further 2 to 3 percent, city growth rates in excess of 5 percent per annum were not out of the ordinary. These rapid growth rates began to slow in the 1970s, and many major cities are now growing only modestly, if at all. But other regional cities, particularly those selected for targeted expansion under the 100 Ciudades Program, continue to grow, especially where the region is experiencing rapid economic development. Since the 1970s the border has been one such area.

Three points emerge strongly from this brief overview. First, the rapidity of the urbanization process. Second, its functional nature, fueled as it was by economic transformation and the demand for cheap labor. Third, the fact that much of this increase in the work force was absorbed into the formal sector at low wage rates. While the petty services sector also began to expand, this was not a dysfunctional urbanization process in which population growth was wildly out of synch with economic growth (Roberts 1978, 1994). Even later studies of the "informal sector" economy have demonstrated the close ties and dynamic interrelatedness between small-scale unregulated activities and services and the larger-scale formal sector. Moreover, these informal activities have also begun to be considered functional for development and not parasitic (as was once the case), providing as they do jobs and access to cheap goods and services for the rich and poor alike (de Soto 1989). In short, urbanization and economic development were natural bedfellows. Even latterly in the 1980s and 1990s as the economic model has shifted toward externally oriented (global) manufacturing industrialization, wage rates in less-developed countries have not shown appreciable convergence with those in advanced economies. However, the more "footloose" nature of economic and industrial activities today provides for growth outside of the traditional urban centers, whose population growth has slowed, so that many provincial cities have begun to experience rapid economic development and urbanization.

A common feature of this urbanization process, wherever its location, was the incapacity of either the private (formal) market or the public sector to provide housing for the expanding work force. Government housing programs in Mexico were extremely limited until the 1970s, and even after the creation of national worker housing banks and funds such as INFONAVIT and FONHAPO, they managed at best only to meet one-fifth of the effective demand (Ward 1990). Low wage rates meant that private housing production was unprofitable, and the lack of a large creditworthy population meant that there was no mortgage market to speak of. From the 1950s and 1960s onward, shantytowns and squatter settlements began to spring up around cities and soon became a feature of the urban landscape, sometimes extending over more than one-half of the built-up area. Government policies typically characterized these settlements as illegal and substandard. Paralleling urban renewal programs and philosophy in the developed world, irregular settlements were frequently eradicated and their residents relocated or evicted in an attempt to improve housing standards (Perlman 1976). In Mexico, given the extent of irregular settlements, such evictions were invariably highly selective of those settlements which were most visible and problematic or which occupied prime sites for redevelopment. Elsewhere the government recognized that there was little it could do to formally generate sufficient housing for its working poor, so it turned a blind eye and adopted a laissez faire approach to continued settlement development (Ward 1982a, 1986; Gilbert and Ward 1985).

From the late 1960s and early 1970s onward, researchers began to assert that irregular settlements, far from being a problem, were— other things being equal—in fact part of a solution to the low-income housing crisis in developing countries (Mangin 1967; Lloyd 1979). Influential policy advocates such as John Turner (1976) argued that what had come to be called self-help housing met the needs of low-income people, and that these efforts should be supported rather than hindered (see also Abrams 1966; Turner and Fichter 1972). The self-build housing process was flexible regarding people's economic capacities and responded to an individual's or a family's priorities in a way that centrally directed housing schemes could not (Turner 1976; but cf. Burgess 1982 and Ward 1982a).

Subsequently, public policy began to support self-help housing through projects such as sites-and-services, core units, settlement "upgrading," and land regularization of "clouded" lot titles (World Bank 1972; Varley 1987; Ward 1984). Since the 1980s the trend has been toward less direct involvement in housing production, and greater government involvement in making the market work more smoothly by providing infrastructure, removing bottlenecks on land markets, improving regularization programs, and creating regulatory frameworks that enhance self-help rather than hinder it (Linn 1983). A major UN-sponsored seminar in 1983 concluded:

> . . . the emphasis of public policy must shift from the housing construction process to the land delivery process, so that governments take responsibility for providing secure land and affordable infrastructure, while individual households or community groups take responsibility for building the shelter's structure. (Angel et al. 1983)

Today the conventional wisdom being promoted by international agencies is to intensify efforts to make the market work more smoothly and to integrate irregular settlements into the property and tax register in order to enhance cost recovery for service provision and to ensure that consumers pay for services received (World Bank 1991). Planning (even retrospective) and "urban management" have become the watchwords of the 1990s, alongside efforts to strengthen municipal government and public administration practices (Rodríguez 1997; Jones and Ward 1994, 1995). In Mexico these ideas have found widespread acceptance as a backcloth to President Carlos Salinas' Reform of Article 27, which allows for the deregulation of the *ejido* sector and the creation of land reserves, and enacted the National Solidarity Program. Although the latter has been recast by President Ernesto Zedillo, the aim continues to be one of strengthening municipal capacity and public participation at the local level (SEDESOL 1994, 1996; Jones and Ward 1998).

Three principal modes of housing production are often identified: private, public, and popular (Schteingart 1989, 117). The private mode is used almost exclusively by upper-income groups, whose housing is produced through legally platted and fully serviced subdivisions, or through apartment and condominium development. Although the rich are not averse to sometimes taking advantage of illegal land development options, most of this housing may be assumed to be legal. Middle-income groups acquire housing in much the same way, albeit on a less grandiose scale and financed through mortgages, banks, and sometimes public housing funds such as FOVISSSTE, FOVI, and FOGA. Active *production* of housing through the public sector is limited, because government investment funds are scarce and the magnitude of the demand would hardly be touched by public supply. Public-sector housing, therefore, has never been an option for a dominant percentage of low-income families (Ward 1990; González Rubi 1984). So-called popular housing (which in my view should also be considered part of the "private" sector) has therefore become the only option for many. Popular housing is based upon three primary principles:

> . . . first, a considerable amount of work provided by the housing occupants themselves; second, the state's tolerance of the illegal status of most housing settlements; and third, investment by speculative private capital operating outside the legal limits through a variety of intermediaries. (Castells 1983, 188)

In essence, popular housing fits under the rubric of self-help, in which the consumer and the builder or controller of the construction process are one and the same (Ward and Macoloo 1992). This means that the consumer has the freedom to translate his/her own priorities into the housing that is produced (Turner and Fichter 1972; Schteingart 1989, 119). Governments have focused on responding to the infrastructure needs of these settlements, and regularizing land tenure in order to spur self-help housing investment (Turner 1976; Linn 1983; UNCHS 1996).

Self-help housing has become the most common means of obtaining shelter in many Latin American cities. Mexico City has seen the proportion of people living in self-help settlements increase from 14 percent in 1952 to 60 percent in 1990 (Gilbert 1994, 82). In tandem with the increase in self-help housing has come an increase in the percentage of individuals who own their home. In Mexico City, owner occupation stood at only 27 percent in 1950–1952, but was 64 percent by 1980–1982. A similar trend can be seen in Guadalajara, where the proportion jumped from 29 percent to 52 percent (Gilbert 1994, 92).

Support for policies which favor self-help housing has not been universal, however. Those on the political left are critical, viewing the lack of housing as a structurally determined by-product of capitalism (Burgess 1982) and arguing that governments have a duty to ensure that workers are properly housed. Even Turner has expressed doubts about how his research has been used (Gilbert 1994; Turner 1982). Other researchers maintain that policies intended to support self-help housing may actually perpetuate a cycle of increasing numbers of irregular settlements and greater inequality in access to housing (Connolly 1982; Pezzoli 1987, 385). Regularization of land tenure and incorporation of land into the formal market, for example, may lead to higher housing costs and detract from successful consolidation (Ward 1982b; Ward and Macoloo 1992).

Within Texas, both the phenomenon of self-help housing and the expansion of colonias may also be accommodated within a similar scenario. Economic activity in the border region has generated low-wage employment, whether in the *maquilas* in Mexico or in service activities on the Texas side. Migration and high rates of urbanization in border cities, in combination with widespread poverty and the inability of either the public sector or the private not-for-profit sector to match demand, have led to settlement development which shares many of the characteristics of that in developing countries. Wages are low and housing is developed privately, and is typically self-organized and sometimes self-built with minimal services—if any at all. But unlike

Mexico, in Texas and the United States there has not been the same parallel shift in the nature of public policy toward colonias. The purpose of this chapter is to describe and analyze the processes of land and housing development in colonias in Mexico and Texas, and to conclude by offering a set of policy recommendations that are informed by the experiences of the border region.

Mexico Land and Housing Production Traditions

Cities in Mexico, as in the rest of Latin America, have experienced extremely high growth rates over the last several decades. Mexico has gone from 35 percent urban to 73 percent urban between 1940 and 1990 (Gilbert 1994, 26). As was outlined in Chapter 1, Ciudad Juárez, and the other border cities to a lesser extent, have shared in this explosive population growth. The *maquiladora* program has brought additional migrants to the border region in search of new economic opportunities, while the economic crises of the 1980s and the 1995–1996 period in Mexico have both lowered average incomes and brought additional migrants to the area. The impact of recession has been less acute along the border than elsewhere in Mexico, given that *maquila* activity was sustained throughout. Nationally, though, these economic crises led to open unemployment averaging around 11.5 percent and to rates of underemployment of over 40 percent during the 1980s (Pezzoli 1987, 375). A similar scenario applied in 1995–1996.

In practical terms, rapid urban growth has meant that only a relatively small percentage of the population can afford to buy a home produced by the formal construction industry (Ward 1990). In Mexico, only about 15 percent of homes are financed by standard home mortgages (*SourceMex*, August 5, 1992). One author sums up the situation:

> Over the past 20 years, less than 15% of Mexico City's families have been able to afford the price or rents required by the formal real estate market. And the limited relief offered through state subsidized housing programs has required levels of income and job stability that could only be met by an additional 15% to 20% of the families. Thus, fully 60% to 70% of all metropolitan families have been unable to obtain their housing units through the formal housing market. (Pezzoli 1987, 34)

The government does provide some public-sector housing units, but cannot meet the demand due to its limited resources (Ward 1990). In 1990, the national housing shortage was estimated at 6.1 million units by the federal government (*SourceMex*, November 7, 1990). Among the border cities, Ciudad Juárez has a "deficit" of about 45,000 units, and there are an additional 9,000 families whom the city would like to move out of so-called high-risk areas.

LAND OWNERSHIP

There are generally three categories of land ownership that are recognized in Mexico: public, private, and communal (*ejidal*). The legal rights and responsibilities corresponding to the first two types of land ownership are roughly comparable to those of the United States. Communal land, however, has a history which begins with land ownership patterns in pre-Columbian settlements. Land was held in common by the village, with individual plots allotted to families and common areas such as forests and grazing pastures shared by all. This land was neither distributed to the *conquistadores* for the assemblage of *haciendas* or *ranchos*, nor appropriated by the Church. As early as 1567 this land was considered inalienable by the Spanish government. There were two types of village land, the *tierra de común repartamiento*, which the village distributed to the families for production, and the *ejidos*, or common lands (Cymet 1992, 102–103). While the original significance of these terms has altered, the significance of *ejidos* grew as a result of the postrevolution Constitution (1917) and the Agrarian Reform Program that was adopted. This broke up many of the large estates and redistributed the land among named peasant families living in what were to be called *ejidos*. These comprise agrarian communities in which peasants have use rights over the land (i.e., it is social property that cannot be sold or alienated in any way). Small settlement areas were designated in each *ejido* where *ejidatarios* and other families offering a service function to the community could reside as *avecindados*. Only the lots in this so-called "urban zone" could be legally bought and sold. Throughout the period 1920–1976 lands continued to be redistributed under the program, and redistribution was particularly active during some (more populist) *sexenio* administrations (Varley 1985). Many of these lands, however, had no agricultural use and were rough grazing or scrub: in these cases especially, the reform was one of political rhetoric rather than agrarian development. However, it did create large areas of land which, by the 1970s, often formed the outskirts of rapidly expanding cities, and the pressures to urbanize them quickened. In the early 1980s President José López Portillo declared the end of the land redistribution process.

In 1992, the Constitution was amended in order to give *ejidatarios* (the named beneficiaries or their families) the right to transfer (sell) their lands if that was agreed to by the *ejido's* general assembly (Austin 1994; Jones and Ward 1998). Even before this legal change, however, a great deal of *ejidal* land had been sold illegally by *ejidatarios* in order to accommodate urban expansion and low-income housing demand. In order to "regularize" those illegal lot holdings, the federal government was obliged to expropriate the land upon which these colonia settlements had formed, and then resell the land to the inhabitants, compensating the *ejidatarios* according to a specified formula. Traditionally, the federal government could always expropriate both private and *ejidal* land, though it had to have a compelling social-benefit reason to do so. Unlike in the United States, the provision of public utilities would be a legitimate reason, as would the construction of public housing (Schteingart 1989). Although the percentage of urban expansion which utilizes communal (*ejidal*) land varies by city, it is worth noting that between 1940 and 1975, about 50 percent of Mexico City's growth utilized *ejidal* or communal land (Varley 1985; Pezzoli 1987, 380). Moreover, as many other alternative forms of illegal land supply began to be more effectively controlled by state and local governments from the late 1970s onward, so *ejidal* land development became the primary form of illegal colonia formation.[1]

LEGAL AND REGULATORY FRAMEWORKS

The Mexican government has promulgated a number of laws which deal with land and housing production. The legal system in Mexico functions in a top-down manner: laws are first enacted at the national level and similar laws may be adopted by the thirty-one sovereign states for application at the state and *municipio* level. The principal laws and their provisions are:

• The Ley General de Asentamientos Humanos (LGAH), or General Law of Human Settlements, which regulates all population centers. The five chapters of the law outline the responsibilities of all three levels of government—federal, state, and municipal—as well as regulating property, land use, expropriation of private land,

and urban housing. Corresponding to the national law are state and local laws patterned after it. The LGAH was passed in 1976, and amended in 1981, 1983, and 1994. Supporting legislation includes the Federal Law of Housing. The aims of this and similar legislation include decreasing speculation and halting new irregular settlements (see Pezzoli 1987, 383).

- The Ley de Fraccionamientos, or Subdivisions (Plat) Law, which also usually has state counterparts and (is supposed to) regulate the way in which residential subdivisions may be formed. It outlines the obligations of the developer, the authorities, and the residents. It describes the sanctions and penalties that apply in cases of noncompliance.

- The Ley de Desarrollo Urbano, or Urban Development Law, which also functions at the federal and state levels. This gives general guidance regarding the role of planning and the guidelines for urban development policy. Urban development plans are prepared at all levels of government. Originally SAHOP (Secretaría de Asentamientos Humanos y Obras Públicas) was authorized to prepare plans for the 31 states and 2,375 municipalities in Mexico. Initially plans were produced in conjunction with state and local government, but since the middle 1980s this function has gradually been decentralized to these lower levels of government.

Established subdivisions for middle- and upper-income groups follow these laws at least in theory, but almost without exception these processes place formal land acquisition beyond the reach of most poor families.

Housing Laws and Programs

National housing policy has seen a succession of programs and agencies. Prior to 1962, Mexico had a federal public works agency, BANOBRAS, which worked in the area of land development and housing. A legal reform in 1962 led to the creation of public funds to supplement the private ones already in existence, as well as the creation of two state funds (FOVI and FOGA) designed to hold money from the Bank of Mexico for "social" (low-income) housing. These funds were designed to cover up to 80 percent of the cost of low-income housing (95 percent with FOGA) and offered good terms with low interest rates. The construction of public-sector housing units increased as a result, but remained woefully inadequate relative to the

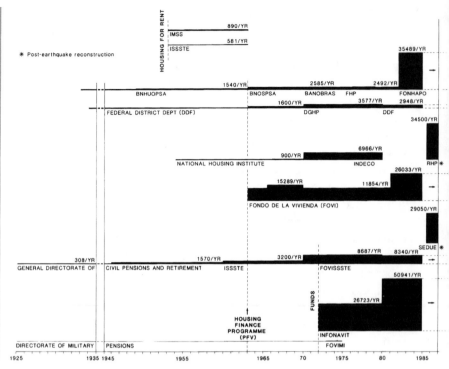

Figure 5. Average annual level of housing production, by principal housing agencies, Mexico, 1925–1987. From Ward 1990, 418.

demand (see Figure 5). Moreover, even the generous funding terms were too stringent for most low-income families, so that in effect these funds financed housing acquisition for the (lower) middle classes. These were complemented in the mid-1960s by the National Housing Fund, which provided for housing production for state employees (FOVISSSTE) and for members of the armed forces (FOVIMI).

Partly in order to compensate for this imbalance toward the middle classes, and partly out of a perceived need to achieve social stability and pacification of the working classes through more aggressive social policies, President Luis Echeverría created a major new Housing Fund Institute for Workers (INFONAVIT) in 1972. Funded as it then was from a 5 percent levy on salaries from workers and employers, INFONAVIT quickly generated a major capacity to intervene in housing production for blue-collar workers. During the 1970s, 55,400 units were produced nationally through INFONAVIT, although its role gradually shifted away from construction toward financing worker-group housing proposals, and was strongly influenced by the Mexican Workers' Confederation, which had come to dominate the Board of Governors. Because unsalaried (informal-sector) workers were not included, a new program (FONHAPO) was created in 1981–1982 to assist them in meeting their housing needs, and made a major on-going contribution during the 1980s, particularly through its self-help support programs, sites-and-services, core units, and upgrading (Figure 5). Major financing was mobilized in 1985 to undertake massive post-earthquake housing reconstruction, principally in Mexico City (see Figure 5). But that aside, the public sector was meeting only 15–20 percent of total housing needs, with the private sector (here I also include the "popular" sector) producing the remainder—much of it informally (González Rubi 1984; Schteingart 1991; Ward 1990).

The national government in 1977 created SAHOP, which in 1982 became SEDUE (Secretaría de Ecología y Desarrollo Urbano), with subsecretariats for housing and ecology. In 1992 this agency became the very powerful SEDESOL (Secretaría de Desarrollo Social) and managed PRONASOL (Programa Nacional de Solidaridad), with its large budget and direct assistance to communities for food support, production, social services, and infrastructure (Dresser 1991; Rodríguez 1995, 1997). The program began operations from the President's Office in 1989 with an official budget of US$680 million, but it quickly grew to many times that size. Solidarity targeted the extremely poor, and functioned simultaneously as a safety net, a means of social incorporation, and, ostensibly, a method of continuing decentralization of government (Dresser 1991, 2–6; Rodríguez 1997). Since 1995 the program has been incorporated into a more generalized "Combat Poverty" initiative (PROGRESA) that is in the process of being decentralized to states and municipalities as part of President Zedillo's "New Federalism" project (Rodríguez 1997; Jones and Ward 1998). In the urban communities of the border, the most important program components of Solidarity were those which gave funds for basic infrastructure, schools, nutrition programs, and land title regularization.

Individual Settlement and Community Responses

Access to Land   In response to limited means of legal access to land, housing deficits, and the inability of the government to supply adequate low-cost housing, citizens have created new ways of housing themselves, invariably through illegal and unauthorized means (Gilbert and Ward 1985). Low-income citizens typically obtain land in one of two ways: illegal subdivision of private or *ejidal* land, and through invasion (of public, private, or communal land). The uncertain status of land tenure at the outset, the illegal method of plat development, and the total lack of services mean that the land is acquired relatively cheaply at prices that many low-income households can afford.

The nature of illegality in subdivisions has several sources. The land may not be legally owned by the seller. There may then be no clear title to transfer to the purchaser, who at some point in the future may complicate the "ownership" sequence by selling the land to another (Friedman et al. 1988, 198). Settlement on certain land may be illegal because it is deemed unfit for habitation (in a floodplain, on a steep slope, etc.). Land set aside for open space, future economic development, or public works is also likely to carry restrictions upon its residential development. Subdivisions may be illegal by virtue of the lack of infrastructure and services and the fact that they do not conform to codes set under the laws outlined above. Most countries, including Mexico, restrict land development to areas which either already have services, or to which services may be delivered. Unserviced land, therefore, is much cheaper because it is not designated for development and is affordable to the poor. The incentives for land developers to promote illegal subdivisions stem from the profitability of the process, particularly given their minimal up-front development costs. Sometimes, too, they are frustrated by planning laws which prevent the development of the lands they hold, so they proceed illegally.

Low-income households may also gain access to land through invasion. Denied access to land through the formal market, people will organize to invade a parcel of land en masse. Invaders may organize to assume control literally overnight, or residents may trickle in over a period of months, or even years, depending upon the level of resistance expected and experienced (Gilbert and Ward 1985). This method of land production has always been fraught with greater risk. Initially, these efforts were met with violence and repression, armed conflict, and the bulldozing of entire settlements (Varley 1989, 163–167). Invasions will take place on marginal lands, thereby lowering the threat of eviction. Sometimes they occur with the active collusion of politicians and political parties. However, invasions are extremely insecure, and scarce resources are consumed by bribes, by payments for

deficient or nonexistent services, and for protection money to unscrupulous leaders (Ward 1989b). For these reasons subdivisions for sale
(albeit illegal) are considered less risky than outright invasions, and
have become a much more widespread form of irregular settlement
development in Mexico.

By and large successive Mexican governments at the federal and
local (state and municipal) levels have failed to take punitive actions
against illegal land developers, be these unscrupulous subdivider/de-
velopers, or *ejidatarios* and their official or informal representatives
(Ward 1984). Rather, politicians and local authorities have turned a
blind eye to illegal land development and only intervened when it is
politically propitious—usually ex post facto, once the land occupancy
process is completed. Invasions which openly flout the law and which
may be strongly resisted by the actual landowner(s) are the exceptions
that prove the rule. In such cases, considerable political capital will be
spent by the land developer in order to persuade local politicians to
evict the squatters. Elsewhere, however, state intervention is almost
always to facilitate the subsequent regularization of the illegal development, a process which invariably requires expropriation and some
compensation to the original land developers for the "loss" of their
land—in effect making a double payment to that land developer.

Throughout Mexico there is ample evidence of *direct* complicity
between state authorities and illegal land developers in the form of
bribes and kickbacks. More often, however, the complicity is *implicit*,
since politicians know that it is not worth challenging developers and
peasant groups engaged in illegal land sales, as these are protected by
higher-level political actors who cannot readily be alienated (Gilbert
and Ward 1985; Ward 1986). The key here has been political stability,
and from the 1960s until the 1980s land and housing were a principal
mechanism for Mexican statecraft to ensure the maintenance of social
stability, and for the PRI to exercise political and electoral influence
over the urban poor (Ward 1986). In contrast to its Texas counterparts,
Mexican officialdom sought to turn the clandestine land development
process to its own political benefit. Even though officials could have
imprisoned the illegal developers they rarely did so: only when a major
urban protest movement threatened to get out of hand would state and
federal officials intervene directly and take sides against the illegal developers (Gilbert and Ward 1985). For a while one state in central
Mexico did sequestrate illegal land developments by forcing developers to foreclose for nonpayment of taxes and fees, the total amount of

which was inflated by the imposition of surcharges and fines for un-authorized development (Ward 1984). But even that policy was con-sidered experimental and somewhat controversial, taking as it did a firm and punitive stand against private developers. Moreover, inter-vention came too late since the developers had completed the settle-ment process and were looking for a way out anyway. Again, their il-legal actions were in effect condoned, although in this instance they received no compensation for the "loss" of their land. Since the mid-1980s federal and local authorities have become more assertive against illegal land developers, and the level of protection afforded by the Agrarian Reform Ministry (SRA) and the National Farmworkers' Confederation (CNC) to *ejidatario*-led illegal land development has waned markedly. Now planning institutions are beginning to exercise paramountcy, and the Reform of Article 27 makes possible the legal alienation of *ejidos* for residential and other purposes (Austin 1994; Jones and Ward 1998).

Land Regularization   If direct action against illegal developers was not considered politically acceptable, state intervention to regularize clouded land titles became the conventional wisdom for policy devel-opment, not least because it offered important opportunities for polit-ical patronage and social control of the poor. All of these illegal means of land acquisition have been supported by policies of ex post facto regularization: the changing of land status from irregular (de facto) to regular (de jure). Public policy has shifted over the past three decades from one of antipathy for illegal settlements to one of grudging accep-tance and even support, such that regularization has become an ac-cepted policy response. The Mexican government in 1973 established CoRett (Commission for the Regularization of Land Tenure), which regularizes settlements on *ejidal* land. The Solidarity program also ar-ranged land regularization on a large scale (SEDESOL 1994). Mexico has been in the vanguard of developing ex post facto responses to illegal land development (Durand Lasserve and Pajoni 1992; UNCHS 1996).

In Mexico, land and housing production have been part and parcel of the political process (Ward 1986). The history of Mexico, with its emphasis on the peasants' right to land, has influenced the govern-ment's response to low-income groups' efforts to acquire land and housing. Moreover, until the late 1980s, the corporatist organizations such as the CNOP and the CNC within the governing party (PRI) had considerable influence over local government responses. However, political opening and the rise of opposition governments in Mexico (particularly in the border region), in combination with the trend to make land and housing development less partisan, have had an important impact in modernizing and raising the effectiveness of local administration responses (Rodríguez and Ward 1994, 1995, 1996). Increasingly, too, intergovernmental relations are being forged between different parties at different levels. For example, from 1992 to 1998 the PAN held control of the municipal administration in Ciudad Juárez as well as the state of Chihuahua, but both city and state must coordinate with the PRI federal government. In part this helps explain why Solidarity, a federal program, tended to be much more visible and active in the cities of Matamoros and Nuevo Laredo, since both remained under the control of the PRI.

BORDER CASE STUDIES

Land Development   Colonias in Mexico are generated through all of the three methods described above, but the prevailing mode of land production differs among the three border cities studied (see Table 11). In Nuevo Laredo, of the 71 new colonias which were formed during the 1980s (a period of economic crisis), 60 formed as illegal subdivisions, often on *ejidal* land, while 11 were invasions. In Ciudad Juárez, where the land market is even tighter, 40 percent of families have irregular tenure, and almost all low-income settlements are formed either by invasion of private land (Colonias Felipe Angeles and Puerto la Paz), or through the illegal sale by landowners and/or developers (Mariano Escobedo, Table 11). In Ciudad Juárez there are very limited amounts of *ejidal* land or territorial reserves, although this was an option in the agricultural area of Zaragoza (in the southeast of the municipality), and led to the state-sponsored sites-and-services scheme of Tierra Nueva. In Matamoros, as Table 11 demonstrates, the primary mode of land production is the conversion of largely unproductive *ejidal* land, although invasions and subdivisions are also a feature.

Along the Mexican side of the border, developers are typically local landowners frustrated in developing their land by a lack of capital or by government development controls. Alternatively, they may even comprise the local community leadership, which cuts an informal deal with the landowner to occupy the lands. These leaders often receive payments from residents, but typically live in the colonias, and often

Table 11. Methods of Land Development and Lot Acquisition in Mexico

City	Ciudad Juárez					Matamoros			Nuevo Laredo		
Colonia	Felipe Angeles	Tierra Nueva	Puerto La Paz	Mariano Escobedo	Sección 16	Solidaridad	Voluntad y Trabajo	Nueva Era	Cavazos Lerma	Enrique Cárdenas	Voluntad y Trabajo
Original land ownership:											
Private	X		X	X	X					X	
Public		X[1]				X					
Community (*ejidal*)							X	X	X		X
Developer:											
Real-estate developer										X	
Community							X				
Popular leader/org.	X		X	X	X	X			X		X
Politician								X			
Government		X[2]									
Acquisition Method:											
Owner sells	X		X	X			X	X	X	X	X
Invasion	X		X	X	X[4]	X		X		X	
Developer sells		X[3]									
Other "purchase"											
Cost	"Fees"	$1,200	"Fees"	"Fees"					$120	"Fees"	

Source: Settlement surveys. Typology taken from Gilbert and Ward 1985.
[1] Private land purchased by the municipality for the subdivision.
[2] The developer is the municipality of Ciudad Juárez.
[3] The municipality provides low-interest loans to families in order to pur-

to US$1,200. Payments were NP$125 pesos per month for the land over four years, and a materials credit of NP$6,400 pesos was payable in thirty installments at a 3 percent interest rate.
[4] The land was purchased by the CTM Sindicato and then subdivided for its

continue to be the popular leaders. One study of colonias in Ciudad Juárez found that at least 25 percent of the residents paid a fee to leaders (Holguín 1994, 7). In the case of *ejidal* lands, the *ejidatarios* may serve as developers themselves. In all of these cases, however, because services are not provided as part of the subdivision and do not impose any up-front costs, the profits can be very considerable for developers. In Ciudad Juárez, one woman earned her living leading invasions, and is said to have organized over 16 colonias. Also in that city the radical Popular Defense Committee (CDP) is represented in some 30 colonias, in which it had a hand in organizing the original invasion (Staudt 1998, 119). In Nuevo Laredo, a Sr. Eugenio Bernal has purchased large parcels of land and subdivided them as colonias.

In Mexico, as already observed, illegally settled land is regularized after a period of time, although the speed with which this occurs depends on myriad factors, including the political party in power, the political affiliation of the colonia, funding, and the degree of social mobilization among colonia residents. The actual manner of regularization also varies by city. In Matamoros, regularization has typically involved the landowner(s), the purchasers, and CoRett (which has aegis over *ejidos*). The regularization process in Ciudad Juárez is encumbered by the need to deal with many individual owners, and the city has its own regularization program which facilitates agreements between invaders/residents and the legal owners. In Juárez, the program managed by the municipality allowed 14,572 families to regularize their lots during 1994, and 42 percent of the land was formerly privately owned (Ayuntamiento de Ciudad Juárez 1994).

The Solidarity program produced changes in land development, servicing, and housing construction practices in many cities. In Matamoros, Solidarity and CoRett developed clearer and more simplified procedures for land regularization, including surveying, platting, and servicing. The percentages of costs to be paid by residents were clearly outlined, and the colonias hired their own contractors for much of the work, managing the process themselves. In the state of Chihuahua, a separate program designed to reduce invasions has begun to focus upon the creation of land reserves to be used for low-income housing (as was the case in Tierra Nueva colonia). In the late 1990s the principal federal housing and urban development agency (SEDESOL) is seeking to strengthen state and municipal administration to expedite the regularization process as well as to promote land reserve development that will cut through the vicious circle of illegal land development–expropriation–regularization (SEDESOL 1996; Jones and Ward 1998).

Housing Production   Once land is obtained, a temporary or provisional dwelling unit is constructed, typically by the new lot owner and his family. Once the household is confident that they are not likely to be evicted by the local authorities, they begin to consolidate a permanent dwelling through self-help, although hired labor may be used, especially for more technical aspects such as concrete roof construction and service connections. Technical advice and instructions can also be obtained from friends, neighbors, and family members. The modal size of house plots varies between 150 and 400 m² (10 × 15, 10 × 20, 15 × 20, or 20 × 20), but unlike their Texas counterparts, it is relatively rare for Mexican dwellings to be set back from the front of the lot, particularly once the consolidation process gets underway. A *barda*, or wall, forms a continuous street frontage on Mexican plots, with the patio located at the rear (Photo 22). This is in part an outcome of tradition (in Mexico patios and yards are interior rather than at both the front and back, as in the United States), but it also results from the greater insecurity of the land capture process: Mexican residents are not concerned about (later) conforming to setback codes, but they are anxious to define their plot boundaries and to avoid any possible encroachment by other families. (Additionally, in Texas buildings are governed by codes which mandate setbacks from the road and prohibit construction on the property line.) The construction of a house commonly begins before services are delivered, but consolidation may be influenced (accelerated) by the provision of services, since this implies that the government plans to regularize land tenure (Varley 1987). Almost all housing in the low-income colonias studied along the border is self-built. One study of several colonias in Ciudad Juárez found that greater than 95 percent relied on self-help construction (Holguín 1994). Collaboration among colonia residents is generally limited to common needs, such as the acquisition of services, the paving of roads, or the construction/improvement of common facilities, such as schools. At the household level, however, each family takes individual responsibility.

Initial living quarters are often a simple one- or two-room structure constructed of recycled throwaways or temporary construction materials such as *lamina de cartón*, etc. *Maquiladoras* provide the cast-off wooden pallets, for example, which can be seen everywhere in

22. *Colonia Paso del Norte, Ciudad Juárez, looking north toward the El Paso downtown. Note the continuous street frontage and mostly interior (rear) yards (see also Photo 6).*

Ciudad Juárez. The boundaries of the plot are clearly defined, and a simple pit latrine is dug. The preferred materials for later dwelling consolidation are concrete block and cement, with a cement foundation (mixed manually on site). For those who cannot afford a concrete roof, corrugated iron or tar paper is used, and increasingly in cities like Ciudad Juárez households appear to be using green-colored roofing felt—good for five to ten years. These construction materials are purchased from stores often located along major roads outside (but nearby) the colonias themselves, or actually in the settlements, where they have a ready market, and benefit as well from the "windfall" gains that accrue to the lot's value as consolidation and integration take place (see Photos 23 and 24).

Consolidation occurs over time according to priorities set by the home owners/builders. The speed of consolidation depends upon many factors, including security of tenure, average income levels, and the provision of services (Ward 1982b). Similar to findings reported elsewhere in the survey cities, the level of home improvement appears to be only loosely correlated with the age of the colonia, and reflects,

23. Construction materials yard at the entrance of Colonia Solidaridad, Matamoros.

24. Construction materials yard at the entrance of Colonia Río Bravo, Webb County.

rather, the household's priorities and resources. It is apparent that both the economic crisis of the 1980s and that of 1994–1996 have taken their toll on the consolidation process. Although local government intervention in colonias has quickened in Mexico in recent years, the residents' capacity to upgrade and maintain their dwellings in a good state of repair appears to have suffered. The rate of home improvement appears to have slowed, and dwellings look rather more dilapidated than they did in the past, when the economy was expanding.

The extent to which housing is regulated by codes differs among the three cities. Housing in Mexico is supposed to meet federal and state standards in order to receive services, but these are inconsistently applied in practice. In Matamoros, for example, the Office of Public Works is expected to review and approve individual house plans, but has generally confined itself to approving the colonia as a unit. In Ciudad Juárez, the municipal government assumes that services will be provided, and in practice factors far removed from building standards govern decision making.

Total costs incurred in self-help housing depend upon the means of land acquisition, the amount paid to the owners and to government officials, and the fees collected by the developers. In Matamoros, the cost of a platted lot of 200–300 m² (2,150–3,228 ft²) ranged between 3,000 and 7,000 new pesos (US$850–2,000).[2] Of course, this did not include the cost of services. The costs of building a minimal dwelling unit would start at around a further 3,000 new pesos and increase depending upon the design of the unit itself. With the exception of FONHAPO-supported housing schemes, self-helpers do not commonly follow a prototype "model" dwelling plan. Instead, they decide the priorities themselves and develop their dwellings gradually.

Financing comes from a variety of sources, and varies between cities (Ward et al. 1993). Bank loans or mortgages are virtually unknown for self-help home consolidation, and personal financing makes up the principal source. Government programs can provide financing mechanisms in the form of allowing residents to pay for land over a period of years (typically three) at a low interest rate. Ciudad Juárez has municipal programs which give credits for building materials distributed by city-run centers. In Matamoros, federal agencies are lenient toward late-paying residents, but can in theory foreclose on their homes. For many projects, including Solidarity, residents had to (but no longer must) raise a portion of the funds themselves.

Turnover among colonia residents seems to be low. Among those questioned in Ciudad Juárez, for instance, it was typical for a resident to have lived in the same colonia since its founding (see also Varley 1987). Lots, which typically range between 200 and 400 m² (2,150–4,350 ft²), are sufficiently large to allow expansion, and increasingly to allow for on-site subdivision of living space (Gilbert and Varley 1991;

Lomnitz 1977). These may be for rent, but more usually they comprise two or three (close) kin-related families living separately as individual units but sharing many of the advantages of an extended household (cost sharing, mutual childcare, etc.). Typically married sons and daughters may set up in the lot with their parents/in-laws; alternatively, a sibling might move in, especially if the owner had been deserted by her husband (Chant 1984, 1996). The use of dwelling space to enhance economic survival strategies for the urban poor is important in Mexico and elsewhere (Chant 1996; Moser 1996). Land and housing investment in Mexico, as in other countries, serves as a form of savings, and has a meaning which goes far beyond its physical attributes (Stickel 1990).

The political context in which development occurs is particularly important in Mexico, although Mexican colonias do not share the jurisdictional conflicts faced by Texas colonias (see following chapters). In Mexico, government officials often encourage or even sanction irregular settlements and invasions as a means of relieving bottlenecks associated with the high demand for housing and with the prospect of garnering votes. Obtaining services often depends upon a colonia's party affiliation or the political ties of the colonia's popular leaders. This was particularly true in the past when housing and infrastructure were much more closely intertwined with government patronage, vote-getting, and partisanship in general.

To sum up, land and housing development processes have generally been accessible to the poor in Mexico, although very low-income populations are often still excluded. In Mexico the challenge is for cities to take a more proactive stance in the area of colonia development in order to provide greater access for the very poor, and to ensure that growth occurs in a way that is more consistent with city development and planning priorities.

Texas Land and Housing Production Traditions

THE LACK OF PUBLIC HOUSING ALTERNATIVES IN THE UNITED STATES

In the United States, as in Mexico, housing supply has been led by the private sector. However, the level of government concern and formal responsibility for housing supply in the two countries differs markedly.

In Mexico, as we have observed above, there is a strong commitment to working-class housing provision in the 1917 Constitution (albeit largely rhetorical, at least until INFONAVIT was created in 1973), and in terms of housing fund provisions, normative planning, and ex post facto intervention to regularize and upgrade, Mexican governments have been highly active at all levels. In the United States, however, the picture is very different.

Federal government involvement in housing activities has been firmly supportive of home ownership for three principal reasons: (1) the nation's immigration and settlement history created fierce resistance and hostility to centralized authority; (2) the political and business coalition saw home ownership as ideologically conservatizing, buttressing principles of stability, thrift, allegiance, nationalism, and so on; (3) ownership was an incentive to fixing investment (Marcuse 1990, 337). Home ownership among whites has risen from around 45 percent in 1940 to almost 70 percent in the late 1980s (tracked to a lesser extent for black households [23 percent and 44 percent, respectively]). In suburban locations home ownership has always been considerably higher. It is also more prevalent among the better off than among low-income groups. At the lower end of the market, mobile (trailer) homes have formed an important niche in the market, rising from around 100,000 units a year in 1960 to around 250,000 in the late 1980s. Within all this, the role of the federal, state, and local governments has been relatively passive and has largely been one of offering incentives to private housing acquisition (federal level) and offering normative and regulatory supports at the state and local levels.

Perhaps the most significant federal government activity has been to pump prime home ownership through demand-type incentives, most notably tax rebates on mortgage interest payments, which evidence suggests are socially regressive, favoring as they do middle and better-off social groups relatively more than lower-income home purchasers. Generally the federal government has shied away from public supply of housing; indeed public housing is stigmatized in the United States. Public housing starts in the United States have always been very modest, and even in their heyday of the late 1960s–early 1970s, they only numbered between 50,000 and 80,000 per year, falling away to an insignificant number during the Reagan years.

The initial post–Second World War years did see a rising concern in the United States for federal government leadership in stimulating adequate housing supply for workers and for veterans, along with urban development and rehabilitation programs (especially for central city areas). The result was the Housing Act of 1949 and its 1954 iteration, which quite clearly sought to place the onus on and direct the incentives toward private-sector involvement (Cole 1979). Suburbanization during the 1950s and 1960s was reinforced by tax policies which favored home ownership, as well as by social construction of the single-family suburban property as the "ideal" home. The housing industry was dominated by progrowth coalitions, which were enhanced by the very loose land-use and zoning controls that have traditionally prevailed in U.S. cities.

Nor did civil rights unrest and inner city disturbances have a sharp effect, although they did lead to several important and quite visible programs. The 1974 Housing and Community Development Act created the Community Development Block Grant system, which provided lump-sum grants to local governments for expenditure within strictly determined federal guidelines. These favored urban areas, and poorer and older cities in particular, but were often socially regressive, as were the later Urban Development Action Grants, when their spatial impact is examined internally (Marcuse 1990, 354). The Section 8 housing program is the nearest that the United States has come to a housing allowance program, and offers a demand-side subsidy to the creation of private-sector-led housing made available at rents that are deemed affordable to poorer groups. Such housing is produced and owned by the private sector (profit and nonprofit), but is subject to limited government supervision (at most for fifteen years and later lowered to five years). Marcuse (1990, 360) estimates that since its inception, Section 8 has led to some 665,000 new or substantially rehabilitated dwelling units, while a further 1.1 million households participate in the existing part of the program that provides housing finance. This total exceeds the total number in public housing nationally, underscoring the relatively limited direct and indirect participation of the public sector in housing provision in the United States.

If the federal government has had only a limited effect in promoting the public supply of housing, state and local governments have been even more ineffectual. State government's role has been predominantly in three arenas: (1) basic legislative standards and sometimes also administrative arrangements and mechanisms for regulating building and housing practices (see below); (2) low-interest assistance to housing development initiatives, sometimes through state finance housing agencies, which can issue bonds for housing purposes; and

(3) experimental programs which have subsequently been taken up at the federal level.

Local government (city-level) actions, however, can be very influential in determining the shape and nature of housing opportunities that prevail, particularly in terms of planning, zoning, the setting of housing and land-use ordinances, as well as in the levying of property taxes—the latter being a major source of revenue for most local governments in the United States. The potential realm of local government intervention in housing is quite large: rent controls, public-private partnerships, landlord-tenant regulations, rehabilitation and urban renewal, as well as planning and zoning, etc.

This short account underscores two important features of housing activity in the United States which differ markedly from practices in Mexico. First, is the lack of a strong federal or formal public-sector role in the *supply* of housing. Second, is the much stronger *regulatory* role of state and (especially) city governments over housing activities. Both features are crucial determinants in the nature of colonia housing production in Texas, to which I now turn.

Concurrent with urban and industrial expansion in Mexico, U.S. labor policy in the 1940s and 1950s sanctioned the flow of Mexicans and other migrant workers into the United States under the Bracero Program. U.S. employers typically provided temporary housing for migrant workers, thereby subsidizing the cost of agricultural labor. As American men returned to the work force after World War II, U.S. demand for foreign agricultural labor gradually waned, and the federal government finally ended the Bracero Program (in 1964). This change in U.S. policy, however, had little impact on either Mexicans seeking employment north of the border or upon American farmers wishing to employ Mexican labor at lower wages. What did change was the practice of employers providing housing to migrant and immigrant workers.

Few Mexicans or first-generation Mexican-Americans working on the Texas border earn enough to afford housing at market rents or qualify for traditional home financing. As we observed in Chapter 1, many of these workers earn as little as between $5,000 and $10,000 a year. Subsidized housing offers little relief: public housing is extremely limited along the Texas border. In the United States, affordable housing for the very poor is a responsibility of the marketplace or the nonprofit private sector. As early as the 1960s, innovative real estate developers and landowners responded to the growing demand for very-low-income housing along the Texas-Mexico border with rural subdivisions now called colonias. As we have observed, in Texas, unlike Mexico, there is no tradition of public sector–initiated housing programs, not even in the border area, where federal (HUD) programs have been few and far between (see below and Chapter 3).

INDIVIDUAL AND COMMUNITY RESPONSES

Developers responded to the low-income housing deficit on the border, capitalizing on four factors: consumer demand; a supply of idle agricultural land; absent or lax land development regulation; and a legal mechanism for land sales called Contract for Deed. The confluence of these factors made the situation ripe for colonia development. A principal difference with Mexico is that these methods of land development are usually *legal*.

Texas law requires developers to provide paved roads, curbs, drainage, and hookups for water, sewer, and utility service when subdividing land for residential purposes *within* city limits. These requirements, while beneficial to public health and safety, have the effect of excluding low-income people from the urban housing market. Because state law, until 1989, had few provisions concerning the subdivision or development of rural land in surrounding county jurisdictions, developers were able to acquire and subdivide agricultural land close to border cities, and to offer for sale unimproved lots at costs that very-low-income people could afford. This situation continued more or less uninterrupted until 1989, when the Model Subdivision Rules began to be more strictly enforced, and after 1995, when Senate Bill 336 introduced a series of provisions that made Contract for Deed less exploitative of purchasers. Also in 1995, a second bill (House Bill 1001) required that basic services be installed on all newly sold colonia land in a number of "affected counties" within fifty miles of the international border (Jensen 1996). These initiatives are discussed below; suffice it to note at this stage that it is expected that the two bills combined will have done much to curtail land sales in colonias since July 7, 1995, but they do not apply statewide. Colonias in Houston and other cities, for example, are not affected. Nor are all colonias in the border region covered by HB 1001.

In some cases farmers or other original owners developed the land themselves. In either case, low-income people who were willing to sacrifice having potable water, sewers, and utility services (at least temporarily) could purchase lots and erect homes in these rural subdivisions for a fraction of the cost of housing in the city. This market response to the lack of low-income housing on the border benefited original landowners, real estate developers, and residential purchasers, each for their own reasons. For farmers or other original owners the growing demand for rural housing meant high prices for agricultural land. In order to persuade farmers to sell, developers could offer double the going rate or asking price and make significant down payments toward the purchase of the land, and then in effect it was the original owners who were self-financing the sale. Developers typically subdivided tracts into half- and quarter-acre parcels and sold off unimproved lots to residential purchasers under the Contract for Deed arrangement. For purchasers, while it was far from perfect as a form of land title and lot acquisition, especially prior to the introduction of some regulation in 1995, the Contract for Deed process and the lack of improvements to the land did enable very-low-income people in Texas to acquire residential plots on which to build homes.

Contract for Deed: Before and after Senate Bill 336 The Contract for Deed arrangement was the key to land development in colonias. Indeed, Contract for Deed is widespread throughout rural and peri-urban areas in the state, as well as nationally (Mettling 1982; Jensen 1996, 106). It originated as a mechanism whereby farmhands could acquire lands without having equity or finance: in short, a poor man's mortgage. However, it is problematic, since the seller is heavily favored, while the purchaser is vulnerable to forfeiture. Over the years, nationally, some commonly known purchaser protection mechanisms have evolved, including: *Notice Requirements*, to ensure procedural fairness in forfeiture processes (guaranteed time elapse, etc.); *Waiver*, in which sellers waive their right to declare forfeiture for whatever reason; *Opportunity to Cure*, which offers a statutory right to allow delinquent purchasers to reinstate their Contract for Deed by making up back payments; *Right of Redemption*, which is analogous to mortgages in that it gives people a grace period to pay off the contract and cure their breach (but the purchaser must pay the full contract price); *Restitution*, which reduces the harshness of forfeiture without denying the seller an opportunity to recover the land, but provides for some equity in the recovery process rather than the purchaser losing all; *Conversion* (to mortgage equivalent), which occurs when some thresholds of payments on a Contract for Deed have been completed; and, finally, *Functional*

Equivalence Doctrine, which assumes that the Contract for Deed is, in effect, a mortgage and is considered such from the outset (i.e., not a conversion along the way). Kentucky, Oklahoma, and Maryland have adopted the latter. The point here is that different states have evolved various levels of purchaser protection within the Contract for Deed.

Until 1995, however, Texas offered virtually no protection whatsoever, and property titles were only conveyed to the purchaser after the entire purchase price had been paid. The purchase price would be paid in installments over a number of years, and the seller retained the legal title to the property until the purchaser had paid in full. In effect, until 1995 a buyer under Contract for Deed had no equity protection. Contract for Deed almost always contained forfeiture clauses which allowed the seller, after a default by the purchaser, to recover possession of the property along with any improvements that had been made, as well as to retain all previously paid installments. Provided the seller was willing to finance the transaction, the Contract for Deed presented a relatively simple one-step process in which transaction costs could be kept to a minimum. Contract for Deed was particularly popular in sales where little or no down payment was made by the purchaser. Sellers were attracted to the forfeiture remedy, seeing it as a way to get property back without having to go through foreclosure. And because generally no third party was involved (such as a bank or title company), and because Contract for Deed purchasers were frequently unfamiliar with Texas law and/or unable to read English, the situation was always ripe for abuse.

This situation changed statewide with Senate Bill 336, which, since 1995, has required greater disclosure information on Contracts for Deed, annual accounting, and restrictions in the recession and foreclosure clauses. As well as these new requirements on disclosure, all transactional documents must be written in English and Spanish. Most important of all is the adoption of the conversion principle: once 40 percent of the purchase price or forty-eight monthly installments have been paid, then forced forfeiture is no longer an option—the heart of Contract for Deed from the developers' perspective. Rather, the Contract for Deed becomes the functional equivalent of a mortgage, and any forfeiture must be undertaken under mortgage law. A major plus for SB 336 is that it applies retroactively, and many existing contracts have fulfilled the 40-percent/forty-eight-monthly-payment threshold. So any forfeiture must take place under the new rules. On the debit side, however, is the fact that these new provisions do not apply uniformly throughout the state, but only enter into full effect within two hundred miles of the border. Although during the Senate hearings there was a call to outlaw Contract for Deed altogether throughout the state, there was strong resistance, it being argued that this would, in effect, make land acquisition virtually impossible for the very poor. Nevertheless, it seems likely that, in the not too distant future, the provisions of SB 336 will be extended statewide (Jensen 1996, 107), although this was not on the agenda of the 1997 legislative session.

In some respects, though, the benefits of Contract for Deed reforms were overtaken by HB 1001 (1995), which now requires that all developers in "certain counties" get county approval of subdivision plats and provide water, sewage, and drainage services. The bill aimed at stopping the proliferation of new colonias. Although it only applies to new subdivisions, it also embraced those unsold lots in existing colonias, as well as any that had been repossessed under Contract for Deed. Thus, if fully implemented, HB 1001 much more than SB 336 will kill further colonia development. However, the principal weakness is that it, too, applies only in designated counties, namely those within fifty miles of the border and which *also* have prevailing socioeconomic conditions that qualify them for the Economically Distressed Areas Program (EDAP). Of the 107 counties in Texas which met the geographical criterion, only 22 also qualified for EDAP assistance, a qualification which was (then) reviewed and renewed annually.[3] A further weakness is that these regulations do not apply to existing ("grandfathered") colonias.

Thus three tiers or levels of tenure under Contract for Deed exist in Texas currently. First, in 22 counties, full regulation of Contract for Deed under the conversion to mortgage principle, but in circumstances where colonia lots are no longer likely to be made available because of the HB 1001 requirements that all lots must be fully serviced before they may be sold and that a subdivision plat should have been prepared. Second, in a further 85 counties (non-EDAP-designated counties, but those within two hundred miles of the frontier), Contract for Deed exists under the conversion to mortgage protection principle. Third, the rest of Texas, where most of the original operating principles of Contract for Deed still apply. It will be interesting to observe the relative effects SB 336 and HB 1001 have upon future development of colonias and lot sales. The possibility clearly exists for colonia developers to slip out of range of EDAP counties where HB 1001 applies, but remain under the aegis of SB 336; or to move out of the two-hundred-mile limit altogether, and focus their activities on colonia developments elsewhere in the state.

Border Case Studies

Land Development   Reference to Table 12 suggests that there is far greater uniformity in the methods that lead from land development to colonia formation in Texas than is the case in Mexico. In Texas the original land ownership is almost always privately held, while developers are the principal agents within the platting and lot sale process, usually under the aforementioned Contract for Deed. Variations on this theme exist (see Montana Vista and Sunny Skies), but they are relatively rare. The generic rules for developing a colonia in Texas were spelled out by Webb County developer Cecil McDonald and are included as an epigraph to this book.

The case of Sunny Skies, in Cameron County, also provides an example of how Contract for Deed facilitates colonia development. The original owners, Roman and Anna Smigiel, acquired the land in 1969, and sold it in four different tracts in 1980. In June 1980, Pete Gonzales, president of World Investments, Inc., purchased two of the tracts (16.664 acres) from the Smigiels under a Deed of Trust for $39,800. Although the land was encumbered by the Smigiels' lien, Gonzales subdivided the land and sold quarter- and half-acre lots to resident purchasers under Contract for Deed. In 1986, Emma and Gumercindo Villarreal, Gonzales' first purchasers, agreed to pay $9,500 for a 0.286-acre lot (= approximately 12,500 ft^2). By Contract for Deed standards the Villarreals made an extraordinarily high down payment of $1,000 in cash, and committed to pay the $8,500 balance in 119 consecutive monthly payments of $112.00 plus a final payment of $152.80. The payments included interest at an annual rate of 10 percent. The total price of the 50 × 250–foot lot was $14,480, not including any property tax assessments, which the Villarreals were also required to pay. In the event of delinquent payments, the contract allowed the Villarreals sixty days to cure the default, after which time the seller was entitled to immediate possession of the premises, any improvements on the land, and all property belonging to the buyers.

Table 12. Methods of Land Development and Lot Acquisition in Texas

City	El Paso		Laredo		Brownsville	
Colonia	Sparks	Montana Vista[1]	El Cenizo	Colonias Olvidadas Hwy. 359	Sunny Skies	Cameron Park
Original land ownership Private	X	X	X	X	X[2]	X
Public						
Community (*ejidal*)						
Developer Real-estate developer	X	X	X[3]	X	X[4]	X
Community						
Popular leader/org.		X[5]				
Politician						
Government						
Method of acquisition Owner divides & sells					X[6]	
Invasion						
Developer sells	X[7]	X[8]	X[9]	X[10]		X
Other "purchase"						
Cost					$8,500	

Source: Settlement surveys. Typology taken from Gilbert and Ward 1985.

Montana Vista includes approximately 22 subdivisions. Our study focused on those subdivisions in the Homestead Municipal Utility District (see Chapter 1).

Land originally owned by individuals living out of state.

Cecil McDonald was the developer.

Purchased from original owners by Pete Gonzales of World Investments, Inc.

One prominent developer was also an important community leader.

Gonzales subdivided "El Jardín" Tracts I and II into 35 quarter- to half-acre lots to create the colonia.

Usually through unfiled Contract for Deed.

Usually through unfiled Contract for Deed.

Usually through unfiled Contract for Deed.

Usually through unfiled Contract for Deed.

Under these circumstances the incentive for developers to acquire, subdivide, and sell rural land under Contract for Deed is clear. Ignoring for a moment the 10 percent interest, at $9,500 per quarter-acre, Gonzales' unimproved lots totaling 16.664 acres were worth an estimated $633,000.

From 1986 to 1988, Gonzales sold 35 lots to at least 26 households. Gonzales promised that water would be piped into the colonia within a few months, and that residents would be able to obtain electricity hookups. Gonzales never provided the water, and a resident, Miguel Torres, helped place a two-inch pipeline down the main road of the colonia with connections on either side. River water was pumped in for a few months until Gonzales found out that no one was paying for the (untreated) water and cut it off. Eventually, a faucet was tapped into a mains pipeline, and residents began to draw their water from it daily. The bill came to the family that lived next to the faucet and was divided evenly among the residents. Until very recently homes at Sunny Skies had no wastewater service. During the months that water was being pumped in, a few people set up septic tanks, although they could not get permits from the county. Most residents used outhouses. Many had electric meters and direct supply, while others jacked lines from neighbors. The main road remained unpaved, although this scenario has since changed dramatically (see Chapter 1).

Some people who originally bought from Gonzales have since moved away because of the lack of amenities, in some cases selling the land to family or friends. Several squatters have lived toward the back of the colonia—some for two years, others for six months—on land that others bought but had abandoned. In several cases, lots have changed hands two or three times. Unfortunately, we have no record of how many times Gonzales repossessed land from buyers who were late in making payments. Indeed, this leads to relatively low densities in many Texas colonias. Although an extreme case, Figure 6, for the colonia of Del Mar Heights, shows dramatically the extent to which occupancy may be very thinly spread throughout the colonia, with less than 10 percent of the 1,700 lots occupied (LBJ 1997, 2:50). But elsewhere, colonias with between one-third and two-thirds of lots occupied are not uncommon. Unlike their Mexican counterparts, relatively few large Texas colonias are built through. The issue of low population densities and absentee lot ownership is an important one in Texas, to which I shall return in detail below and in later chapters.

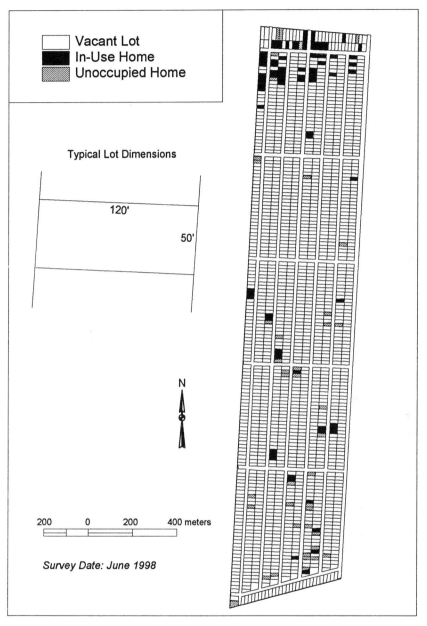

Legend:
- ☐ Vacant Lot
- ■ In-Use Home
- ▨ Unoccupied Home

Typical Lot Dimensions

120'

50'

N

200   0   200   400 meters

Survey Date: June 1998

Figure 6. Typical colonia plat map and occupancy: Del Mar Heights, Cameron County.

LEGAL AND REGULATORY RESPONSES IN TEXAS

In the 1960s and 1970s, colonias were few and relatively distant from cities. This meant that cities were able to ignore what were perceived to be rural self-built housing developments and subdivisions. Out of sight was out of mind. But in the 1980s, colonia development mushroomed and began to encroach on urban areas. Sometimes, too, cities' outward expansion meant that they began to encroach upon what had formerly been distant colonias. Whichever, border cities sought to place responsibility for colonia problems upon counties whenever possible. Brownsville, for example, deliberately drew its city limits to avoid annexation of Cameron Park. However, because counties both lacked the legal authority necessary to prevent colonia development and rarely enforced the limited land development regulations available to them, further colonia growth was inevitable. Ultimately, health problems bred by unsanitary living conditions in the colonias threatened to spread to non-colonia populations; probably more than any other factor, this prompted a more concerted legal and regulatory response by state and federal governments.

While the federal and state governments' first response was to blame colonia developers, it was apparent that local authorities (cities and counties) were themselves also to blame for not having prevented colonia development. Given that it was primarily environmental and health problems that spurred government action in the first place, state and federal responses have focused upon water and wastewater service provision and financial aid. Only latterly has a second focus emerged: to increase land development regulation and enforcement, and to undertake litigation to recover from developers the costs of installing water services. On the whole, funding and regulation have been the primary tools that the federal, state, and local governments have used to address colonia problems.

At the federal level major appropriations have been provided for water and wastewater projects through the Environmental Protection Agency (EPA), the former Farmers' Home Administration (FmHA, now the Rural Economic and Community Development Agency [RECDA]), and the U.S. Department of Housing and Urban Development (HUD). Through Section 306c, the FmHA contributed grants to individuals for the construction of bathrooms that met state minimum requirements in an effort to increase the number of colonia households connected to approved water and waste services. The

Cranston-Gonzalez National Affordable Housing Act of 1990, passed by the U.S. Congress, stipulated that 10 percent of all HUD Community Development Block Grants (CDBG) to states bordering Mexico must go to colonia projects. Although available for improvements in housing, CDBG money has been used almost exclusively for water and wastewater service provision.

Perhaps the most important role that the federal government has played is in pressuring state and local governments to take action. The message sent to Texas from D.C. was that Congress was reluctant to appropriate money for colonias without some reassurance that steps were being taken locally to prevent more unregulated developments: hence the legislation enacted by the state in 1989. In the late 1980s, as colonias were becoming more and more noticeable along the Texas border, governments at all levels were called upon to take steps to prevent further colonia growth. Different state agencies answered this call by designating special offices to deal with the colonia issues. Governor Richards' office created the Governor's Border Working Group (GBWG) to bring together all state government actors to discuss problems along the border, including colonias.

Significantly, while the early discussions about colonias noted the various aspects leading to substandard development, the most prominent definition of a colonia came to be an area in which water supply or sewer services are inadequate to meet minimal needs of residential users, and in which resources are insufficient to meet those needs.[4] On the basis of this definition, the state began to develop programs that would help distribute funds to ameliorate these substandard conditions. For example, the Texas Department of Housing and Community Affairs (TDHCA) established programs to fund colonia projects specifically (largely through federal Community Development Block Grant [CDBG] appropriations). Again, while some TDHCA funding is used for housing, public facilities, and economic development, most of the money has been used for the prioritized water and wastewater projects. This fixing of the definition of what constitutes a colonia to the absence of adequate water and wastewater services is highly illustrative of how the problem is conceived in Texas. First, it underscores that the "problem" is constructed exclusively in terms of infrastructure, rather than according to social, cultural, or income criteria—points to which I shall return later in this book. Second, it erroneously suggests that once services are installed, the neighborhood is no longer a colonia. As one elected state representative put it to me at a public committee hearing in April 1998, ". . . if services were present then it wouldn't be a colonia!" My point (and my reply) was that, on the contrary, it would continue to be a colonia by virtue of the housing production processes and the patterns of social and cultural organization embedded within these self-help settlements.

EDAP and Model Subdivision Rules   The earliest state action that had the strongest impact on the development of colonias is Texas Senate Bill 2 (SB 2), passed in 1989. The legislature intended to prevent the future development of settlements without appropriate infrastructure. SB 2 had two major components: one programmatic and the other regulatory. The first established the Economically Distressed Areas Program (EDAP), to be run by the Texas Water Development Board (TWDB). Through the EDAP program, counties along the border that meet certain requirements can access state and federal (EPA) funds through the TWDB, and these funds can be used to finance water and wastewater projects in colonias that existed prior to June 1989. County eligibility is tied to the second major component of the bill, or the Model Subdivision Rules (MSRs). The MSRs essentially regulate residential subdivision development, and counties must adopt and enforce MSRs in order to access EDAP money.

The MSRs require that land subdivided into tracts of five acres or less must provide adequate water and sewer infrastructure (in the original bill, the MSRs only applied to land that was subdivided into one acre or less, but this was modified in 1991 by HB 1189). To ensure that the conditions pertaining to MSRs are applied, the county engineer and the county commissioners court are required to approve subdivision development plats and record those plats with the county clerk. Without a certificate to verify that the plat has been approved and recorded, utility companies are prohibited from providing services to residents of the development. Plat approval is contingent on the developer's presentation of a plan for water and sewer service provision and appropriate setbacks. In addition to an engineer's certification that the infrastructure meets minimum state health and safety standards, a plat must also be signed by various county and sometimes city officials verifying that all relevant ordinances have been met. Other pertinent regulations within the MSRs include a restriction of one single-family dwelling per plot, and a prohibition on county commissioners with a vested interest in a development voting on plat approval. The rules applied to any land sold *after* county adoption of the MSRs and any land that was sold before but replatted after MSRs adoption.

In theory, the MSRs should have allowed counties to stop developers from unscrupulously selling land to unsuspecting buyers without the appropriate infrastructure. However, while SB 2 provided some enforcement mechanisms, it did not provide the full range of enforcement authority necessary. This issue was partially addressed in 1993 with Texas House Bill 2079, which enabled local governments to ask the attorney general's office to get involved, and to develop a database that would facilitate their enforcement activities.

Targeting the Developers Because counties have very limited resources with which to pursue developers who fail to comply with the MSRs, the Office of the Attorney General of Texas (AG) stepped up its involvement in colonia litigation. In September 1993, Texas Attorney General Dan Morales created the Colonias Strike Force with the purpose of slowing colonia growth and improving conditions for colonia residents. The primary targets of the Strike Force quickly became the developers themselves, and some 13 Starr County colonias were sequestered in 1995 on behalf of a speedily created nonprofit organization intent upon providing utilities to the colonias for $21.6 million (Davies 1995, 38). The Strike Force was actually composed of only two lawyers, but lawyers in the Consumer Protection and Natural Resources Divisions, as well as lawyers in regional offices, also contributed to the effort. The Strike Force received an EPA grant to hire a third lawyer in the Harlingen office to work strictly on colonia issues. At that time these lawyers prosecuted mainly under the Water Code, the Health and Safety Code, and the Deceptive Trade Practices Act (DTPA).

The DTPA was the primary litigation tool, and it was used in cases where residents had been promised infrastructure services but developers had never fulfilled their obligations. Most of the suits were civil lawsuits, though a few were criminal. In the final analysis the amounts of money that have been won were minimal; however, the AG's office hoped that the time and expense of dealing with a lawsuit would in the future dissuade developers from selling land without adequate infrastructure. Even out-of-court settlements were seen as victories because they often involved the installation of services and improved conditions for colonia residents.

One of the most notorious cases brought by the AG was against

Cecil McDonald, who as already noted had developed some of the largest colonias in Webb County, including El Cenizo (one of the study settlements). The AG filed suit against McDonald, claiming that the developer deceived residents because services had not been provided. The DTPA was invoked because the land was developed before the MSRs, and therefore was not covered by SB 2. McDonald declared bankruptcy in order to derail the suit. While the suit did not result in service provision, colonia residents gained valuable information about the land development and sale process, and the state renegotiated the residents' Contracts for Deed into Deeds of Trust, to be repaid into a state fund to finance service provision. In El Paso County, the AG sued the Homestead Municipal Utility District and imposed a moratorium on all water hookups in 1992 (see Photo 25).

Contract for Deed was another issue of colonia development that has only recently begun to be addressed (from 1995 onward, see earlier discussion). Community groups such as the Border Low Income Housing Coalition had stressed the importance of Contract for Deed reform. For its part, TDHCA started to investigate refinancing Contracts for Deed into Deeds of Trust. But as we have seen, the biggest push came during the 1995 legislative session with a bill that provided basic consumer protections to Contract for Deed purchasers and reforms that required disclosure in Contracts for Deed of utility services available regardless of whether the land was located in a floodplain, or even if the property was encumbered by a lien. Most importantly, the legislation (the Fair Land Sales Act) required the recording of Contracts for Deed, and turned the Contract for Deed into an effective mortgage once 40 percent of the total land price had been paid (Jensen 1996).

Housing Construction and Building Codes   Like their Mexican counterparts, Texas colonias also display a great variety of house types and levels of consolidation. Nevertheless there is somewhat greater uniformity, given that many households start with a trailer home and extend from that. The quality and size of trailers vary enormously, however, as does the middle- to long-term goal of families to replace the trailer with a consolidated home (Photo 26). Shacks and shanties are far less common at the outset, though sometimes these will exist as lean-tos alongside the trailer. Even loosely defined, self-help consolidation is less ubiquitous. Many dwellings do appear to be following

25. Montana Vista (El Paso County), 1992 moratorium imposed against Homestead MUD to prevent new water hookups and to discourage new lot sales. Note signs by realtors selling lots (including Century 21).

the household-led expansion and upgrading processes, the work being undertaken on weekends and in residents' spare time. These homes are generally rather more modest (Photo 27). Equally, though, many other homes appear to be much more substantial and have clearly been constructed by a professional builder (Photo 28). Sometimes one observes a hybrid arrangement, as though the money ran out and building activity has been temporarily suspended, or held over to be completed by self-help (Photo 29). Whatever, even though the extent of direct self-build input may be less obvious than in Mexico, colonia

26. *Typical trailer and self-built consolidating home on adjacent lots in Río Bravo colonia (Webb County [Laredo]).*

housing in Texas continues to be firmly self-managed. I shall return to the issue of collaborative mutual aid at the colonia-wide level among residents in Texas in Chapter 4.

Lot plans tend to be much more open in Texas, as well as being inherently larger. Also the greater security of the land acquisition process means that it is unnecessary to clearly demarcate and protect one's lot boundaries, although many households do enclose their lots with fencing, and occasionally with walls. Dwellings—whatever form they take—are invariably set well back from the road. Trailers tend to run at right angles to the road, while permanent homes will be parallel to it with front door facing outward. Often there is a yard or garden at both the front and the back.[5] On-lot densities appear to be much lower in Texas, and clear-cut "sharing" of lots is far less visible (in large part because it is prohibited by law). Because public transportation is often nonexistent, many households will have private cars or trucks, and these will be parked on the lot itself. In Mexico car ownership is far less common, and parking is usually on the street in front of one's home, rather than secured behind the lot's walls.

With respect to housing production, however, the state has done very little. Cities have the authority to enforce building codes, but counties' power is very limited. Texas HB 1817, introduced in the 1993 session, would have given the county both zoning and building code enforcement authority, but it was defeated. Any proposals to increase counties' zoning or land-use planning powers in unincorporated areas face significant opposition. Some legislators are uneasy about empowering county commissioners, who are often perceived as corrupt. Others fear counties would not have the resources to implement additional authority. Indeed, community groups themselves oppose county enforcement of building codes in the unincorporated areas because of the nature of the self-built housing. Given the nature of incremental home building in colonias, most colonia homes cannot meet codes and would be subject to demolition. In effect, almost any regulation that deals with the housing would fall upon the shoulders of the colonia residents themselves, and efforts to address substandard

27. *Consolidating home in Río Bravo colonia showing partial (temporary) home at rear with slab prepared for the final dwelling. Note water standpipe in front of the trash box.*

28. Professionally built custom house in Montana Vista. Although the house has been occupied, the sidewall brick cladding and chimney stack have yet to be completed—"lower-middle-income self-helpers."

29. Home in Río Bravo colonia (Webb County [Laredo]) in various stages of completion. Note the frame second-floor structure and the bricks in front of the house.

housing through regulation have gone nowhere. However, there are some positive changes: in El Paso, Edinburgh, and Cameron Counties, for example, there has been some attempt to allow family partition of lots in contravention of the MSRs, which ostensibly require lots to contain a single-family residence.

At the county level, there have been some efforts to change attitudes toward colonias. All three counties included in this study, Cameron, Webb, and El Paso, adopted the MSRs with the hope of stemming future colonia growth and obtaining state and federal EDAP funds. These counties have been able to control most of the larger land developments and to ensure compliance with the MSRs, but because of insufficient staffing, smaller developments may still be produced illegally without the county's knowledge. However, there is widespread anecdotal evidence that colonias have continued to be created in Starr and Hidalgo Counties, in contravention of the MSRs legislation.[6]

Moreover, few cities have taken any steps to enforce building codes in colonias which fall within their ETJ, instead continuing to leave that responsibility to the county. In the case of El Paso and Webb Counties, this has meant that there has been no enforcement of building codes in the colonias. Cameron County has tried to take another approach since the early 1990s, when the county realized that the Public Utility Act allowed it to prevent utility hookups to residences that had not met county ordinances. The building inspector's office has taken steps to enforce plumbing, foundation, and electrical codes in the colonias, but has been hampered by limited staff and county power. Lately this has caused a serious problem, since Cameron Park received water and wastewater facilities but the county refused to give permission for individual hookups because of the substandard condition of a majority of the homes. In short, colonias found themselves in a Catch-22 situation, a point to which I return in Chapter 3. Overall, while some of the goals of the MSRs and funding programs are being met, government responses have often resulted in unintended consequences, and have never begun to address the root causes of colonias' creation in the first place: poverty.

The Weakness and Inadequacy of Legal and Regulatory Responses in Texas to Date

As outlined previously, one of the principal differences between Mexico and the United States is the way in which state and federal legislators in the latter have attempted to address the problems of colonias, focusing primarily on disaster relief, water and wastewater services, and rural land development law, instead of seeing the phenomenon as a structural problem of modes of housing production and of poverty. Moreover, because border cities have turned their backs upon the annexation of colonias into their ETJ, responsibility for colonia problems has fallen on counties' shoulders. Unlike cities, however, counties in Texas have traditionally had no planning or zoning authority, and until 1989 assumed the role of innocent bystanders to colonia development.[7] Consequently, the shift in responsibility for colonias from city to county effectively precluded the prevention of colonia development, and forced state and federal action.[8]

As stated above, Senate Bill 2 in 1989 sought to prohibit colonia development through regulation. The legislation required border counties to adopt and enforce Model Subdivision Rules (MSRs) and denied EPA funding for colonia water and wastewater service installation to any county that did not comply. In short, MSRs required developers to plat and record with the county any land subdivided for residential purposes into lots of five acres or less in unincorporated areas of the state. However, the MSRs applied only to subdivisions platted after 1989 and not to the large numbers of colonias that were already "grandfathered." In theory, because county adoption of a plat depends on the inclusion of *plans* for water and wastewater service provision, it was believed that SB 2 would prevent the proliferation of unimproved subdivisions. In practice, however, colonias continued to be developed and inhabited. Unscrupulous developers could quickly subdivide and sell unimproved lots without the county's knowledge by locating subdivisions in remote rural locations, advertising across the border or in other jurisdictions, and submitting a plat with no intention of ever installing services, as Cecil McDonald's "recipe" outlined in the epigraph. Although such subdivision is illegal, many developers have been able to escape the law, in part because counties lacked the will and necessary staff for enforcement.

The problem of new colonia development on platted subdivisions approved prior to 1989 was also addressed by SB 542 (1995), which provides counties with a mechanism to *cancel* subdivisions that are likely to be developed without infrastructure, and to apply the MSRs once replatting occurs. Naturally, adequate notice and public hearings must be provided, but this does offer an important precedent to cancel earlier approved developments. It is indicative of the tougher and more aggressive stance that is required toward developers in the future.

However, small-staffed county planning offices are hard pressed to verify on-site the compliance with all relevant regulations of even those developments for which plats have been submitted. Interviews with county planners during the study revealed that, in many cases, officials often certified compliance without physically inspecting a site. A Cameron County engineer explained that his office simply doesn't have the personnel to patrol the county, "policing" colonia development. Nevertheless, he occasionally receives calls from purchasers of lots in subdivisions that the planner's office has not approved inquiring about service provision, thereby confirming the continued development of colonias and sale of unimproved lots. Although it's not part of his job, whenever possible the engineer notifies the county attorney of violations of the law, but he has learned that the information has no bearing on the plat approval process in the county commissioners court. This is unfortunate since the county commissioners court is the county's sole source of regulatory power.

Despite counties' assumed role of innocent bystander, prior to SB 2 they were often cognizant of colonia development and rather like their Mexican counterparts turned a blind eye toward developments. Developers would sometimes seek approval for subdivision development from the commissioners court. Because developers frequently contributed to commissioners' political coffers, commissioners courts were often predisposed to approve certain land developments, particularly when county commissioners themselves were owners or investors in the developments. SB 2 attempted to remedy this problem by requiring commissioners, with a vested interest clause, to refrain from decision making related to that development. While the legislation may have curbed abuses, it has no effect on campaign finance or political loyalties, both of which almost certainly continue their impact upon land development.

The focus of SB 2 on water and wastewater services has also proved to be off the mark. No one denies that the health and safety problems caused by inadequate services in the colonias need to be addressed. However, it is not clear that the installation of water and wastewater facilities alone is the solution (see Chapter 3). Nevertheless, the disproportionate share of state and federal dollars targeted to colonia projects for water and wastewater infrastructure poses several problems. Although funding for water provision is politically attractive because it promises to prevent the spread of colonia health problems to non-colonia populations, it is at best only a Band-Aid solution. To illustrate, Cameron County, after adopting the MSRs, qualified for and received a demonstration grant from the EPA through the Texas Water Development Board to install water and wastewater facilities for Cameron Park colonia. Although portrayed as a model effort, in 1995 only 5 of the nearly 1,200 households in Cameron Park could afford to hook up. In order to be serviced, homes must meet minimum state standards *with respect to building codes.* Because Cameron Park is in a floodplain, homes must be elevated on piers 18 to 22 inches above the ground, depending on the location of the home in the subdivision (Photos 15 and 16). Homes must be properly insulated, wired (no exposed wiring), and plumbed. Consequently, major investments in water and wastewater infrastructure have failed to translate into homes with water service provision, or to greatly improve living conditions in the colonia. Indeed, policy that focuses solely on the installation of water and wastewater facilities may represent an inefficient and ineffective allocation of public resources. This issue of sequencing infrastructure and code compliance is a crucial one. In Cameron County officials have been relatively assiduous to enforce housing codes, and at the request of the commissioners court, the engineer's office sought to develop a compliance schedule by which homes in Cameron Park would be brought up to standard and thereafter allowed to hook up. However, the plan was rejected by the influential NGO Valley Interfaith, which wanted people to be allowed to hook up without being up to standard. It is imperative that such an impasse be avoided, and it is to be hoped that the county will agree to adopt looser standards in the future—at least for an interim (specified) period.

Of course, such policies are not made in a vacuum; politics and bureaucratic restrictions often dictate policy priorities. For example, HUD and RECDA funds cannot be used to rehabilitate housing, nor can loans be secured unless adequate water and wastewater services exist. Even if the funds might be more effectively spent on housing, federal regulations prohibit it. Similarly, county officials responsible for enforcing MSRs fear financial liability and legal prosecution by the Texas attorney general. Originally intended to improve living conditions for those with very low income, MSRs put counties in positions of potentially bankrupting financial risk (liability) and cause county officials to deny substandard homes utility service. In essence, the proliferation of bureaucratic responses and a lack of policy coordination at the state and local level may quickly compound colonia problems and sharply reduce the effectiveness of public resources and expenditure.

Other elements of MSRs, such as increases in the minimum plot size for rural subdivisions, plus prohibitions on multiple dwellings per lot, unapproved water supplies (e.g., drinking water delivered via truck), and the use of pit privies, have all exacerbated the problems of colonias. Such action increases the cost of land and housing, thereby encouraging in-filling and illegality. Bills proposed and (fortunately) defeated in the 1995 session of the Texas Legislature would have criminalized substandard housing in EDAP counties and allowed counties to terminate utility services to homes unable to comply with local codes, thus punishing the poor for their poverty. Nevertheless, despite the defeat, these kinds of actions do demonstrate that some Texas policymakers continue to shy away from regularizing and continue to seek to criminalize irregular settlements instead.

I will return to this question of appropriate standards later in this chapter and elsewhere in this book. Suffice it to say that setting an unrealistically high bar of code requirements is a self-defeating policy that can only inhibit self-help home improvement, while at the same time "outlawing" such improvements. In Mexico, the authorities turn a blind eye, at least during the first few years of colonia consolidation, when no one is in compliance. In Texas, some level of provision for a temporary period of permitted below-code status, during which time residents could consolidate their homes and leverage services unencumbered by code considerations, would be both pragmatic and desirable. As we have observed above, colonia organizations and residents would almost certainly support such an initiative, provided that colonias were not being *permanently* designated as substandard zones. A below-code time frame (say ten years) could be set in agreements with residents, at the end of which dwellings and settlements would be expected to conform to local code requirements. The concept of a temporary period associated with development rights is nothing new, of course; it is the basis for enterprise zone designation for economic development programs. Why not extend the concept to housing areas in Texas? Some countries have experimented successfully with designated Special Social Interest Zones (ZEIS, Assies 1994), and individual colonias or parts thereof, and even inner-city neighborhoods scheduled for upgrading, could be designated as Social Interest Development Zones (SIDZs). Indeed, the precedent for this already exists in Texas, since EDAP counties are, in effect, special-development-designated counties. The SIDZs proposal would differ in scale (i.e., it is very localized), as well as in the focus upon codes and the time frame. Were they to be approved in principle, SIDZs could be designed to limit liability for jurisdictions that adopt them, and would need to allow for a differential (probably slightly higher) rate of state-sanctioned insurance premiums to be levied during the period of lower than normal code designation.

Adherence to unrealistically high code requirements at the outset prevents any possibility of experimentation in Texas with site-and-service-type self-help programs such as that adopted in Tierra Nueva colonia in Ciudad Juárez, described earlier in this chapter and in Chapter 1. Site-and-service projects have formed part of conventional wisdom housing policies in many less-developed countries since the mid-1970s (Ward 1982a; UNCHS 1996). In essence, these are housing agency platted developments that are provided with a minimum level of services (water, wastewater, and electricity), then sold to low-income residents, who are required to take up early occupancy and who take responsibility for dwelling construction through self-help and for colonia-wide improvements through mutual aid programs. The level of ongoing state support can vary: sometimes the initial servicing levels may comprise a "wet core" such as bathroom/w.c. and perhaps a kitchen. This option has been adopted where local authorities are concerned to ensure that the dwelling environment conforms to a minimum level of service and health standards, and I assume that were sites-and-services to be permitted in Texas SIDZs, some version of the core unit model would be required.

In short, what sites-and-services do is to take a leaf from the developers' book, but they do so in a way that ensures that land is made available with services from the outset, at sufficiently low cost to make them attractive to low-income residents who are willing to add their sweat equity in home building and tolerate austere levels of servicing (e.g., unpaved streets), at least for a number of years while the colonia improves. Although a good idea in theory, sites-and-services have only had limited success in practice in less-developed countries. The primary reason for this is cost. The up-front costs of paying for the land and services from the outset, while at the same time consolidating the home, have meant that such projects invariably are only affordable to the third and fourth deciles of the income distribution, and not the lowest 20 percent. Nor have attempts to offer "grace" periods on repayment or to reduce the costs by reducing the "quality" (e.g., offering sites without services or very small serviced lots) proved attractive and viable (Ward 1982b). Low-income residents have preferred the lower-cost and larger-lot alternatives of land acquisition such as invasion and illegal land purchases, which have much lower initial economic costs, albeit higher social costs associated with tenurial insecurity and lack of services. However, the important difference is that in Texas sites-and-services *would be affordable to the majority* of prospective colonia residents. As we observed in Chapter 1, although Texas colonia residents are relatively worse off compared with the state average, their actual incomes are on average between three and four times higher than those of Mexican colonia residents. Were code requirements to be waived under a SIDZ-type arrangement, then sites-and-services could provide an attractive public- or private-sector alternative form of supply to the housing demand in Texas. But it does require temporary adjustment of housing standard and subdivision codes.

The root causes of colonias are the structural characteristics that cause poverty (such as low levels of educational attainment and low-wage employment) and a shortage of decent, safe, and affordable housing options for the very poor. None of the policies discussed above has addressed these problems directly. And, by not addressing the structural causes of colonia development, colonia policy misses the mark and fails to prevent colonia growth. In short, public policy addresses the symptoms (often ineffectively), and not the causes.

Senate Bill 2, for example, provided funding for the construction of water and wastewater facilities. Through their participation in the construction and installation programs, colonia residents could have received job training, thereby improving their employability and income. Yet because of bonding requirements and legal liability, county officials chose instead to contract with top-dollar San Antonio engineers and contractors. Similarly, FmHA Section 306c grants required the use of professional contractors to install bathrooms that met state codes, rather than employing local labor and injecting job training and the grant money itself into the community in need.[9] These kinds of compromises on policy objectives for bureaucratic and legal reasons seriously hamper efforts to inhibit new colonia development and to upgrade existing colonias and homes.

Texas and Mexico: Differences and Similarities in Colonia Development

Throughout this chapter I have explored the nature of land and housing processes that are prevalent on both sides of the border. In this concluding section my purpose is to underscore the more relevant differences and similarities in those housing processes in an effort to offer insights about the broader possible policy options that might be applied in the Texas colonias, to be considered in Chapter 6.

As I have observed, the socioeconomic background which fosters colonia development is similar in many ways. Neither side has developed policy responses that provide sufficient access to formal land and housing acquisition for the very poor. Colonia residents on both sides of the border are the working poor: they are firmly integrated within the labor market, not excluded from it as many middle-class policymakers would have us believe, a point that Janice Perlman aptly made more than two decades ago in her book *The Myth of Marginality*. However, the principal nature of that job insertion is different: a larger proportion of Mexican workers is engaged in manufacturing enterprises, especially in the *maquiladoras*, which sometimes also draw upon a population of their Texas counterparts. But generally speaking, the latter are more likely to be employed in low-grade service activities. While Mexican-side wages are higher than the national (Mexican) average, Texas colonia residents earn much less than the state and national averages. Relativities aside, the key point to appreciate is that on neither side is the working wage sufficient to sustain access to formal land and housing alternatives provided by the market. Although the border offers jobs, it does so on wage terms which stifle effective demand for formal housing alternatives.

Nor have state and local authorities been capable at promoting alternative state and/or "not-for-profit" housing supply. While the Mexican federal, state, and local authorities have a long tradition of low-income housing production, supply has never kept pace with the demand, especially in fast-growing urban areas such as those we are considering here. Texas has not begun to develop a strategy of providing cheap worker housing at prices that the poor and very poor can afford. Thus, for these two reasons, low wages and the lack of formal alternatives, the working poor in the border region as a whole have had no effective recourse but to seek cheap and often illegal land acquisition alternatives. On the Mexican side the illegality of land acquisition and the lack of infrastructure at the outset reduce the cost of lot purchase to a level that makes it more or less affordable; while in Texas affordability is a function of rustic ("rural") site conditions and location, a lack of services, and a Contract for Deed arrangement which traditionally has been highly advantageous and preferential to the interests of developers. On both sides of the border, the process is extremely profitable for the land developers and agents involved, while bureaucratic inefficiencies and graft have frequently conspired to facilitate the process.

A large proportion of Mexican and Texas colonia residents are migrants: either from the interior and from other parts of the state in the case of Mexico; or from nearby cities in the case of Texas. Some Texas colonia residents are immigrants from Mexico, although very few appear to be undocumented. Most are first- or second-generation citizens, and many will have lived in Texas for many years before moving into a colonia.[10] This migrant provenance has important implications for the creation of a sense of community, as we shall observe in Chapter 4, but for both Mexican and Texas colonia residents, putting down roots by acquiring a home is crucially important. Colonias are not worker dormitories; they are homes for worker families. The meaning of owning a home of one's own is paramount in both contexts. Residential land acquisition and self-help housing represent hope and stability. They are patrimony for the family (*patrimonio para sus hijos*), and they represent a major investment and commitment. "Sweat" equity is invested in the dwelling and the lot through self-help, and over time the home acquires significant exchange value, which may be mobilized by sale in the marketplace (even if the plot is still illegal or has payments outstanding on a Contract for Deed). Granted, in Mexico, the equity component of colonia residence is higher, and the speed at which it appreciates and may be sold informally in the marketplace through a *traspaso* is much more rapid. But in both contexts, home ownership offers stability and a foothold in the property market. As elsewhere in the world, in colonias the "house is the haven" for the family (Rainwater 1966).

In both contexts colonia house construction is basically left up to the residents themselves. This has led to a wide practice of self-built housing that, if high building standards and codes are adhered to, will automatically be deemed substandard. In Mexico there is considerable laxity about enforcing building codes: in essence, these are not an issue in colonias except for public or large-scale commercial buildings. The aim is to get people registered in the property base so that *in the future* planning and building norms may be applied more forcefully, but few planners realistically expect this to be pursued vigorously while the housing deficit remains substantial. Priorities require planners and officials to turn a blind eye at least to on-site lot and construction regulations. In Texas the opposite is true. There is much more concern about these conditions on the Texas side because of the emphasis upon the enforcement of building codes. This has led to problems for colonia residents in accessing other services and funding, as well as creating some anxiety among housing and other agencies for fear of overreaching their jurisdiction.

In terms of house design and construction, there appears to be great variation in both countries in the type of homes that are built. No modal plan is evident in the Texas colonias, and the decision about what to build, house style, whether to include part-prefabricated trailers, etc., depends upon family size, income, place of work, and other circumstances. The larger lots also facilitate great variation. In Mexico, too, family income and the disposable surplus are the key criteria governing the level and rate of consolidation of self-build, and almost every house is unique. However, within that uniqueness there is a general pattern of substitution of recycled throwaways for bricks; of clear demarcation (fencing or wall) of one's lot; of metal doors and window frames; of horizontal expansion first, and later to add a second story, etc. The smaller lot sizes tend also to make for homes fronting directly onto the street, and almost always there is a patio or yard at the rear.

Overall in terms of land production, too, there are important differences. In Mexico there is a commitment in the 1917 Constitution for employers and the state to provide decent housing for workers, a commitment that neither has kept, but which has led to the creation of a raft of federal housing production and/or financing agencies from the mid-1970s onward, and of local and state agencies since the mid-1980s. However, the combination of dramatic population growth, rapid urbanization, the need to concentrate productive investment in industry rather than in housing, and so on, has meant that those agencies have never received the investment that would bring them close to meeting the demand. So Mexico left it to the informal market to develop land for worker housing, albeit illegally, and to individual family home builders to construct their homes through self-help. But since the early 1970s Mexico has been highly *interventionist* in responding to irregular settlement (Ward 1986). Over more than two decades policy-making at all levels has evolved to improve the responsiveness of the authorities to colonias: through site-and-service programs such as Tierra Nueva in Ciudad Juárez, through land title regularization, through the provision of basic infrastructure and public utilities and improved transportation, and through the creation of housing credits for self-help. Granted, this state intervention has had a strong political (sometimes partisan) content in Mexico, a point to which I will return below, but colonia housing supports have been a central policy and funding issue for more than two decades. At the beginning of that period policy creation was tied to a patrimonialist state, whereas today policy is being formulated by a state that is much more liberal and market-oriented, and that seeks greater project replicability and recovery of housing and infrastructural investments from beneficiaries and from consumers (SEDESOL 1996). Although Mexico is a developing country, it has sought to provide essential services to irregular settlements, initially at heavy subsidy, which severely impeded its ability to make programs replicable, but later demanding copayments (albeit often on generous credit terms). Today, many cities are using land regularization as a means to achieve integration of the low-income citizens into the planning, land registry, and urban taxation process. The point, here, is that the Mexican state has been *firmly engaged* in supporting colonia production and reproduction processes throughout its recent history.

This is not the case in Texas, where all levels of the state apparatus have tended to be negligent, ignoring the problem. Formal housing production has been minimal, and there has been little systematic attempt to develop imaginative housing and land production alternatives or credit schemes for the working poor, especially those living in the colonias along the border. As in Mexico, the market has been left to provide residential land and was able to do so legally through Contract for Deed. The result was the proliferation of colonias, at least until the Model Subdivision Rules began to be implemented after 1989. Subsequent colonia developments which do not conform to these rules are therefore illegal, and have begun to be pursued by the state attorney general's office, although experience suggests that litigation can be time-consuming and relatively ineffective.

Unlike their Mexican counterparts, which are effectively "incorporated" into a municipality from the outset (even though they may be beyond the city's urban edge), Texas colonias begin as unincorpo-

rated areas of the county, outside of the city limits, although sometimes within the ETJ (where city intervention is discretionary).[11] By
placing them in this "no man's land" between city and county, land
can be developed cheaply without interference from the more watch-
ful city authorities, who would otherwise be concerned about down-
line infrastructural needs and costs of newly subdivided colonias.
Whereas in Mexico the local authorities actively seek to regularize in
order to integrate these settlements, in Texas the colonias are by-
passed, and are sometimes quite literally sidestepped once the city limits reach them—as was blatantly the case for Cameron Park. Apart
from waiting to be formally annexed by a nearby city (all too often a
forlorn hope), their only other option is to seek to incorporate themselves as municipal or independent "city" jurisdictions. While there
is little fiscal advantage in so doing, it does give the colonias greater
autonomy for self-servicing, utility district creation, etc. More usually,
however, they remain in jurisdictional limbo under the aegis of the
county.

   Another important difference springs from the scarcity of urban
residential land in Mexico and its higher unitary cost (which is often
higher than in adjacent counties of the United States [see Siembieda
1995]). For example, in Matamoros the cost of a lot ran at US$850–
2,000, depending on size, compared with average costs of $1,000–
2,500 for substantially larger lots under Contract for Deed in Texas.
These relatively high land prices in Mexico, combined with the relative insecurity (at least at the outset) of the land capture process, make
for much smaller average lots (modal size is 200 m², or 2,152 ft²), for
a much faster settlement process, and for larger populations in each
settlement. In Texas, colonias are smaller (total size averages around
twenty-five acres, with a much smaller total population), and the modal
size of lots is three to four times as large (6,000–8,000 ft²). Moreover, many lots in a colonia are not occupied but are owned by "absentee" households, many of whom are poor Mexicans and Mexican-
Americans who live elsewhere in the United States and who have
invested in a lot in the Texas border area upon which, ultimately, they
intend to settle (Davies and Holz 1992). Such low colonia density has
major down-line implications for much greater unitary costs of servicing colonias in Texas, as we shall observe in Chapter 3. Moreover, lot
renting and internal petty-landlordism are becoming features on both
sides, albeit for different reasons. In Mexico they are precipitated by
the scarcity of land and high land prices, while in Texas the adoption

of Model Subdivision Rules also creates a scarcity of demand for new lots, leading to pressures to in-fill on existing lots instead (an *illegal* arrangement under MSRs, which prohibit more than one family per lot). However, in light of the subsequent amendments to the MSRs making any fresh lot sales or replatted developments contingent upon services already being installed, it seems inevitable that in-filling will take place primarily on *existing* approved and occupied lots (albeit illegally and outside the MSRs). Alternatively, a submarket of illegal lot sales will begin to quicken. In either scenario, paradoxically, regulation begets illegality.

But in Texas the state failed to take an *interventionist and responsive* stance, delaying until 1989 the development of regulatory guidelines for subdivisions, and until even later (1995) significant guarantees to Contract for Deed purchasers, albeit only in certain border counties. Unlike Mexico, Texas failed to take action that would provide for colonia development *on its terms*, that would facilitate policy design and implementation either through preemptive land developments such as sites-and-service, core units, etc., or through ex post facto housing supports such as minimum-norms legislation for selected areas (akin to my SIDZs proposal), more equitable contracts, maximum plot size controls to facilitate lower unitary costs of servicing, etc. At all levels (state, city, and county), colonias were construed as an aberration, rather than as a mode of housing production for the working poor. Thus, there has never been the commitment to a housing strategy that would seek to integrate them into the city fabric as there has in Mexico. Instead, they have been the focus of occasional task force and basic infrastructural initiatives, which are often themselves impeded by regulatory restrictions at the county and city levels. Not until 1989 and then again in 1995 did the state government begin to take concerted action, but even then the rationale was to *restrict* colonia development, not to guide and facilitate it as a form of housing policy for the working poor.

Of course, these fundamentally different perspectives on colonia housing policy are not accidental, but are born of the political environments in which colonia production are embedded. Overall, there is a marked difference between how the colonias are viewed by Mexico and Texas. In Texas, as was underscored in the Introduction, there is a sense that the "colonia problem" is largely one of health concerns. The fact that the colonias represent "Third World conditions in a First World country" presents an embarrassing situation. The result is that residents are marginalized, and addressing the issues in colonias is perceived as a burden upon local and state authorities. This is reflected in the unwillingness of local administrative areas to take responsibility for servicing colonias. Moreover, the fact that the colonias are not seen to constitute a significant voting power has further allowed governments to ignore colonia issues.[12] On the other hand, in Mexico, colonia residents make up a large portion of the urban population (sometimes more than half) that politicians must answer to. This has led to a different dynamic in which both the PRI and the emerging opposition parties (the PAN in Ciudad Juárez, for example) have made efforts to reach out to the colonias. In addition to the voting power represented by this population, the colonias' large size makes the enforcement of strict regulations at best unfeasible, if not impossible. The government is, in essence, obliged to normalize these substandard units. Public perception of the colonias therefore takes on a much less negative connotation than it does in the United States.

The responses by Texas and Mexican governments to the colonias have taken different routes. Because of the already more positive attitude toward colonia residents on the Mexican side, there has been more willingness to help colonias along the regularization process. Mexico has also responded by intervening to support the workings of the market. Texas, on the other hand, has opted for increased regulation focused on the developers, and on funding for infrastructure. Overall, the responses have taken a much more top-down approach than in Mexico. The emphasis at the U.S. federal and state levels has been to provide disincentives for the creation of colonias, rather than providing housing production incentives to the colonias. While the colonias have the greatest impact at the local level, it is the federal and state governments that have become most heavily involved either through funding for, or putting pressure on, the county and city levels. Also, the simple fact that there are two possible entities that can be held responsible for the colonias in Texas (city and county) complicates matters in a way that does not exist in Mexico.

The Implications for Policy in Texas

The aim of this concluding section is to offer some pointers about how state and local government in Texas might move forward in developing a more coherent and effective policy response to colonias.

There is no single policy recipe, nor is the intention to advocate one solution over another. Rather, the aim here is to highlight the bottle-necks that exist and to offer some ideas about how these might best be confronted. Nor am I considering at this stage whether such policy changes are politically feasible, simply suggesting that they should be considered. As stated in the Introduction, one of the aims of the origi-nating Policy Research Project was to learn from government achieve-ments on both sides of the border, and to identify policy approaches that might usefully be adopted in each country. However, given that a primary anticipated readership of this work will be public officials in Texas, I have decided not to rehearse policy implications for their Mexican counterparts, except to point out where lessons from Mexico suggest directions in which Texas should probably *not* go. To that extent, therefore, I will be implicitly identifying areas of Mexico's re-sponse to colonias which require some policy shift, but without mak-ing explicit the policy changes that might be invoked.

Of course, the art of successful state intervention is in developing strategies and policies that will respond positively to a given prob-lem, and not make it worse. But unless one properly understands the underlying processes, and correctly diagnoses the structure of the problem, intervention may quickly make conditions worse, not better. For example, it is imperative that we understand the ways in which informal-sector housing responses serve and meet people's objective needs: points which Turner and others made clear starting in the late 1960s, which were later integrated into self-help conventional wisdom (Mangin 1967; Abrams 1966; Turner and Fichter 1972; Turner 1976; World Bank 1972; UNCHS 1996), and which have since been redis-covered and rehearsed by national government advisers such as Her-nán de Soto (1989). But by the same token, in dismantling informality and embodying its principles in formal policy solutions, many of the cost-reducing elements may be lost, making the solution unworkable (Ward and Macoloo 1992). In part, this proved to be the case with site-and-service projects adopted and promoted by the World Bank during the 1970s, which by short-circuiting the illegal and unserviced routes to residential land ownership, created immediate up-front costs which, in part at least, had previously been avoided under informal modes of land acquisition.

Moreover, state intervention may articulate the entry of agents, actors, and economic groups that previously were excluded, but which now are provided with legitimate access to self-help, again raising the costs substantially and/or criminalizing formerly unregulated activities (Ward and Macoloo 1992). This is not to advocate doing nothing (though in some circumstances this may be preferable), but it does require that policy should be fully sensitive and nuanced to local conditions and needs. Failure to do so will heighten the probability that the cure will be worse than the ailment.

A good example here is regulation and codes. With the best of intentions, the State of Texas has adopted the premise that colonias should enjoy the same level of regulatory norms and codes as model subdivisions and other residential markets. Fearful of litigation and claims against them, local government has eschewed (or probably not seriously considered) lowering the bar on minimum-norm legislation, which would allow for a much more realistic and achievable set of standards to obtain. Minimum-norm legislation is nothing new (Mabogunje et al. 1978), but it does require two things. First, that government accept, at least on a temporary basis, the existence of dual standards (for rich and poor). Second, that it recognize that it has a serious problem and be willing to confront it. My sense is that for Texas legislators the idea of dual standards is anathema. And as I have argued, the prevailing social construction of the colonias problem is one of technical, sanitational, and health shortcomings in rural areas, rather than a structural problem of urban poverty and exploitation. Thus Texas has not made much progress toward developing a more realistic minimum-norms policy for colonias, even though city officials increasingly recognize its pragmatic merit.

Below, five areas of policy attention are identified. These are: (1) politics, intergovernmental coordination, and regulations; (2) land and housing access; (3) land and housing finance; (4) support for self-builders/individual consumers; and (5) structural problems. For brevity, each set of recommendations is provided in bullet-point form, and is followed by a brief statement of the rationale underlying the policy proposals.

1. Politics, Intergovernmental Coordination, and Regulations

Aims: To revise the basic premise of existing building and subdivision code regulations; to extend and enforce regulations concerning developer responsibilities and consumer protections; and to enhance intergovernmental cooperation at all levels, especially local.

Recommendations

- Revise regulations in cities and counties to reduce acceptable standards for designated colonias and ensure that these are enforced. Such designation might be tied to Social Interest Development Zone status for individual colonias, with special liability and insurance waivers.
- Improve enforcement in county jurisdictions by ensuring adequate county staff with the proper expertise. (This could be funded through state programmatic funds such as extension service funds or through TWDB grants. An alternative would be to contract with the city or private individuals.)
- Consider merging city and county roles in regulating land and housing development (as has been considered in the El Paso area).
- Allow planning and zoning in the counties such that county commissioners and other county officials are responsible and accountable for long-term development in the county.
- Shift responsibility to developers by requiring bond guarantees for subdivision construction.

Rationale The colonias in Texas have evolved within a regulatory context that is unworkable, given its adherence to high standards and codes on the one hand, and poor functioning and enforcement on the other. The latter is due to a lack of appropriately trained staff and a lack of political will and/or leadership. Thus, to the extent that steps have been undertaken, these have usually been largely the result of actions initiated by the state. While the framework for addressing colonia development already exists in some Texas counties, it fails because of poor administration, such that residential subdivisions are falling too easily through legislative and administrative loopholes, to the continuing advantage of developers who profit from the ignorance or trust of buyers. The MSRs, HB 1001, and the revised Contract for Deed provisions have strengthened the hand of the local authorities, but more effective implementation and follow-through are urgently required.

Texas colonias have been created and perpetuated by cities' and counties' failure to find solutions congruent to the problems facing their citizens. It is clear that the subdivision plat approval process does not result in a comprehensive regulatory framework as it should, in part because intergovernmental communications are often nominal at best, and absent at worst. Responsibility for development in the county must lie with the county and its elected officials in such a way as to enhance and empower the role of planning at that level. The same can be said for the city. If the county or city is mandated to approve development (as they are), then they should also have the capacity to seek a "big-picture" approach in order to make effective development approval decisions.

In Mexico municipalities have such powers in theory, but implementation has often been ineffective due to poor financing, partisanship and corruption in decision making, and poorly trained officials. However, in the past decade many of these weaknesses have begun to be addressed. Today, many cities, especially in the border area, are demonstrating major advances in the administrative capacity and effectiveness of planning, housing, and land-use controls. In general, Mexican administration focuses upon pragmatic minimum standards that are locally sensitive and achievable, particularly in the residential environment. Public buildings and commercial establishments, on the other hand, are more heavily regulated, usually by federal and/or state agencies.

2. LAND AND HOUSING ACCESS

Aims: To introduce measures that will raise access to land and housing for very-low-income groups, perhaps by allowing counties and cities, in coordination with local nonprofit organizations, to establish mainstream or alternative long-term development solutions. In order to develop a more rational and efficient use of urban land, these policies might act proactively to develop new residential land developments, or be reactive to existing colonias and subdivisions.

Recommendations

- Rescind the "grandfathering" of previously platted subdivisions, in order to open up this land (and contracts) for modern development controls implemented since 1989. (In large part this already has been achieved in certain counties under SB 542 and HB 1001.)
- Increase existing low-income housing stock, by sponsoring nonprofits or public-nonprofit partnerships.
- Through the above, experiment with sites-and-services and core-unit housing promotions either on "greenfield" sites or within

existing colonias that have been sequestrated for noncompliance under the MSRs.
- Use "informal" interventions to oblige greater responsibility among developers (see Ward 1984 for a full range of those contemplated in Mexico).
- Provide financial and fiscal incentives to densify land sharing and use, to encourage in-filling and smaller lot sizes, etc. (Hidalgo County is pursuing this idea.)
- Adopt actions that may be used in conjunction with future proactive land and housing developments. Inter alia, these might include: government purchase of land (for land "banking"); cross-subsidies, to be passed on to adjacent colonia housing projects, derived from approvals and permissions on land for commercial and industrial land uses; lot swaps and/or resident incorporation into site-and-service projects, or into colonias that are in more proximate city locations that are more easily serviced.
- Rescind those parts of legislation (MSRs and HB 1001) that prohibit lot sharing and multilot occupancy.

Rationale Increasing the stock of affordable housing is perhaps an obvious recommendation, but thus far very little has been done to facilitate the construction of truly affordable housing that can effectively compete with the low-cost lure of colonia development. Several projects are underway in Webb and El Paso Counties to support nonprofit organizations' efforts to build homes. However, in order to make the housing truly affordable, local governments must play a more assertive role in acquiring capital and in encouraging (or compelling) private industry to contribute to this endeavor. Also within the purview of local governments is the possibility of direct action to acquire currently unoccupied land and to hold it in trust with a nonprofit organization, in order to both provide alternative land supply (sites-and-services) and forestall land speculation. Other approaches seek to densify existing colonias, thereby reducing the unitary (per lot/household) costs of servicing and other infrastructural improvements. Such measures also reduce scarcity and keep land prices low. But many of these measures require a fundamental shift in legislated standards. Furthermore, they require a more proactive approach, such that the government becomes the land developer and the financing arranger. This will not be cost-neutral, but it will afford greater regulatory control over urban growth.

3. Land and Housing Finance

Aims: To improve the poor's access to alternative as well as mainstream financing tools, and to improve existing financing programs to better suit the needs of the very poor.

Recommendations

- Provide financing and refinancing and alternative financing assistance, especially relaxing construction and subdivision standards for RECDA and other agency financing.
- Apply the new (1995) Contract for Deed regulations to all colonia areas irrespective of geographical and EDAP qualification criteria.
- Intensify and extend funding of down-payment assistance programs such as that provided by the TDHCA.
- Revise the Mortgage Revenue Bond program qualifying criteria for colonia housing so that more residents may receive first-time home owner mortgages, and increase the number of participating lending institutions (although this will probably depend on the Fair Land Sales Act and other measures to ensure that residents do have secure deeds and/or have gone beyond the 40 percent/forty-eight monthly payments on a Contract for Deed).
- Reform the Low Income Housing Tax Credit—for cashing out, "pooling," and technical assistance in poor and hard-to-reach areas.
- Create a guarantee program to allow the state to set its own credit underwriting standards, better suited to the needs of lower-income families in the border region.
- Enhance outreach about refinancing and financing to residents and potential residents.

Rationale   Current practice is for original financing of land purchase in Texas to be left almost exclusively to the discretion of developers, who are often the only possible source of financing for the poor. Notwithstanding the substantial improvements in Contract for Deed achieved by Senate Bill 336, the changes do not go far enough, nor do they apply uniformly across colonias. Research is urgently required to examine the impact of the 1995 legislation in curtailing colonia sales in those counties where it came fully into force, and to explore whether or not the new legislation has simply displaced new colonia development to and intensified lot sales in the non-EDAP and non-SB-336-designated counties. Detailed research is also required to determine past lot sales and to identify the status and residence of absentee lot holders.

Current programs to assist colonia residents with housing, land purchase, and improvements are too inflexible to provide adequate coverage. Funding is assessed using criteria that do not allow for informal or substandard dwellings, producing a "Catch-22" loop whereby financial aid may only be leveraged if the structures meet certain criteria that cannot be achieved without financial support. The effectiveness of programs will continue to be sabotaged if these circular requirements persist. Now that the Texas Homestead Law has been revised (from 1998 onward), this should open up greater opportunities for small-scale credits for home improvement against the lot and dwelling equity.

Nor can one look to Mexican colonias for guidance here, since until recently at least the country had a very poorly developed mortgage market, which even now has almost negligible impact in colonias. In Mexico, as in Texas, financing is primarily from wages and from small-scale savings for the down payment. However, even the most rapacious land developers in Mexico had nothing like the Contract for Deed to facilitate their lucrative business. Nevertheless, programs of regularization of "clouded" titles have made it possible to use residence as equity on small loans: some of the major housing funds (INFONAVIT and, to a lesser extent, FONHAPO) have thereby provided credits for home improvements. A big plus in Mexico is that credits are not tied to dwelling or plot standards, with the exception of land title requirements (and even these may be waived). Secular nongovernment organizations have played an important role in advising and assisting colonias throughout Mexico.

4. Support for Self-builders and Individual Consumers

Aims: To enhance legal rights and education about legal rights for low-income buyers. To develop technical assistance for self-help. To recognize the worth of self-help or self-built housing alternatives, and seek solutions that allow for a broad range of building techniques, including "low-tech" solutions.

Recommendations

- Take further actions to establish consumer protection in land sales, and ensure that contracts for property be properly recorded even before full title deeds are obtained.
- Provide credit for the refinancing of existing Contracts for Deed, through RECDA funds or bond financing.
- Increase information to buyers and enhance outreach to residents and potential residents concerning legal rights under land purchases.
- Support public and private (NGO) technical assistance programs, at-cost construction materials yards exclusively for colonia residents, and modular self-build plans for home and infrastructure improvements.
- In codes pertaining to building in the counties, allow for innovative technology or "low-tech" solutions.
- Support development of less costly housing designs specifically adapted to the border region and provide technical assistance.
- Look to Proyecto Azteca and the Mission Service Project in Hidalgo County, and to the Lower Valley Housing Corporation in El Paso County, as sources for model self-help and low-income housing programs (perhaps in conjunction with site-and-service-type alternatives).

Rationale   In part at least, preventing many of the problems of colonias lies in giving people the tools and information to help themselves. Greater dissemination and understanding of legal rights are the cornerstone of a policy for long-term colonia independence. Some of the most blatant abuses by developers could have been avoided if the colonia residents had been protected earlier, and if they had received at least nominal consumer protection against fraud and unjust contractual arrangements.

Some of the most interesting and meaningful insights gleaned from our field research in colonias involve the construction of housing. While buildings are officially coded unfit for habitation, the highly innovative uses to which materials are put speak to the enormous resilience of people determined to hold sway in the creation of their own dwelling space. Although some minimal safety standards must clearly exist, these should seek as far as possible to be the absolute minimum (perhaps to avoid life-threatening exigencies). Policies regarding housing should allow for the flexibility that low-income households require in financing and building their homes, rather than requiring that middle-class norms apply. Granted, such flexibility should be contingent upon the capacity to gradually implement changes in the interest of safety and health, and the ultimate convergence toward more widely applied norms. The need for double standards in colonias should be viewed as a temporary expedient, albeit probably a long-term one of ten to twenty years. These recommendations require acceptance of the reality that the colonias and colonia housing within them are rational and acceptable responses to the basic need for shelter. This is a fundamentally new mindset, to which legislators and policymakers need to be able to adjust. Equally fundamental and novel is the final view, that the origins of the colonia problem are structural, rather than being either conjunctural or contingent.

5. STRUCTURAL PROBLEMS

Aims: To begin to consider possible solutions that tackle the structural causes of "problems" in colonias.

Recommendations

- Require area industries and commercial establishments that employ low-wage workers to grant housing bonuses or other housing services.
- Require those enterprises to pay a livable wage.
- Link housing production with job training and job creation programs.

Rationale   Colonias are a manifestation of poverty. That they exist in Mexican cities and in the U.S. border region reflects the extant high rates of poverty and the lack of development resources. They are not the product of backwardness, nor of a different system of values. Nor are they a cultural aberration. Thus in the long term, sustainable solutions for residents of colonias must, necessarily, address issues of education and training, employment, wage rates, and discrimination. To that extent they require integrated regional development programs that must derive from state and federal initiative, which once on line may, of course, be harnessed or hindered by the quality of local government. But as this chapter has sought to clarify, much may also be achieved by more effective and concerted policy development at the state, city, and county levels: in particular by developing a more appropriate integration of roles and responsibilities at the various levels. Simply viewing colonias as future housing solutions and opportunities will be an important first step. Subsequent steps will require many of the above-mentioned proposals to be implemented in tandem and in a way involving coordination among jurisdictions. There is no single solution or silver bullet to effective land and housing development. If there were, we would have found it many years ago, probably in Mexico.

Three

Servicing No Man's Land: Ambivalence versus Commitment in the Texas-Mexico Colonias

A basic lack of physical infrastructure, including water, wastewater, pavement, and electricity, characterizes colonias on both sides of the Texas-Mexico border. Land in colonias on both sides of the border is settled before basic infrastructure is constructed, and residents often must wait many years for services. The response on the U.S. side to this situation has been qualitatively different from that on the Mexican side. In Texas, a maze of overlapping and sometimes contradictory regulatory and jurisdictional frameworks masks a larger public-sector ambivalence already identified in this volume. Typically infrastructure provision—of water, for example—into border colonia areas has been extremely limited and piecemeal, particularly up until the mid-1990s.

The lack of political will to confront the problems created by colonias was only transcended in 1986 when a crisis situation began to be recognized by principal leaders such as Governor Mark White, Lt. Governor Bill Hobby, Comptroller Bob Bullock, and State Treasurer Ann Richards (Wilson and Menzies 1997, 249). Crises at that time, such as the threat of a cholera outbreak, were viewed as dramatic health hazards, and there was political embarrassment at the spotlight being turned on so-called "Third World" conditions in one of the richest states of the developed world. Combined with this crisis view was the growing recognition among legislators that Texas would continue to be denied federal funds for colonias until it convinced Congress that it was taking action to prevent the proliferation of colonias. This it began to do only in 1989. Despite the concerted effort to improve levels of infrastructure in the colonias since that time, there is considerable evidence that ambivalence remains: within the Texas

Legislature,[1] among federal and state bureaucracies, within implementation programs, among water development "sponsors," and within local jurisdictions such as cities and counties. While such ambivalence persists, colonias and their resident populations continue to suffer the hardships and social costs associated with Third World housing conditions.

In Mexico, however, despite its relative poverty, federal, state, and municipal levels of government have shown no such ambivalence, and have directly addressed the problems represented by colonias in a much more coordinated and systematic manner, over many years. The proactive and responsive nature of Mexican policy makes for both more effective and more economical solutions to the dilemmas posed by colonias. Physical infrastructure in Mexico is provided by the public sector, while in the United States the private sector has traditionally been expected to fill existing service gaps. In Mexico, colonias are viewed as a self-help response to a chronic housing shortage in the rapidly growing border region. Regularization of settlements paves the way for future taxation and cost recovery for service provision. In Texas, the government primarily plays a role in regulating housing and infrastructure provision without addressing the larger needs of affected populations. Regional authorities work within federal and state criteria in providing assistance to colonias, with limited commitment to resolving the larger issues affecting the border region.

Many variables shape the process of service provision, including geography, settlement structure, the level of capital investment required, the cost to providers, the legal and institutional framework, and of course, political will. Marked contrasts exist between the context of, and approaches to, service provision on the two sides of the border. These factors affecting service provision are discussed below.

Factors Affecting Service Provision

Adequate physical infrastructure is essential to human and environmental health. A lack of water and sanitation services, in particular, results in both disease and environmental degradation. In addition, research has focused on the relationship among service provision, productivity, and economic development (World Bank 1991). Colonia residents obtain services through both formal and informal means—

30. Two-part trailer home in East Montana (El Paso County) showing the water tank and propane tanks. Note also the beginnings of a lean-to extension at the rear of the dwelling.

the former referring to provision through standard utility networks. Research in Mexico has found that even when water and water drainage systems are provided by the formal sector, these systems have sometimes been so unreliable or inadequately maintained that the poor may end up paying for *both* formal and informal methods of supply (Ward 1986). The "informal" cost of service provision is generally considerably higher than the formal cost. In the Texas colonias, for example, residents often buy water from tanker trucks and store it in large heavy-duty plastic storage tanks, paying $22 per 1,000 gallons (Photos 30 and 31). A resident hooked up to a network in a nearby city would pay only about $1.50 for the same amount of water (Russell et al. 1988, 193). Many colonia residents in Mexico, as in other countries in the developing world, also hook up to existing service networks illegally, and pirate services. This is particularly true of electricity, since it is the easiest service to obtain in this manner.

GEOGRAPHY

Geographic location can make service provision difficult regardless of policy initiatives. A principal problem presented by colonias is that they may be established in locations which make the introduction of

31. Household water trailer rig in San Enrique (Webb County [Laredo]). This tank is replenished every three weeks at a nearby Shamrock gas station.

physical infrastructure prohibitively expensive. This can be due to topography: in Ciudad Juárez, for example, city officials have made it plain that they will not provide services to settlements located on steeply sloping land at the western edge of the city (Prieto 1995). Instead, the city intends to relocate these inhabitants. In Texas, as we saw in Chapter 2, many residents have built their homes in the floodplain, creating a situation in which services may legally not be provided. Geography can also hamper service provision if settlements are developed far from existing service networks, since this increases the cost of providing the primary service links to established grids.

SETTLEMENT STRUCTURE

Settlement structure is another major factor which affects service provision. Characteristics including population density, settlement size, and the number of colonia residents relative to municipal or county population are all aspects of settlement structure. The level of population density relates inversely to the cost of service provision. Higher densities mean that lines will service larger numbers of people, making servicing more cost-effective. This rationale works to the advantage of Mexican colonias because residents tend to live in and are willing to accept higher lot density conditions.

The opposite applies in Texas, where developers deliberately sell noncontiguous plots, a process known as leapfrog development (see Figure 6 in Chapter 2). Larger plot sizes in Texas may also allow developers to avoid some regulations.[2] A smaller population means fewer individuals paying into the system, which is particularly crucial in leveraging services such as water and wastewater, where substantial revenue is required to support construction, operation, and maintenance costs. Smaller settlements are also easier to ignore and are less important politically.

LEVEL OF CAPITAL INVESTMENT

Services can be roughly divided into two categories, the so-called "lumpy" and "nonlumpy" services. Lumpy services are those which require a large initial public investment and extensive public works to provide primary and secondary networks before any individual customers can be serviced. Water and wastewater are examples of lumpy infrastructure since the treatment plants and primary networks are expensive to construct and install. Public markets, street lighting, and electricity provision are comparatively nonlumpy kinds of infrastructure. On both sides of the border, infrastructure provision becomes dramatically more expensive and problematic if it is brought on line ex post facto, i.e., after residents have moved onto their property and already begun to construct housing. Even a comparatively less lumpy service like electricity may become considerably more expensive to provide if it is installed after settlement, and in increments to a few customers at a time. The cost of service provision can be greatly increased by this kind of piecemeal approach.

Cost levels and the way in which residents are charged for services can both affect residents' ability to pay. Research from Mexico indicates that there are important reasons for why the costs of service provision quickly become too high for colonia residents. One reason concerns the type of payment plan involved—that is, whether payment is obtained through a one-time charge, or is spread over a period of time as consumption costs, and as surcharges on consumption costs. High payments for services may also have important repercussions upon the residential mix, affecting the economic heterogeneity of households living within the settlement. As I commented more than a decade ago (Ward 1986, 105): "Significant hardship is likely to be experienced by some families during a relatively short phase of the settlement's development. The very poor . . . face major and inflexible monthly repayments and must either sell out or attempt to meet these additional costs in some other way."

Once a plot receives services, the property becomes more valuable, which in turn can lead to the initiation of or sharp increases in property tax payments. Although research on population displacement out of colonias is not conclusive, higher commercial values on plots may persuade owners to cash in on their equity and move elsewhere, once again affecting the demographic profile of the settlement (Ward 1982b). In Texas we know very little about how people mobilize resources in order to pay for infrastructure and service improvements, how this affects household budgets, and the mechanisms adopted to overcome such costs (population displacement, lot sharing, and so on).

Legal and Political Factors

In Texas, the issue of responsibility for colonias is complex due to the considerable ambiguity surrounding government and service provider jurisdictions. Cities and counties disagree about who is responsible for regulation of development and about responsibility for service provision in a city's ETJ, where colonias are sometimes located. Colonias that lie outside a city and its ETJ fall under the jurisdiction of comparatively weak county authorities, who may not have the political will or desire to expend limited resources on improvement of colonia infrastructure.

Texas law makes it the responsibility of the developer to provide services, but developers have often been able to escape the requirement because of the failure of authorities to properly regulate their activity. The situation is further complicated by jurisdictional confusion pertaining to service providers. Public or private entities must obtain legal authority from regulatory boards or agencies, such as the Texas Natural Resource Conservation Commission (TNRCC), before providing services. The complexities and the disputes which arise regarding the issue of service provision can deter potential providers, and halt or delay projects that are in the works.

In contrast, Mexico's *municipio* combines the functions of county and city. Traditionally independent and autonomous, *municipios* have been weak and resource poor, subjugated to the state and federal levels of government. However, reform efforts in recent years, most notably the changes in Article 115 of the Mexican Constitution in 1983, have begun the process of giving municipalities the authority and the responsibility for many services, including water, street lighting, and solid waste (garbage) collection (Rodríguez 1997; Ward 1995).

Mexico's Solidarity program is a particularly significant example of this phenomenon. Begun in 1989 under the auspices of the Salinas de Gortari *sexenio*, or six-year term, PRONASOL was a presidentially sponsored internal program of relief to poor communities and internal development. Solidarity (PRONASOL) provided the political clout required to link the different levels of government in a coordinated effort to address the problems of service provision in the colonias. Significantly, the government provided a major part of the funding for projects in colonias, insisted on contributions at the state and *municipio* levels, and asked residents to provide a portion of the cost, either in cash, materials, or labor (Rodríguez 1997).

A key difference between service provision in Mexico and Texas is underscored by this integration of different levels of government and service provision falling under different jurisdictions. Municipal responsibility for paving, for example, and decentralized federal responsibility for electricity may thereby be coordinated. In Texas, the fragmented hodgepodge of private and public providers of such diverse services as proper drainage and electricity creates a situation of very uneven and poorly planned coverage.

In Mexico, regulations appear to be fewer and more flexible than in Texas. Land regularization agencies, such as CoRett, can be extremely flexible in accepting petitions for legalization of title. Also, agencies often have their own criteria for determining whether or not a colonia gets serviced, and act almost independently of other agencies and of municipal authorities. In contrast, Texas regulations prevent service provision when residents and dwellings do not comply with setbacks, housing codes, floodplain requirements, or city-county health regulations. Regulations in Texas also govern the type of infrastructure which can be provided, thus limiting the alternatives that can be offered by service providers. In addition, a legal inability to assume debt prevents many subdivisions from supplying services to colonias.

Colonos (colonia residents) in Mexico have a greater voice in the service provision process and in the polity as a whole, although until the late 1980s this derived largely from political patronage from the PRI and from local politicians. In Mexico, moreover, *colonos* are sources of city revenues and votes for politicians. Provision of services has often, therefore, been highly politicized (Gilbert and Ward 1985). During the Salinas administration colonia leaders negotiated with municipal representatives under the auspices of Solidarity committees (Contreras and Bennett 1994). Notions of "social justice" are central to Mexican political culture, and the *colonos* provided a natural constituency for populist politics during the 1970s and 1980s and were mobilized politically to a high degree. Since 1995, and in many northern cities since the early 1990s, such overt partisanship surrounding service provision has declined, and servicing decisions have become more routinized and systematic (Ward 1993, 1995).

In contrast, the ability of colonia residents in Texas to impel government to respond to their problems is severely constrained by their lack of financial resources, their lack of voting strength, and the (erroneous) public perception that they are often illegal immigrants. In fact, patterns of political patronage in Texas have traditionally worked against colonia residents. Local officials have often been slow to enforce legal statutes, favoring instead the position of developers. Participation of citizens in elections is low due to the social, legal, and geographic isolation of colonias. When colonia residents do vote, their local impact is restricted to counties, where elected officials have few resources or authority to solve their problems, since resources and service providers are more likely to be concentrated in the cities. In addition, community organization is lacking in many Texas colonias—a point to which I will return in the following chapters.

Although Texas and Mexico face similar problems when it comes to providing infrastructure, each side has its own perceptions as to who and what constitute a colonia. As we have observed, in Mexico, colonias are considered to be a normal housing option, so that policy concentrates upon improving their dwelling environment rather than on trying to eradicate them and prevent their densification and development. In addition, colonia residents do not face the same social stigma as their U.S. counterparts—hardly surprising given that, in some Mexican cities, over half of the population resides in colonias.

In Mexico, spontaneous mobilization for land acquisition and schemes such as Solidarity have assured that a certain level of community organization exists in colonias, albeit often under government control. In Texas, developer control over many settlements, the public perception that colonia residents are illegal aliens, and geographical and cultural barriers all serve to deter community involvement.

Infrastructure Provision in Mexico and Texas

Variables affecting provision of physical services are often inter-related. Geography may affect the decision of providers when they consider offering a particular service, as well as the prospects for cost recovery. Concerns about health issues may influence local authorities in their decision to make water available to a local colonia, or confusion over jurisdictions may prevent any effective local action from being taken at all. Comparative case studies examining the management of the provision of water and wastewater, electricity, street lighting, and transportation show how these variables manifest themselves. In turn, cross-border comparison points to the strengths and weaknesses of policy approaches on both sides of the border and toward directions for future initiatives.

Water and Wastewater in Mexico and Texas

In both Texas and Mexico, health issues arise because water obtained from the principal sources is likely to be of poor quality and unsafe. Groundwater sources are frequently contaminated by agricultural run-off and by the seepage of sewage. Water storage tanks and drums, wells, and irrigation ditches may be similarly contaminated. The general scarcity of water and disputes among the city, irrigation districts, and water supply corporations about water rights can cause supplies to be expensive and uneven. The poor quality and irregularity, unaffordability, or total lack of treated water creates serious health risks and negatively impacts the *colonos'* quality of life. High levels of hepatitis, shigellosis, and other waterborne illnesses are closely associated with unpotable water, contaminated storage and distribution systems, and inadequate waste disposal.

In Mexico, the provision of water and wastewater service is viewed as a political and community development issue, while in Texas the lack of water and wastewater infrastructure is viewed primarily as a health and environmental hazard. This difference in attitude is further reflected in the way governments in both countries intervene to deal with the issue. In Mexico there is no question that the government is required and expected to provide water and sewer service irrespective of whether it is financially and geographically feasible. In Texas, colonias have primarily been forced to find the services through private sources—at least until 1989, when Senate Bill 2 began to provide for federal funds to be leveraged alongside state funds for the extension of publicly subsidized water services to colonias. From the outset, state policymakers have focused on addressing the health issue in the most cost-effective manner. This has resulted in a top-down approach centered around two types of actions: regulation to stop the proliferation of colonias, and the provision of technical solutions to the lack of adequate infrastructure. The policy approach does not try to achieve integration of colonias into mainstream society, but rather seeks to tackle the health and environmental issues while letting colonias remain in relative isolation, often in jurisdictional limbo. Even today, many jurisdictions are skittish about taking responsibility for extending infrastructure to colonias.

The Provision of Water and Wastewater in Mexico   In Mexico the official process of obtaining water service is relatively straightforward and involves cooperation between the municipal government (often with federal and/or state inputs) and colonia residents. For example, the latter were required to assume some responsibility for raising money from the community for service provision, particularly where this came through the Solidarity program (1989–1994). Under this program, the government responded to a formal request for water provision backed by the legally stipulated funds. The colonia residents were responsible for raising 50 percent of the funds necessary for water provision. If the money was there, governments made it clear that they would provide water. In actual fact the 50-50 requirement was often waived. So long as local communities were organized and were willing to make some contribution, federal and state resources were usually found (SEDESOL 1994).

PRONASOL appears to have had an important impact in many cities. Water provision has expanded in Matamoros and Ciudad Juárez, and has remained about the same in Nuevo Laredo, during the early 1990s. According to municipal representatives Matamoros currently has approximately 85 percent coverage of potable water, Nuevo Laredo, 85 percent, and Ciudad Juárez, 88 percent. However, these are almost certainly overestimates and ignore some realities of service provision. The quality of water provision, for example, is not discussed. Is the water available twenty-four hours a day? Are there shortages at times? What is the water pressure—a trickle or a substantial flow? In addition, the type of water distribution system varies greatly. At this point it is unclear how much water is piped into individual homes or to community water tanks, or pumped into a community spigot that may be a substantial distance from the homes of some residents. This is exemplified in the colonias examined in this study, in which four had mostly indoor faucets (with some intermittently low pressure), three had community spigots or a community tank, and three received water by truck.

Approximately 40 percent of the colonias in Matamoros, Mexico, are hooked into the municipal wastewater system, while the majority of the remainder make do with some sort of on-site system: usually a rudimentary *fosa séptica*. Nuevo Laredo is said to have nearly 75 percent drainage coverage, while the master plan of Ciudad Juárez states that 82 percent of the city has drainage. Again, these percentages may be misleading. Nowhere is the nature of drainage infrastructure or the adequacy of the system defined. It may range from the crudest of pit privies, to various types of septic tanks, to having a municipal hookup for sewage and wastewater. Most of the case study colonias had some sort of on-site system, ranging from pit privy to septic tank. Only one had full municipal hookups.

Factors Affecting Water and Wastewater Provision in Mexico As noted above, an important factor affecting service provision in Mexico is politics. The official process can easily become sidetracked by partisan considerations. Colonias are seen as sources of votes, and so political priorities may have a profound influence on servicing decisions. In Ciudad Juárez, for example, the three *trienios* of opposition (PAN-ista) city administrations (1989–1998) have had tenuous relations with PRI colonias, and the latter therefore may not receive infrastructure, just as "opposition" (PAN) colonias did not when the PRI governed city hall (Staudt 1998). Some Mexican colonias, on the other hand, are founded for political reasons, on land given by a politician or administration—and these colonias would usually be at the top of the servicing hierarchy. Traditionally, colonia residents in Mexico often mobilized public demonstrations as a means of motivating political officials to provide services (Montaño 1976; Gilbert and Ward 1985; Bennett 1995).

According to many individuals questioned, however, Solidarity did make a significant difference in the way infrastructure was provided in Mexico. Community involvement was essential in order to secure water provision in Mexico since residents were required to organize in order to provide part of the cost of servicing. Nevertheless, although there is a consensus in Mexico that services should be provided to the *colonias populares*, there is still some confusion at the level of policy implementation, and the efficiency and speed with which any service is provided differ according to the kinds of service (Gilbert and Ward 1985). In the case of water, for example, there are overlapping agency responsibilities at different levels of government.

In Mexico, one main obstacle to service provision pertains to geography. If a colonia is far removed from the existing grid of primary water lines under the city, it may be necessary to wait until areas between the city and colonia are serviced before it is physically possible to deliver water. However, the right of citizens is recognized and water is allocated as quickly as possible, given existing resources. Water tanker trucks owned by the municipality are a common sight in the Mexican colonias, and they provide water in colonias lacking the proper infrastructure. Private sources may also provide water for sale to *colonos*, who store the water in large discarded industrial drums.

The failure to treat wastewater in Mexico has been a serious problem for many years. Until very recently there were no wastewater treatment plants along the Texas-Mexico border, and so even if colonias were hooked into a wastewater system, the border environment was still being degraded, and downstream inhabitants who drew water from the river were being affected. Ciudad Juárez and Nuevo Laredo (whose wastewater systems became functional in 1995) have both opened sewage treatment plants or plan to do so in the near future, and a high percentage of funds allocated to the new North American Development Bank is designated for water and wastewater infrastructure. Even so, the levels of capital investment required are extremely high, and it is doubtful that this problem can be adequately addressed anytime soon. Nor has the NAD Bank to date had much success in making major loans available for environmental projects.

The Provision of Water and Wastewater in Texas   In Texas the onus has traditionally been placed upon the private sector to provide. City laws require developers to construct water and wastewater infrastructure. The problem lies in the fact that these laws have not usually been applied beyond the city limits, where the majority of colonias lie. As was outlined in Chapter 2, county zoning and subdivision regulatory power are virtually nonexistent, and there is no legal basis for zoning. The state government has recently begun efforts to remedy this situation by increasing the regulatory powers of counties, and now requires paved streets, drainage, and utilities to be provided in MUD (municipal utility district) subdivisions, and that lots be a minimum of 7,000 ft^2 (70' × 100'). However, enforcement continues to be lax due to a lack of resources and political will (Davies 1995). At the same time, the effort to increase regulatory power often still does not address the thousands of acres platted prior to these new laws (notwithstanding SB 542 [see Chapter 2]), and thus many colonia residents are forced to obtain services elsewhere.

Although once established, water and wastewater service providers are often government owned or government regulated, provision of infrastructure and the provision of service itself are viewed as a private-sector matter. Local governments perceive infrastructure construction to be the responsibility of the subdivision developer. For this reason, although the extension of city service lines is typically the cheapest method of service provision, Texas colonias must primarily obtain water from other sources, such as nonprofit rural water supply corporations (WSCs). WSCs currently service over half the colonias in Texas (Texas Water Development Board 1995). Where WSCs are not an option, developers or residents will drill wells and/or establish their own municipal utility districts. If a water hookup is not available or is not affordable, water is obtained from shallow wells, coin-operated tanks, tanker lorries, or neighbors, or sometimes even collected from irrigation ditches. Even where a water hookup is available, inadequate plumbing is a critical problem. According to the Texas Department of Human Services (1988), 24 percent of Texas colonias lacked treated water in their dwellings (see also Table 13).

Very few colonias in Texas are hooked into wastewater collection systems. Residents primarily build their own septic systems, latrines, pit privies, or outhouses to dispose of waste. Fifty percent of the dwellings in colonias use septic systems (often rudimentary), and 35 percent use cesspools (Texas Department of Human Services 1988). In one study of Del Mar Heights colonia, one-quarter of homes had a septic tank with soil absorption, 14 percent had a septic tank without a drain field, 44 percent had pit latrines, and 10 percent had a cesspool (TWDB, cited in Davies 1995, 45). Virtually all of these systems are substandard and inadequate. Septic tanks are potentially a viable option, but those constructed in colonias rarely meet state criteria for adequate absorption field operation because of poor drainage and small lot size (Reed 1994). Flat terrain and occasional torrential rains lead to poor drainage and frequent flooding, causing septic tanks to fail and sewage to rise to the surface. This situation also threatens

Table 13. General Characteristics of Colonias

	Cameron, Hidalgo, and Willacy Counties	El Paso County	Combined
Number of people	71,478	68,395	139,873
Number of households	14,643	12,045	26,688
Number of colonias	435	537	972
Number of colonias with 15 or more households	277	162	439
Average age of residents	18.5	26.3	21.8
Average number in households	4.8	4.3	4.5
Average annual household income	$6,784	$11,497	$9,137
Proportion Hispanic (%)	99	96	97
Proportion Anglo (%)	1	3	2
Proportion Black (%)	0	1	1
Residents born in U.S. (%)	61	68	64
Residents born in Mexico (%)	39	32	35
Primary language Spanish (%)	83	89	87
Household heads not proficient in English (%)	71	49	60
Residents with no health insurance (%)	72	57	65
Family heads not completing high school (%)	86	62	75
Unemployment rates, 16 or over (%)	47	33	41
Work for minimum wage or less (%)	48	25	38
Colonia home ownership (%)	87	84	85
No treated water in house (%)	21	26	24
Outhouse or cesspool (%)	20	66	44

Source: Texas Health and Human Services Commission 1995.

health and water quality where there is the possibility of effluent seeping into water sources.

The Texas State Government Response   Media attention generated most recently by NAFTA, and by an increasingly powerful Hispanic political constituency in Texas, along with the decade-long activities of community organizing groups such as Valley Interfaith and EPISO, has recently focused on the so-called "Third World" living conditions and provoked what has become an unprecedented high-level government response in the area of infrastructure. This concern appears to have begun around 1986, when Valley Interfaith organized a visit for Governor White and Lt. Governor Hobby that led to the TWDB making a commitment of $100 million for colonias (Wilson and Menzies 1997, 249; Bath et al. 1994). Some two years later, then–Texas Comptroller Bullock recognized that financing wastewater and water would require a combination of loans and grants, and he proposed creating a $500 million subsidy program. Although the legislature failed to approve the proposal, it did lead to Senate Bill 2, which provided for: (1) a $500 million issue in new water bonds (of which $100 million was earmarked for water to colonias), (2) the creation of designated EDAP counties, and (3) the introduction of Model Subdivisions Rules, designed to prevent the proliferation of colonias and thereby make Texas eligible for federal assistance in the colonias. This legislation designated the Texas Water Development Board as the administering agency for funds approved in a statewide election to design and construct infrastructure projects in colonias. Federal government funding from agencies such as the EPA and Farmers' Home Administration (now RECDA) has also been made available to TWDB and used to create separate assistance programs.

TWDB requires that a legally recognized political administrative area (county, city, nonprofit water supply corporation, or municipal utility district) must sponsor a colonia. This means that colonias must be adopted by a legally recognized body, and they cannot act alone or independently. The administrative entity must submit an application to the EDAP program and hire an engineer to conduct a facilities engineering plan. A team of engineers, financial analysts, and environmental experts then evaluates and approves a proposed project. According to the EDAP estimates, some $142 million and $448 million are required to meet water and wastewater needs, respectively, in twenty-eight counties (Table 14), while other sources put the total costs at around $1 billion (Davies 1995, 39). The distribution of some $125 million of federal funds for colonias by program and by source for the period 1989–1993 is shown in Table 15. However, although an overall total of $344.5 million in funding (federal and state) had been allocated toward colonia infrastructure since 1989, only four projects had been completed by 1995. Seventeen others had received committed construction funds and forty-three were in the facility planning process (Texas Water Development Board 1995).

Table 14. Estimated Cost to Meet County Water and Wastewater Needs

Texas County	Water (in $Millions)	Wastewater (in $Millions)
Brewster	0.0	0.0
Cameron	2.8	46.9
Dimmit	19.0	5.4
Duval	0.2	0.4
Edwards	1.3	0.8
El Paso	70.3	84.9
Hidalgo	5.0	157.8
Hudspeth	0.0	1.6
Jeff Davis	0.0	1.4
Jim Hogg	0.2	0.2
Jim Wells	1.7	8.7
Kinney	0.2	0.9
La Salle	8.8	9.3
Maverick	0.7	25.2
Newton	1.6	6.0
Pecos	0.6	5.4
Presidio	2.7	4.7
Red River	0.5	2.5
Reeves	0.0	0.7
Sabine	0.6	0.5
Starr	1.2	26.5
Terrell	0.0	1.9
Uvalde	0.1	6.3
Val Verde	7.2	11.5
Webb	14.5	25.5
Willacy	0.6	3.7
Zapata	0.0	3.9
Zavala	2.5	5.6
Total	142.3	448.2

Source: Texas Water Development Board, Economically Distressed Areas Program (Davies 1995, 46).

Table 15. Federal Funding of Colonia Water and Wastewater Systems

Program	Source of Funds	Dollar Amount (in millions)	Implementing Agency	Eligible Activities	Eligible Areas
Colonia Wastewater Treatment Assistance Program	Environmental Protection Agency (EPA)	50	Texas Water Development Board (TWDB)	Design and construction of wastewater system	Colonias
Colonia Plumbing Loan Program	EPA	15	TWDB	Connection fees, indoor plumbing, maximum loan $4,000/household	Colonias
Texas Department of Housing and Community (TDHCA) Colonias Fund	Housing and Urban Development, Community Development Block Grants (CDBG)	18.6	TDHCA	Public water or wastewater improvement	Colonias
Water and Waste Disposal Loans to Entities	Rural Development Administration (RDA)	15	RDA	Water and wastewater system	Entire state but priority to colonias
Water and Waste Disposal 306C Colonia Grant	RDA (Transferred to FmHA)	2	FmHA	Connections and indoor plumbing	Colonias
Water and Wastewater Disposal Loans and Grants	Farmers' Home Administration (FmHA)	24.3	FmHA	Construction or improvement of water and wastewater system	Rural areas and towns up to 10,000 population in entire state

Source: Texas Water Development Board, *Providing Water and Wastewater Service to the Colonias: A Shared Responsibility,* SAO Report Number 3-150 (October 1993), pp. 26–31.
Taken from Wilson and Menzies 1997, 259. Reprinted by permission.

Recent field visits to case study colonias suggest that many have received water services since 1995 (LBJ 1997, vol. 2). According to the TWDB, these projects will address the needs of 60.5 percent of the estimated colonia population. The TWDB speculates that more funding will be required to meet remaining needs. The estimated average unitary cost of providing a piped water service into a colonia, together with "tap fee" (average $350–750 for each connection), is around $2,500. In addition, there are internal plumbing costs ($1,000–2,000), and often a standing charge of $25–30 per month in order to retire the bond (Davies 1995, 40). Indeed, during the 1990s monthly water user fees in El Paso County were almost double those of the city ($26), and were expected to triple by the year 2000 (Staudt 1998, 114). These are very substantial costs for very poor colonia residents and make additional credit supports imperative.

Factors Affecting Water and Wastewater Provision in Texas   It is often difficult to discern which agency should be responsible (city, county, state, WSC, or MUD) for service provision in Texas. This confusion alone deters eligible political administrative areas from applying for funding. If a utility provider chooses to apply for EDAP funds, that provider must possess or acquire a Certificate of Convenience and Necessity (CCN) from the TNRCC authorizing that provider to provide a water or sewer service to an area. According to the TWDB (1995), disputes have arisen between EDAP applicants (i.e., sponsoring administrative authorities) and other already established utilities in a given service area. Nonsponsoring utilities do not want to jeopardize their water rights or lose potential revenues. This problem has delayed many projects. Laredo is a prime example: here the TWDB worked with the city, county, and Public Utilities Board for over two years before an agreement could be worked out about how to service colonias. Similar delays occurred in El Paso between its Public Services Board (PSB) and the Homestead MUD (for Montana Vista colonias), and between the PSB and the local specially created Lower Valley Water District Authority (Sparks colonia).

Ownership of water rights and jurisdictional authority to provide service have also generated conflicts. Concern over jealously guarded water rights has presented a problem in El Paso, where water scarcity is a particularly critical issue. Owners of water rights have been reluctant to sell water rights to authorized service providers. In El Paso the nonprofit Lower Valley Water District Authority was created to access government funds for infrastructure, and to provide a service to those areas unserviced by the Public Services Board (PSB). The LVWDA was forced to negotiate with El Paso Water Utilities and to buy water from its PSB, since the latter does not want to service the colonias directly. This has dramatically increased the cost of service provision.

In Texas, even when jurisdictional issues can be worked out, a variety of other factors deter potential sponsors from applying for funds, including the complexity of the funding process, a lack of financial and technical resources to develop a facilities plan, a lack of expertise, and a lack of political will. A number of agencies provide funds and have differing eligibility criteria, making it difficult for potential sponsors to identify the appropriate funding source. Also, counties and small rural water supply corporations (WSCs) usually do not have expertise in constructing or managing this type of large-scale infrastructure (Reed 1994). In particular, WSCs have no experience in wastewater systems, and because of the expense, few are interested in developing their experience beyond water provision. Additionally, sponsors worry about their legal liability, and sponsors may not have the authority to assume debt to repay loans, as is also the case with many counties. Another obstacle is the requirement that sponsors agree to manage the system; many eligible sponsors simply do not want that responsibility. Water scarcity, and the fear that infrastructure provision encourages the future growth of colonias, may also further discourage cities and counties from taking concerted action.

In Texas, the top-down, expert-driven approach to design and approval for TWDB projects creates a bias toward traditional "lumpy" and high-cost infrastructure. Although the TWDB requires that applicants for government funds consider innovative and alternative approaches, this mandate has largely been treated as a technicality. Engineers and experts tend to be overly biased toward large-scale traditional urban infrastructure. The Texas Water Development Board, moreover, has been reluctant to fund any innovative and alternative approaches such as on-site septic system management, even though properly managed septic systems might serve the needs of colonias.[3] As a result, colonias near cities have been the primary beneficiaries of the government policies, and almost all of the projects approved for funding thus far have involved the extension of city or other utility lines (Reed 1994). This prepares those areas for eventual annexation at the expense of the federal and state governments. Sparks colonia in El Paso is a prime example. This colonia is adjacent to valuable land that the city would like to annex, and this incentive for the city means that Sparks became one of the first colonias to have a project completed with the assistance of the TWDB.

More remote colonias with less favorable locations have been neglected (LBJ 1997, vol. 2). Distances from the cities make it cost-prohibitive to service these areas by extending city lines, and population densities are too low to enable the communities to sustain separate systems. The biases mentioned above have prevented TWDB from giving adequate consideration to other approaches for these areas. Additionally, because of a lack of outreach, eligible entities in rural areas may not even be aware of the resources potentially available to assist colonia development.

The relative lack of political strength of colonias in Texas compared to their Mexican counterparts contributes to the perpetuation of a situation of poor-quality servicing. Prior to the intervention of federal and state governments, a Texas colonia's best hope for city-provided infrastructure and services was annexation. Cities rarely pursued this option, however, because potential tax revenues from colonias are low. Tax revenues cannot cover the cost of infrastructure, nor down-line costs of requirements for compliance with city codes, such as the construction of paved roads.

Where cities can legally extend service outside city limits without annexing a community, other factors have deterred them. For example, developer-controlled utilities have resisted serving colonias in order to save the scarce resource—water—for wealthier developments. El Paso is a case in point, where the affluent Horizon City was serviced, but not neighboring colonias such as Sparks. EPISO representatives attribute the El Paso Water Utilities' historical reluctance to service colonias to developer influence on the Public Services (Utilities) Board. Also, some institutional memories go back a long way: El Paso's annexation of Ysleta in the 1950s cost the city far more in service provision than it was able to recover subsequently in revenues and taxes. In short, low tax revenues, lack of resources, liability issues, and other obstacles have prevented counties from providing infrastructure.

The value of a strong political voice can be seen in cases where colonias have successfully organized to lobby government officials for services (Bath et al. 1994; Staudt 1998). State intervention occurred in part as a response to the growing political voice of colonia residents. Community organizing groups such as EPISO and Valley Interfaith work with residents in lobbying government officials and attracting media attention (Wilson and Menzies 1997). These actions are frequently credited as one key impetus for government response. For example, the 10 colonias along Highway 359 in Laredo, under a "Colonias Olvidadas" (Forgotten Colonias) banner, successfully lobbied the government for provision of water lines.

In Texas, city and county requirements, including those related to floodplains and building codes, can preclude the provision of infrastructure and can prevent residents from hooking up to service networks. For example, liability constraints may prevent a city from extending lines to an existing water distribution system if the system does not conform to city regulations. Floodplain regulations and lack of compliance with housing and health codes can also prohibit servicing (see Photos 4 and 25 in earlier chapters). In Cameron Park, for example, the City of Brownsville received $6.65 million (most of it as a grant) to provide water and wastewater, yet only about 150 of 1,100 homes were connected to the completed system because many dwellings did not comply with housing codes and because 20 percent of the homes were located in the floodplain. State and local government should have identified these legal obstacles in advance and produced compromises or other adjustments (less stringent codes, for example). Another example of such a regulatory obstacle is the existence of local laws which limit the amount that service providers can charge for service connections and consumption fees; these regulations can prevent a city from effectively recouping the cost of service provision. Also, new regulations imposed by SB 542 may actively preclude the introduction of services for families who have been resident in the colonia for many years. Specifically, homes cannot be provided with new gas or electric services unless there are adequate water and sewer services installed. The law is, in effect, locking people out of utility provision.

EDAP legislation has given the county more power to regulate subdivision development in order to prevent the proliferation of colonias. According to the Model Subdivision Rules (MSRs), a developer in a county must provide basic infrastructure to tracts of five acres or less (in effect most colonias). Unfortunately, counties often have neither the resources nor the political will to enforce the MSRs. The same is true of health regulations. Similarly, cities can require compliance with MSRs in their ETJs, but many approve subdivisions without water service as a concession in order to get orderly development. If they don't, then developers, recognizing that cities don't have the resources to enforce MSRs, will develop land in the ETJs without even platting it. As we have seen in Chapter 2, 1995 legislation extended the purview of the MSRs and strengthened their enforcement. (Service lines may not be extended to a colonia that has no approved plat plan.)

TWDB's top-down technical approach has also paid little attention to residents' economic ability to connect to infrastructure. The government has instituted some programs to deal with this problem, including the Colonia Loan Plumbing Program, but major funding gaps exist. TWDB estimated a need of $80.8 million, twice what is currently available, for connection fees and indoor plumbing.

In conclusion, even though Wilson and Menzies (1997, 260–261) argue that "The Colonias Water Bill, enacted by the Texas Legislature in 1989 and expanded in 1991, represented a comprehensive approach to addressing the problem of the colonias," and that this represented a serious commitment, they also highlight several major problems that have emerged in delivering funds and in achieving implementation on behalf of the intended beneficiaries. They argue that these difficulties are compounded by the existence of two state agencies with primary responsibility (TWDB and TDHCA), along with two federal agencies (FmHA and the U.S. Rural Development Administration—see Table 15). Moreover, different programs have different eligibility criteria, so that seeking funds means finding one's way through a complex bureaucracy. In addition, Wilson and Menzies (1997, 261–264) identify several other problems that have impeded implementation and resolution of the colonias' water problem. Specifically these include, inter alia: slow materialization of the funds; difficulties in identifying a suitable sponsor for water projects and a host of associated obstacles that this creates; occasional gaps in funding for plumbing and hookups; delays in project construction; and the failure of some border counties to adopt MSRs (and therefore gain eligibility for EDAP funds). Returning to my chapter title, one might ask whether the failure to do more with the considerable resources that have been mobilized represents ambivalence, inefficiency, or incompetence, or perhaps some mixture of the three.

PROVISION OF PUBLIC TRANSPORTATION SERVICE IN MEXICO AND TEXAS

Field research in all three Mexican cities reveals that transportation is supplied primarily by the private sector. Although the use of private automobiles is higher in Mexico along the border than in other cities, mass transit is still much more intensively utilized than in Texas. In Ciudad Juárez, for example, about 50 percent of travel is by bus (González-Ayala 1995, 4). In Matamoros, Ciudad Juárez, and Nuevo Laredo, privately owned buses and taxis compete for contract routes, and the cities have not devoted funds to public transportation, nor have they regulated the private providers. In most cases this practice has created short, indirect routes which are inefficient and costly for colonia residents. *Colonos* in Ciudad Juárez state that their commutes may take as long as two hours each way between their homes and their work at the *maquilas*. Getting to work requires them to take several different buses, possibly a taxi at some point, and long walks to reach their destinations. In addition to individual frustration with the existing system, there is the tremendously high opportunity cost involved (i.e., the high cost of needless time and effort expended because of system inefficiencies and inadequacies).

In Texas, most cities run their own bus service. In Brownsville, for example, the city runs its own bus system (the Brownsville Urban System), but this comprises only twelve buses to serve a city of approximately 100,000 people. However, ridership levels in Texas are much lower than in Mexico (in part a self-fulfilling trend, given the lack of public transportation). In El Paso, only about 5 percent of the population uses public transportation (González-Ayala 1995, 4). Buses run to some, but not all, of the colonias, and generally do not run through them because the roads are not paved. In El Paso, the city's long-term strategy is to create a City-County Transit Department. This is primarily a result of pressure from the colonia community outside the city limits. Unfortunately, however, the City Planning Department believes that because of the current political and economic situation in El Paso, it is unlikely that such a department will be established.

The difference between transportation services in Texas and Mexico is that in Mexico, *colonos* can access at least some transit service. Texas colonia residents invariably have no means of public transport and must rely upon private car ownership or friends and family for their transportation needs. This makes it difficult to enroll in night classes, or in some cases to hold a job, because one cannot be certain that transportation will be available on a regular basis. Perhaps in part because the United States is regarded as a car-owning democracy, and partly because there is no alternative, many colonia households in Texas have a private vehicle. However, whatever their motive for car ownership, the cost of purchasing and maintaining a vehicle diverts valuable resources away from self-build and home consolidation. It also creates access inequity *within* households.

Once again, these transportation differences between Texas and Mexico stem from factors already discussed, including geography, settlement structure, and political considerations. Texas colonias are often located far from existing transportation routes, and population densities may be too low to generate an appreciable level of service demand and operating revenue. In contrast, Mexican colonias usually lie close to major municipal arterials, and private bus or combi-transport can be a very profitable business.

Street Paving in the Colonias of the Border Region

Paved roads on both sides of the Texas-Mexico border are necessary for the same reason—to provide access, and to protect the public health and well-being. In the densely populated colonias along the border, especially in Mexico, a fire can easily get out of control and devastate an entire block if emergency vehicles are unable to reach the area. Without accessible roads, police and ambulances cannot respond in a timely manner to emergency calls.

However, street pavement is generally a low priority for cities. In some colonias, paving is not even an option because it makes no sense to lay it until after water and drainage systems have been installed. In addition, paving is very costly and requires a large investment and ongoing maintenance. It is not surprising, therefore, that only main access streets are likely to be paved in the colonias along the Texas-Mexico border. Lack of funds is the primary reason that cities fail to pave streets in Mexico, but in Texas developers often try to avoid this cost even where funds are available. There is little that can be done in Texas to force developers to pave streets.

Nevertheless, the proportion of paved streets in the Mexican border cities has increased over the past two to three years; estimates place the percentage of paving in colonias at anywhere from 5 to 30 percent of all streets. In Texas, this figure appears to be even lower, although it, too, is growing. With the exception of the main access road running through the colonia, few of the study settlements had extensive paved streets. In some areas the county had laid down some caliche. However, many roads wash out after a rainstorm.

The experience of Ciudad Juárez exemplifies the approach some

Mexican border cities are taking to address the issue. The city's priority is to link up existing roadways as opposed to constructing entirely new ones. The reason for this is that building a major new road requires cooperation among all three levels of government, while the city can connect existing ones on its own. The municipal government has also decided to move away from asphalt as a paving surface and has started to replace it with *concreto hidráulico*. The advantages of concrete are several: it lasts twenty-five to thirty years, whereas asphalt lasts only five; it does not develop potholes like asphalt; it does not buckle under intense usage; and it is more water-resistant.

ELECTRICITY: WHO ENSURES SERVICE?

Electricity is commonly the first requested physical service in the colonias of the United States and Mexico. It is nonlumpy, thus making it easier to provide and less expensive. Coverage on both sides of the border is reasonably good, although important gaps in coverage still exist. Competition between different regional providers creates a situation of uneven coverage on the U.S. side, while the influence of a strong federal authority allows for provision on the Mexican side to be better coordinated. For their part, colonia residents on both sides, particularly in the early days after settlement establishment, have responded to the lack of provision of electricity by tapping existing lines. Recent trends include increased cross-border cooperation between U.S. and Mexican electricity providers and the decentralization of the Mexican federal authority, consistent with broader currents of decentralization in Mexican government.

Electricity and Power Supply in Mexico   In Mexico, provision of electricity is largely a technical matter dependent on the availability of resources (Ward 1986). The Comisión Federal de Electricidad (CFE), administered by the Secretaría de Energía, Minas y Industrias Parastatales (SEMIP), is the responsible federal agency. In the past, only the CFE has had the right to generate electricity under Mexican law. However, the CFE has been affected by the larger trends toward decentralization and privatization in Mexico, which have included the recent privatization of Teléfonos de México. The Public Electric Power Law, passed December 23, 1992, permits the private sector to generate electricity, which it may then sell to the CFE or export.

32. Pair of gas tanks in Cameron Park.

In Mexico, colonia residents were able to petition the CFE for provision of electricity directly through PRONASOL. Funding followed the common Solidarity model of division among federal, state, and municipal sources, with a portion to be provided by residents themselves either in money or in labor. As in Texas, electricity is commonly both the first requested and the first provided of physical services. Hookups for electricity provision are provided in all of the Mexican colonias we surveyed. The capital costs incurred by the CFE are recouped through utility bills, which are remitted bimonthly irrespective of whether land regularization and cadastral taxes have been determined.

With the exception of certain colonias in Ciudad Juárez which have a piped gas supply, the normal method of gas supply is from pairs of standing propane tanks purchased from private companies which service colonias by truck (Photo 32; see also Photo 21). Gas is used mostly for cooking and for heating water.

Electricity and Power Supply in Texas   Electric companies in the United States have offered alternate payment plans to make service affordable. These agencies, both public and private, are basically re-active. They will provide service to anyone who can pay for it under one of these alternate payment plans. Applicants must also meet city or county requirements (permits, etc.). Power consultants work in particular areas to assess the costs of provision, but they do little outreach in terms of supplying people with information about how to get service provided at a lower cost.

Agencies are funded by user fees and installation charges, which can be assessed under several different plans according to specific criteria, including revenue-justified payment plans and revenue guarantee agreements, in which the customer pays the projected deficit up-front. If the price of a connection is $3,500, for example, and the customer is expected to use $1,000 worth of electricity over the next four years, then a customer would pay $2,500 up-front (refundable if revenue is higher than projected). If a line is extended (the bulk of the higher cost) and several neighbors hook up, then the cost is distributed across customers and the individual fees are reduced, possibly to the point where the service can be revenue-justified, and no up-front payments are then required.

In terms of policy, the power companies appear to be accommodating by providing different payment plans and accepting numerous forms of payment: cash, letter of credit, insurance bond, collateral (e.g., a CD). The long-term problem, again, is leapfrog development, which makes the supplying of electricity to individual lots very expensive. Providing service on a customer-by-customer basis makes costs much higher than if the entire grid were installed at the beginning. The issue of service provision, however, may also be complicated by the exigencies of regional utility policy and politics.

In El Paso, electricity was the first service provided to both Sparks and Montana Vista. Electric poles reach most parts of the colonias researched, so anyone in those colonias who can afford electricity can receive it. If a resident wants electric service in an area where a service line has not been provided, the best thing to do is to coordinate with neighbors who also want the service, so that the cost can be divided among the group, and most likely they can qualify for the service under a revenue-justified agreement. The problem, however, is that many neighbors do not know each other and do not feel comfortable joining together in this effort, issues that I will return to in Chapter 4. For those that must provide some sort of collateral up-front in order to receive service under a revenue guarantee agreement, the electric company will work with them to find collateral or financing.

The colonias surveyed in the Brownsville area face more serious problems. Cameron Park is triple-certified for electricity, meaning that three different utility companies have installed lines. That each street has lines from a different company is an indication of the "as needed basis" by means of which lines were installed, in contrast with the more rational practice, whereby one provider installs the lines before the houses are built.

As in Mexico, cooking is mostly done by gas supplied privately through propane tanks. At first, these are the upright transportable tanks, but once established, households install a single, much larger permanent tank which is filled periodically by propane truck suppliers (Photo 1). Occasionally, where gas lines are extended to a major utility (a school, for example), lots alongside the feeder line are offered the opportunity to hook up (Photos 18 and 35). Both Montana Vista and Sparks in El Paso have one or two such streets, as does Sunny Skies.

Street Lighting in the Colonias

Colonia residents on both sides of the border are concerned about the escalating crime rates in their cities. One method of preventing crime and making streets safer is to install street lighting. Well-lit streets deter crime and enable police officials to better perform their jobs. Many border residents stated that increased public safety is a primary goal, and for this reason, street lighting may be a high priority for some. Nor is a high density of coverage required. Except for on principal thoroughfares, the main concern is public (pedestrian) safety at night, not the free flow of traffic. Therefore, street lamps every second or third post is often adequate to provide minimal lighting. This is sometimes referred to as an "austere" (*austero*) level of service in Mexico.

On the Mexican side, street lighting comes under the remit of the city (municipality), which may contract with the CFE, using their poles and paying the costs of initializing service, and then maintain the lamps themselves (Photo 33). Costs are recovered from property taxes. Given the fact that fiscal concerns are the main barrier to the provision of this service, it is interesting to note how Ciudad Juárez has dealt with this issue. The city has found a cost-effective way to provide street lighting that could work for cities on both sides of the border. Juárez has converted its streetlights to sodium-based light bulbs. These produce 25 percent more light while using 50 percent

33. Colonia Felipe Angeles (Ciudad Juárez), showing low network sodium street lighting provided by the municipality.

less electricity. Thus, in 1994, the city spent half of what it used to for lighting and was much better lit, with light poles having increased from 27,107 in 1992 to 34,271 in 1994 (Ayuntamiento de Ciudad Juárez 1994).

In Texas, it appears that formal street lighting is extremely rare in the colonias, although some households do place a heavy-duty lamp either in front of their lot or within it, thereby offering a minimalist service, primarily for their own benefit. Part of the problem is that it is a collectively consumed service (everyone benefits), but there is no easy way to spread the costs among all beneficiaries, since not everyone is contracted to a single company, nor does the city or county have the wherewithal to recover "consumption" costs through local tax revenues. Also, as for public transportation, there is a much lower *demand*, given the low colonia population densities in Texas. Though desirable, street lighting is a low priority in Texas. This is a pity, since publicly sponsored street lighting provision would be relatively inexpensive to provide, particularly if counties and cities were to recover the costs from local property taxes.

Policy Implications for Infrastructure Provision in Texas

Until recently, Texas city government basically ignored the problems of the growing population of the poor residing beyond its periphery and providing cheap labor for its industry and economic development. Counties lacked the resources, authority, and political will to respond to the problems associated with the lack of infrastructure suffered by their colonia populations. The Texas state government did not act until national media attention created public awareness of the "Third World" conditions in its own backyard, and until politicians became aware of the voters and increasingly vociferous organizations that existed in border region colonias (Davies 1995; Wilson and Menzies 1997).

Considering the financial austerity of Mexican local governments, the system of service provision in Mexico seems to work remarkably well, particularly in the past decade, as the formerly high social costs associated with living in serviceless communities and the need to spend long hours lobbying officials has been reduced, and as service provision has become more streamlined administratively, less partisan, and more routinized (Ward 1993; Rodríguez and Ward 1996). Of course, the greater empowerment of municipal authorities also reduces the likelihood that colonias will be ignored or will slip between the cracks of ambivalent or competing jurisdictions. If settlements get ignored in Mexico, it is more likely to derive from their being noticed but not favored by the party or politician in authority. It may result from politics, but not from ambivalence.

Once again, Texas officials probably have more to learn from Mexico than vice versa. One suggestion is to decentralize decision making. This can be as simple as ensuring that residents are also included in discussions about the acquisition of services that will be both affordable and accessible. Another suggestion is that more alternative (low-tech) approaches should be considered for service provision where applicable. Similarly, it would be worth trying to develop projects that incorporate greater self-help, mutual aid, and public participation into servicing programs. However, none of this will have much effect without the political will on the part of Texas officials to make change work for the populations which inhabit the Texas-Mexico borderlands.

Government alone, however, should not be expected to shoulder the burdens of responsibility in the border region. Nonprofits could be used for outreach and community organizing to get services in alternative ways. A key role of outreach to communities would be to create links with eligible sponsors and to inform colonia residents about the programs that are available.

Change, though, will not come about without an impetus at the level of policy which redirects resources into the hands of those best positioned to aid colonia residents. As mentioned in Chapter 2, more resources for regulation enforcement should be made available at the county level. Federal or state agencies must act as facilitators in connecting affordable housing and infrastructure. Service provision needs to be made more attractive to political subdivisions such as cities and counties by offering incentives or by reducing regulations regarding housing codes, liability, etc. The government could institute a policy of in-filling existing colonias by settling new residents in areas where infrastructure is or will soon be provided. Consolidating city and county jurisdictional authority for colonias would reduce the confusion over responsibility. Making regulations more flexible in Texas to account for the differences in situations, and allowing for more "low-tech" and "self-help" approaches, could also assist *colonos* in obtaining services. This would require that officials find ways to skirt legal issues that inhibit innovation.

However, rather than promoting a comprehensive policy approach to address the myriad issues of the colonias, the action on the part of policymakers has been directed toward solving only segments of the problem: namely, the threat to public health and the proliferation of colonias. In this sense, Texas government has treated the colonias with ambivalence. The government ignored the existence of colonias until compelled by the threat of an impending health crisis and by public outrage to address the situation. Mexico, on the other hand, has demonstrated a commitment to the residents of the colonias that recognizes their intrinsic importance to society. Within this broad clarion call, there are a number of specific recommendations that I would wish to highlight:

1. Water and Wastewater Management and Provision

Aims: To tap resources that will allow for these "lumpy" services to be extended into colonias. To resolve ambiguities and overcome ambivalence among the political jurisdictions, thereby empowering and mandating them to coordinate more effectively in undertaking service provision.

Recommendations

- Revise EDAP criteria so that programs apply more widely in counties with significant colonia problems. Also, once counties are assigned EDAP status, lengthen the overall period of designation to, say, six to ten years.
- Provide incentives for political authorities (jurisdictions) to access EDAP and other funds on behalf of colonias.
- Revise HB 1001 and SB 542, and any other legislation with similar provisions, which inhibit or slow down on-lot development and densification.
- Eliminate the requirement that water and wastewater sponsors can only be political jurisdictions, such that colonias and nonprofits may apply directly for funds.
- Simplify the application process (*ventanilla única*) and have one coordinating agency for all grants and loans.
- Consider innovative and alternative solutions for colonias, particularly in the arena of "low-tech" and low-cost sewage and wastewater removal schemes.
- Decentralize decision making to include active community participation and incorporate self-help and local human resources in infrastructure development projects.
- Extend infrastructure cost share to include absentee lot owners, either by direct ongoing charges or by "deferred" assessment (i.e., a lien on future sale/inheritance [see Shoup 1994]).
- Increase the amount of funding available to reduce or pay the cost of hookup ("tap") fees, and for internal plumbing grants and loans.
- Consider innovative financing schemes which postpone repayment (e.g., deferred assessments [Shoup 1994]).

Rationale   The aim here is to extend the powers and opportunities of political jurisdictions, NGOs, and colonias in order that they may leverage funds for water and wastewater provisions; and to minimize the extent to which projects fail (or don't get started) because of lack of political will, inappropriate or "Catch-22" regulations and standards, or prevailing low colonia block occupancy rates (absentee owners). In addition, new approaches need to be conceived that will reduce the overall unitary costs of infrastructure, through low-tech and/or minimum-standards solutions, and the costs to beneficiaries, through "tap" fee grants and waivers, complementary credits for hookups and internal plumbing, etc. Failure to do so will incur major opportunity costs, as well as additional hardship to "beneficiaries." If grants and subsidies are nonstarters, then deferred assessments and other innovative schemes should be introduced.

2. Street Paving and Public Transportation Services to Colonias

Aims: To raise accessibility in and out of settlements. To raise the level of effective demand. To make public or private transportation more cost-effective. Generalized street paving is probably not a general high priority, nor should it be.

Recommendations

- Use more cost-effective paving (concrete rather than asphalt).
- Prioritize principal arterial access street(s) only, and leave side streets unpaved or "austere" (caliche or hard core).
- Engage community mutual aid in street leveling/improvement campaigns.
- Develop guidelines with respect to the minimum road conditions necessary for emergency vehicle access, perhaps modifying vehicles to make them more rough and ready (four-wheel drive, all-terrain tires, etc.).
- Provide regular transportation at peak times, perhaps using robust buses; double up (shared) ridership on school district buses, etc.
- Issue shared taxi concessions to run specified routes (as in Mexico microbus *peseros*).

3. Electricity and Street Lighting

Policy Recommendations

- Outreach programs to community organizations informing them of ways to contract for electricity and avoid pitfalls of multiple-company certification in a single neighborhood.

- Extend infrastructure cost share to include absentee lot owners, either by direct ongoing charges or by "deferred" assessment (i.e., a lien on future sale/inheritance [see Shoup 1994]).
- Provide grants and credits for installation costs and hookups.
- Promote "austere" street lighting, on principal arterial access roads, and occasional placement elsewhere (corners and midblock [or nearest adjacent occupied lot]).

This chapter has drawn our attention to three policy areas associated with the provision of infrastructure. First, the high costs of providing what are often "lumpy" (high up-front charges) utilities and the need to find ways of spreading those costs among beneficiaries and over time. Second, the jurisdictional conflicts, resistance, and ambivalence associated with servicing in no man's land. Third, the weak level of demand in many colonias, given the very-low-density populations that live there, itself a result of high levels of absentee lot owners and the practice of "leapfrogging" lot sales in order to promote colonia spread and the appearance of widespread colonia development. In the first two areas we have sought to identify a series of possible ways forward. This third point, however, the low density of people in no man's land, is a major problem, not just because it represents low demand and leads to higher unitary costs of service provision, but also because it isolates families physically, and reduces the propensity for neighboring and for collective (community) action which, in Mexico in the past, has often proven to be the single most important determinant of colonia upgrading. Not only do protest group "squeaky wheels" sometimes get the grease, but active community organization can be important in other ways: information sharing, effective negotiation, reduced dependency, a better prioritization of internally generated needs (vs. externally imposed perceived needs), public collaborative mutual aid works, child-minding, and informal support groups. For this reason "social infrastructure," and its propensity to develop, are also vitally important in colonia development, and are discussed at length in the next two chapters.

Four

Settlements or Communities? Social Organization and Participation in the Colonias

Introduction: Horizontal and Vertical Integration

Analysis of the informal social infrastructure in colonias on both sides of the border quickly alerted me to a crucial difference in the nature and density of patterns and levels of social organization. Almost always in Mexico, colonias are possessed of a relatively high level of social organization, much of which relates directly to the activities of acquiring land and services, defending the fledgling settlement, and undertaking mutual aid for settlement improvement programs. In this way settlements quickly attain a level of community participation, albeit this is often a rather instrumental form of self-organization for the purposes of settlement development and upgrading. But out of such interactions the dynamic patterns of friendships and ongoing networks are often forged. This feature of relatively high levels of social mobilization and organization in young irregular settlements is not unusual in Mexico; nor is it unusual to observe a tendency toward a decline or atrophy of participation and community efforts over time, once the settlement has achieved its development goals, become physically integrated within the city, and often changed its residential makeup to include a large (minority) proportion of renters, who are less vested in community upgrading (Handelman 1975; Gilbert and Ward 1985). But it does seem that these initial activities create the basis for formation of a genuine sense of community. Of course, the informal social infrastructure will differ from one community to the next, but in Mexican colonias at least, a sense of community exists from the outset and even after social relationships are no longer tied to the settlement per se.

In Texas, colonias exist much more as settlements, and only relatively rarely as communities. For a variety of reasons that I will touch upon below, the settlement process in Texas colonias does not foster a strong community spirit. Part of the problem lies with the individualized contracting between developer and settler, which makes redundant the need for collective negotiation—so often the case in Mexico (albeit mediated through leaders). Another problem is the lower population density, since many lot owners are absentee owners, and occupied homes are spread around the block rather than being associated with cheek-by-jowl neighboring and propinquity. The lack of collective action is also a product of a lack of a perceived common outside "enemy": as we observed in Chapter 3, there is no palpable political jurisdiction, level of government, or agency to get mad at, or to lobby for support. Nor do the developers' unfulfilled promises serve to galvanize residents into action against them; instead, relations between developer and colonia residents are often cozy. The point here is that there is very little informal social infrastructure at the outset in Texas, and if a sense of community is to be forged, then it will take time and patience, and it will probably require some facilitator to make it happen rather than develop spontaneously.

In the context of colonia development, what is meant by *informal social infrastructure*? For the purposes of this study it refers to the networks of communication and the habitual contacts between individuals within a community or settlement. *Formal* social infrastructure, by contrast, differs in that it refers to the institutional structures that are created externally in order to meet settlement social needs—health, education, recreation, development, etc.—structures which are considered in greater detail in Chapter 5. In order for a strong sense of community to emerge it is imperative that horizontal and ongoing social linkages, or informal social infrastructure, among settlement members be fostered, often in conjunction with vertical social linkages to supra-neighborhood organizations, although these appear to be less critical.

Two further concepts require introduction. First, *horizontal integration* describes the amount of interaction at the local level among individuals within the community or settlement in order to access resources. Second, *vertical integration* describes the level of interaction and number of contacts between the community or settlement and organizations and powerful actors outside of the immediate area (i.e., in the city, region, or state, and sometimes even in federal govern-

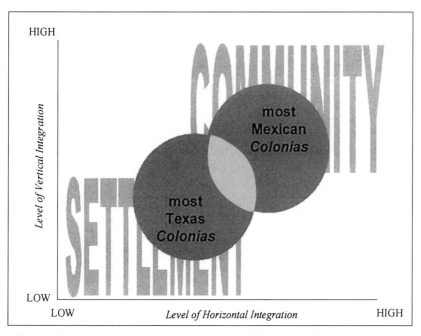

Figure 7. Dimensions of informal social integration in Mexican and Texas border colonias.

ment; see Figure 7). Vertical integration is important because it affords access to supra-local resources, i.e., those beyond immediate availability to colonia-based community groups. Both forms of integration are important, but horizontal integration must take place before effective vertical integration can truly begin to enhance the reality of the community at large. Otherwise, it may just act to advance the interests of one or two individual leaders whose interests are primarily external, without impacting upon (and sometimes without reference to) the settlement population (Eckstein 1988).

Community participation is another important aspect of colonia social interaction patterns. *Participation* can be described as colonia residents' awareness of, and involvement in, the decision making process in the colonia, particularly insofar as these decisions impinge upon colonia development (Skinner 1983). The emergence of a sense of community is most likely to be successful if there is active participation, as well as multiple levels of horizontal and vertical integration. Overall, the colonias in our study exhibited varying levels of horizontal integration and participation, but generally speaking, those which had accessed more services also tended to demonstrate a correspondingly higher level of vertical integration. However, both types of integration appear to be necessary in achieving self-sufficiency: comprehensive colonia improvements can occur only after colonias are horizontally integrated and begin to access resources as a unified body. In other words, widespread colonia improvements will only occur after effective bonds have been established within the entire settlement, as well as with appropriate outside entities.

Reference to these notions of vertical and horizontal integration, and to community participation, help to clarify the idea that there are important differences between a settlement and a community. A *settlement* is usually defined in demographic and spatial terms, without any assumption about the characteristics of any particular social infrastructure. The concept of a *community*, on the other hand, transcends spatial and demographic definitions (although both are implicit), and makes some assumptions about the group's norms, shared goals, and values that govern social behavior and organization. Generally speaking, when it comes to physical development projects and initiatives, settlements are likely to be highly dependent upon supra-local decision making on their behalf, whereas communities have a greater capacity for self-help and mutual aid that is likely to yield positive outcomes of upgrading and improvement irrespective of the degree of external involvement (although this, too, is usually enhanced by intra-settlement social mobilization). Thus, communities are more likely to be proactive in developing an internal settlement development agenda and links with external agents.

As the chapter title suggests, this distinction between settlement and community is important since it "flags" important differences that I observe between Mexican and Texas colonias. It also indicates the rather different mindsets of the ways in which colonias are perceived by supra-local authorities and nongovernment organizations. On the one hand, if colonias are viewed as settlements, then their social construction is primarily one that is developed in demographic and physical terms without reference to or acknowledgment of social and cultural patterns of organization, or leadership structures. This facilitates an analysis and policy approach which focuses upon demographics and physical infrastructure and which implicitly assumes that development initiatives must be promoted from outside *onto* the settlement surface—what, in Chapter 5, I will refer to as an "ends-centered" approach. In these circumstances policymakers may focus upon short-term responses to what are perceived to be temporary problems. Physical services will be provided by government entities, with no real effort to help make the colonia a socially self-sufficient entity. As we have already seen in previous chapters, this perception (of dependency) is the one that has traditionally been fostered by Texas authorities.

On the other hand, if colonias are viewed as communities with some level of internal cohesion and commonly shared goals (even if these are not uniformly shared but comprise several competing substructures or factions), or if some level of community organization is the desired end result, then policy recommendations are much more likely to take a more holistic approach, and to focus upon ways of working with the social (community) structure in order to improve physical infrastructure. Working with the informal social infrastructure of a colonia in this way is likely to require much more time and effort than an instrumental interventionist approach (i.e., in-and-out to provide x service), but it also raises the possibility of a number of other positive outcomes: namely, those of improving the match between physical infrastructural outcomes and resident-specified needs; a reduction of overall costs; and greater acceptance and commitment in terms of cost recovery and ongoing maintenance (Skinner 1983). In developing countries community participation has become a sine qua non of government development projects (Moser 1989; UNCHS 1996).

In Mexican colonias horizontal integration is invariably high at the outset since this is a necessary precondition if the (illegal) land capture process is to be a success, and if adverse government response (namely eviction) is to be avoided. It is also paramount for the politicking and pressure politics needed to begin to address some of the lack of services, settlement inaccessibility, regularization, etc. Traditionally this horizontal mobilization is soon followed by aggressive steps toward achieving some level of vertical integration as settlement leaders seek official recognition and support for the colonia, and as supra-local authorities maybe seek to co-opt neighborhoods, and as local actors cultivate political constituencies and personal bases of support (Cornelius 1975; Ward 1986). Thus, the colonia quickly achieves some level of community self-organization and participation, even during the earliest stages of development. In contrast, in Texas there are very low levels of both horizontal and vertical integration at the outset, and the pressure toward some significant level of self-organization may take many years to emerge, if ever. Texas colonias, viewed here as settlements, therefore have low potential to become communities.

This chapter examines the propensity for social development in the colonias of Texas and Mexico in terms of vertical and horizontal integration, and focuses upon the issues of participation, leadership, and the involvement of external entities. Individual colonia improvement and development trajectories tend to reflect where that colonia falls on this spectrum between settlement and community (see Figure 7). While colonias on both sides of the border demonstrate a tendency toward the creation and re-creation of social infrastructure through the development of horizontal and vertical integration, the pace of and propensity toward cultivating these defining elements of community remain much weaker in Texas than in Mexico.

Traditions of Settlement, Traditions of Community

The reasons for this differential level of informal social infrastructural development may be explained by comparing the originating environment in which colonia formation takes place. These are examined briefly below.

MIGRATION PATTERNS AND SETTLEMENT FORMATION

Migration analyses traditionally focus almost exclusively upon regional migration patterns and flows. In addition, in the Mexico–United States context it also prioritizes transborder flows of international migration, documented and undocumented (Butterworth and Chance 1981; Cornelius 1992; Bustamante 1992; González-Aréchiga 1992). As was indicated earlier in Chapter 1, most of the Texas colonia resident population are Mexican-American U.S. citizens, or they are legal Mexican-origin migrants. In the Mexican border cities, colonias are populated by those born in that same city and by migrants from elsewhere in the Republic, although the majority are from relatively nearby areas in the same state, or from adjacent states. While there may be important differences in patterns of provenance on either side of the border, it seems unlikely that this will impact significantly upon colonia development in Texas, with the single exception of the criterion of legal immigration status in Texas. To the extent that it exists (and we have no clear data), the possibility that one's neighbors, relatives, and friends may be undocumented Mexicans is likely to inhibit the development of community interaction and popular participation, whether for fear of being found out (if one is undocumented), or through fear of being penalized by association. Although little is known about how the Immigration and Naturalization Service (INS) operations on the one hand, and the social construction of illegal migrant status on the other, actually impact upon the colonia-resident psyche, there seems little doubt that they inhibit easy cooperative social interaction and the willingness to participate. There is widespread anecdotal evidence of fear among recent Mexican immigrant households that other households living nearby may report or denounce them on the basis of rumor or suspicion. One should not underestimate how pervasive is the stereotype that many colonia residents are illegal, nor ignore the extent to which it may raise suspicion and act as a barrier to community development.[1]

Compared with the literature on regional migration patterns, there is far less analysis of people's intracity mobility patterns between residential neighborhoods in cities and counties (i.e., their recent moves between different places of residence in the same locality). This is especially true in the United States, where little interest has been expressed in intraurban migration since Rossi's (1955) seminal work in Philadelphia tied most residential decision making to criteria related to one's stage in the life cycle. Yet there has been virtually no research on the intracity residential search behavior of Mexican-American or Mexican migrant populations within cities in the United States. In Mexico, there have been various surveys of intraurban trajectories (Turner 1968; Brown 1972; Ward 1976), while more recent studies appear to demonstrate that moves are closely tied to the dynamics and affordability of land and housing markets (Gilbert and Ward 1982; Ugalde et al. 1974; van Lindert and Verkoren 1986). In Mexico, colonia residents' last place of residence was usually a rented room in a center-city or nearby tenement, or in a kinsman's home, again often relatively nearby. Very rarely are they migrants who have just arrived in the city and chosen to "own" a plot in the periphery (Gilbert and Ward 1982). It seems likely that this is also the case in Texas colonias, but we know virtually nothing of these *colonos'* former residential life histories. Once again, a fear of raising questions that might appear to impinge upon their citizenship status probably explains why researchers have avoided this research arena.

Nevertheless, knowing how people move into colonias has considerable relevance for understanding the development of the horizontal interactions among residents, such that important differences exist between Mexico and Texas. Specifically, in Mexico, the widespread demand for land for self-help, combined with the much greater insecurity associated with the land acquisition process (especially invasions, although not exclusively so), means that most prospective residents arrive in the colonia en masse within a relatively short period of a few months (and sometimes within only a few days—in invasions, for example). As mentioned above, they move into the newly developing settlement from the downtown tenements and from nearby established colonias where they may have been living with kin or as renters (Gilbert and Ward 1982). This sharp and rapid influx generates a common experience over a short time span and results in much higher levels of early community participation and mutual aid programs.

In Texas, we have very limited data about previous place of residence for new colonia arrivals. Staudt (1998, 99 [Map 4]) offers a rare glimpse into migration trajectories for new periphery colonias in El Paso (County), and although the spatial categories are unnuanced, the data suggest that, as in Mexico, nearby colonias are also important jump-off points for new colonia formation (32 percent of new residents in her study). A further 41 percent were reported as coming from the city itself or from a formerly annexed area (Ysleta). Thirteen percent came from out of state, while 14 percent came directly from Mexico. Whatever their trajectories, Texas colonia residents tend to settle on an individual basis, buying plots from a developer in a process which is legal—as we observed in Chapter 2. Moreover, the overall demand is lower, and the settlement process may take many years to complete. Also, some residents appear to purchase lots as an eventual homestead, but do not occupy the plots for many years, since they have moved on to cities elsewhere in the United States. Thus, they are sojourners rather than settlers (Cornelius 1992). Unlike in Mexico, where plots are quickly occupied, in Texas, plot occupancy is often highly dispersed, militating against propinquity as a basis for neighboring (as Figure 6 sharply demonstrates). The point is that neither the legality of land acquisition, nor the nature of the settlement process, is conducive to in-group community formation. There may be some level of familial cooperation, but on the whole participation is low. In contrast, in Mexican colonias the nature of information flows between kinsmen, or between families from the same state or village, can lead to small-scale clustering of households within the settlement, further contributing to ongoing social interaction (Lomnitz 1977; Ward 1978).

The Level of Poverty

The level of poverty is also likely to shape community formation, particularly insofar as colonia residents do or do not form a societal mainstream. The largest group in Mexican society is the working class, many of whom live in colonias and form the bulk of the electorate; whereas in the United States and Texas, the middle class is the majority, and the impoverished do not have a powerful voice. As a result, the residents of Mexican colonias are much more likely to be viewed as legitimate voting members of society, and as part of a mainstream. Legitimacy and recognition afford greater participation to the *colonos* due to the more open vertical channels of participation provided by the political process, whether this is democratic or authoritarian in nature.

In Texas, colonias and their residents are much more likely to be isolated geographically and socially, and their smaller relative numerical importance marginalizes them, sometimes fostering a sense of inferiority and illegitimacy, particularly given the stereotyped notion that colonia populations are largely made up of undocumented Mexicans. That stereotype aside (most are citizens and/or legal residents), low voter registration and relatively small numbers do not make them part of a mainstream political voice for possible capture by ambitious politicians. Except for in those counties where they do represent a conspicuous and sizable population and/or where major organizations such as Valley Interfaith or EPISO have managed to raise the public profile of colonia deprivation, few local politicians have sought to court colonia residents as a source of voter support. This is because they are often unregistered as voters, and because local power elites are generally unsympathetic toward colonias. Opportunities for broad participation built around political mobilization have therefore been limited.

Influence of Local Leadership

This dimension refers to the role played in community development by the principal local patron or mobilizer of the colonia. In Texas,

this patron may well be the land developer himself, who sells and fi-
nances the plots of land purchased by Texas *colonos*, and who often
maintains a personal and individualized relationship with each colonia household. Some notable colonia developers in Texas have been
able to nurture a positive relationship with colonia residents and land-
holders. The developer may present an image of himself as the person
who has made the "American dream" possible for struggling low-
income families. Often, too, he will demonstrate his goodwill toward
colonia residents by offering lightweight community supports such as
a park (as in Webb County's El Cenizo), or by making other minor
concessions, as was the case in Sparks (El Paso County), thereby reducing any dissatisfaction and adversarial response that might otherwise develop among *colonos*.

There is a clear asymmetric social class and power relationship between the better-off land developer and the resident, one which is
likely to be carefully sustained by the developer, who will not take
kindly to any challenge to his authority. Indeed, his almost total control over the land acquisition process through Contract for Deed and
the very limited rights that this afforded to purchasers, has meant that
he could usually head off any threats to his paramountcy. Moreover,
there is considerable potential for discretion that the developer may
actively exercise over the colonia development process in terms of
land sales. Whereas a formal institution such as a bank might repossess
land for lack of regular payments (as could the colonia developer), he
will usually renegotiate payment plans which condone one or two
missed payments, further cementing the dependent patron-client relationships between himself and colonia residents. Indeed, the very
fact that he does not usually assiduously pursue foreclosure at the first
opportunity further cultivates this dependency. Through these and
other measures such as the provision of occasional lightweight services
and/or modest improvements on their behalf, developers may actually
endear themselves to the colonia residents—as did Cecil McDonald in
Webb County, for example.

Moreover, another strategy developers use to cultivate a positive
image of themselves is to construct antagonistic relationships with city
and county organizations, portraying them as indifferent to colonia
issues. Because of the nature of these land deals and the sizable profits
which accrue, developers take steps to protect themselves from would-
be adversaries (especially the state) by ensuring strong bonds between
themselves and the colonia residents. Thus many developers have suc-

ceeded, at least until very recently, in promoting themselves as the sole defenders of these communities (Myerson 1995). In short, developers may be an important barrier to the emergence of community self-empowerment and to direct vertical integration between settlement residents and supra-local organizations or authorities. Thus the opportunities for community-based independent leaders to emerge are circumscribed.

In Mexico the opposite is true. Land developers and vendors hardly ever figure after the initial deal is struck, and certainly do not become ongoing intermediaries around whom community mobilization may cohere. Instead, local leaders quickly emerge, motivated in different ways: some are authoritarian bosses (*caciques*) eager to make money from extortion and from kickbacks tied to the illegal land invasion or land development process (Cornelius 1973; Ward 1989a). Others are self-serving minor would-be politicians who are cutting their political teeth within the lower echelons of the PRI, and who hope to benefit from party patronage—what I refer to as "positional" leaders (Ward 1989a). Leaders may also be (relatively) honest brokers whose efforts are informed by a wish to expedite colonia development for them and for their families. Church leaders are also sometimes important positional leaders, although their role is usually one of offering moral and pastoral support rather than being in the vanguard of colonia mobilization (see Ward 1989b).

The impact of Mexican community leaders may significantly shape *colonos'* levels of participation, as well as the settlement's physical development trajectory. As Cornelius (1973, 136) noted:

> . . . anyone who does extended fieldwork in squatter settlements or related types of low-income zones in a Latin American city cannot fail to be impressed by the importance of leadership differences in accounting for the development trajectories of each settlement. There appear to be strong relationships between leadership performance and differences in the outcome of demand-making experiences, the length of time needed to accomplish certain developmental objectives, the quality of relationships maintained between a settlement and political and governmental agencies, and the level of internal organization within a settlement over time.

Local leadership, therefore, is often crucial in fostering both horizontal and vertical integration. In order to be effective a leader needs to be known by a large number of residents and have their support, so s/he serves as a catalyst for decision making and organization around local development projects, serving to meld settlement residents into a group with a strong sense of community. And, as a "broker," the leader serves to link the community to the outside authorities, acting as a conduit for negotiations and liaison (Cornelius 1975; Ward and Chant 1987). Nor is it uncommon, given the larger size of Mexican settlements, for several competing leadership factions to exist, although this may equally work against successful outcomes, since it leads to internal conflicts between neighborhoods, each allied to different leaders, thereby undermining the effective authority of any one leadership group.

Access to Land, Land Supply, and the Institutional Environment

The ease and legality of access to land for self-build are an important factor shaping the level of participation by colonia residents. In Texas, notwithstanding the MSR legislation applicable in certain counties from 1989 onward and prior to SB 336 in 1995, land was obtained easily and legally, albeit under conditions which favored developers. This highly individualized process severely reduced the need for or likelihood of collective action by colonia residents to resist developer interests or developer-imposed conditions. Contracts were essentially developer-family, and no other actor or agency was involved around which collective mobilization might gel. Rather, collective response was only likely to emerge from a crisis situation which impinged upon the whole settlement (e.g., natural disasters). Moreover, as we observed in Chapter 2, developers deliberately sought to spread lot sales *across* the colonia in order to foster a more highly developed visual impression, but this, too, reduced the formation of close-knit neighboring. Thus, the process of settlement may take a long time: In Cameron Park, for example, settling of the plots has occurred over a period of approximately twenty-five years. Nor does a developer's failure to fulfill promises of service provision appear to have galvanized protest movements before or after Model Subdivision Rules came into effect. Most households made improvised arrangements and, unlike their Mexican counterparts, were fairly passive in seeking systematic improvements or in taking the initiative to press their case with city or county officials. Where improvements came, they tended to materialize from a complex raft of agencies in local, state, and federal government and, as we saw in Chapter 3, were riddled with "Catch-22" impediments to implementation. Unless a strong community organization existed, little was likely to emerge from the community level—at least not spontaneously, and not from the bottom up. Instead, as we shall observe below, it was wider (often religious) organizations that began to mobilize on behalf of the colonias (Wilson and Menzies 1997).

In Mexico, whatever route is adopted to acquire land (invasion or purchase), the process is illegal and often highly insecure, especially in the early phase of invasions, which, if they are to be successful, must be collectively organized and rapidly effected. Thus, either the land capture process itself (in the case of invasions), or the subsequent regularization of "clouded titles" to convert land rights from de facto to de jure, necessarily requires some level of collective organization. Moreover, neither land developers nor *ejidatario* vendors (the usual sources of illegal land sales since the 1980s) are cast as villains. Once land is acquired, *colonos* recognize the need to settle their claims with government agencies, and it is these agencies that become the target of community collective action. The same applies with regard to services provision, road paving, markets, schools, health centers, and so on (Gilbert and Ward 1985; Ward 1986). Resources are scarce and needs are pressing, such that squeaky wheels tend to get greased first—at least that was the case until a decade or so ago: since then governments have become rather more systematic and routinized (Ward 1986). Colonias that mobilized most aggressively and/or those that managed to cultivate powerful political backing tended to jump the queue and receive priority attention. Community mobilization was, therefore, a sine qua non for colonia improvement and development. Indeed, community organizations and, even more, local leaders had become so influential by the early 1980s that in order to systematize the regularization and servicing procedures, agencies deliberately sought to undermine collective action and sideline leaders by insisting upon individual households contracting with the authorities. This shift from collective to individual contracting was accompanied by important shifts and streamlining in the allocation of powers and responsibilities for colonias: Agencies became more effectively empowered and resourced, and both policy-making and implementation processes were made more simple and less bureaucratized. Notwithstanding this shift toward individualization of property and citizen rights, some agencies such as PRONASOL made community organization mandatory both in the solicitation and implementation of development programs, though these continued to be carefully stage managed by the state and mediated through approved-of leaders (rather than *caciques*).

A further barrier to community organization is the tenure mix within the colonia. As we observed in Chapter 2, tenure is almost uniformly that of owner occupancy in Texas, as it is in Mexico in the early stages of colonia formation and expansion. However, Mexican colonias, as they age and densify, do so in part through the creation of rental opportunities by small-scale landlords (often colonia residents themselves utilizing additional plots for rental accommodation; see Gilbert and Varley 1991). Ultimately, renters and other nonowners may form a large minority (or even majority) of the colonia population. The important point is that this higher ratio of renters to owners reduces the common goals that underpin community mobilization and participation, since renters have little vested interest in pressing for colonia-wide improvements in which they have no financial stake, and which may even come to penalize them through higher rents. However, it should also be noted that by the time renting reaches this threshold level, community organization around settlement servicing and regularization issues has usually dwindled, since most sought-after services have been secured already.

Access to Information

Access to information and the flow of information also affect the level of participation by colonia residents. In Mexico, good information is essential: first, to correctly identify institutional pressure points; second, in order to hustle effectively for resources. This has meant that colonias traditionally have tended to show much higher levels of political awareness even compared to other low-income housing market populations, where there is less need and propensity for collective action (housing projects, for example; see Cornelius 1975). Moreover, their forming part of society's mainstream (at least in terms of population) means that media attention and coverage will be greater, and both public and nongovernmental agencies are more likely to target them with information about development initiatives and opportunities. Also, information flows in low-income communities are often highly personalized, informal, and through word of mouth; thus, the greater the population density and level of social interaction among *colonos*, the greater likelihood that a sense of community will emerge and will be perpetuated.

In Texas, there are severe information barriers which result in a low level of participation. It is to the advantage of the developer to *prevent* information concerning social, economic, and infrastructural development from reaching the *colonos*. This makes them dependent on the developer and shields him from what would otherwise be their legitimate complaints. Nor have government authorities, with one or two exceptions (the TDHCA, for example), done enough to promote the information flow to colonias. County officials in particular have been reticent to raise colonia expectancies unduly, or to alienate local political support among non-colonia populations. In addition, language in Texas may limit access to information given by outside sources, since most residents speak Spanish as their first language and a minority are unable to speak or read English well. Although this means that language is not a major barrier to horizontal integration and interaction, it may be an impediment to vertical integration, especially if this is individualized rather than being articulated through clearly identified leaders.

POLITICAL RECOGNITION AND THE LEGITIMACY OF COLONIAS AND COLONIA ORGANIZATIONS

As I have observed, the stance taken by the various levels and branches of government toward colonias is another critical factor in the community development process. Since the 1970s, Mexican governments have viewed colonias pragmatically both as settlements in which the bulk of the work force is housed, and as a major political constituency of electoral and other forms of possible governmental support. In the past, this constituency has been the key to maintaining both the political hegemony of the PRI and social stability through mechanisms of co-optation, divide and rule, routinization of demand making, etc. (Eckstein 1988; Ward 1986, 1989b). More recently, with electoral and political opening, colonias continue to provide a large proportion of the votes through which parties get themselves elected into power, and the PRI's hegemony and even dominance have declined as a result. Major electoral registration campaigns in the early 1990s, in combination with substantive electoral reforms in Mexico, have led to high levels of voter participation in contemporary elections (as high as 78 percent in the 1994 presidential elections). Today, this more open electoral environment has meant that the party that secures the working-class (colonia) vote will probably win the election. This was certainly the message sent by Cuauhtémoc Cárdenas' victory over the PRI in the first-ever elections for Jefe de Gobierno for Mexico City's Federal District in July 1997, and it will almost certainly be the case in most other contemporary city elections (Ward 1998b). But whether as in the past when patronage politics prevailed, or today when more clean and highly contested electoral politics are the order of the day, colonia populations have always enjoyed considerable influence. This political influence has done much to encourage their participation in government-sponsored programs.

In Texas, however, until the late 1980s most levels of government and many political jurisdictions failed to recognize the legitimacy of colonias, and they certainly did not encourage the development and improvement of colonia settlements. To some extent this continues to be the case, particularly away from the border, in areas which do not have a major colonia problem and whose priorities are therefore different. But even some border jurisdictions are reluctant or unable to undertake responsibility for and a commitment to colonia programs.

Although the state legislature and senior officials have begun to address the colonia problem in the past decade, and while county and state politicians are more cognizant of the modest but increasing significance that colonia populations offer as electors, the political priority accorded colonia development remains relatively low. In Mexico housing policy and low-income residential infrastructure are national mainstream issues of concern to all levels of government everywhere. In Texas they are spatially and sectorally constrained, such that any major initiative must seek to become a statewide imperative: either by including legislative proposals that may potentially be leveraged elsewhere and not just in colonia-dominated border counties, or by shaming the state into serious action (Wilson and Menzies 1997). While political embarrassment is important, pragmatic politics requires that colonia initiatives must be placed *alongside* (and sometimes *within*) wider legislation—as we saw in Chapter 3 regarding the so-called Colonias Water Bill. The point is that to date, there has probably still not been sufficient political or electoral concern for colonia residents to galvanize collective consciousness and community organization within colonia neighborhoods. Rather, community organization has been vested at a non-neighborhood level—within church-based regional or city coalitions such as Valley Interfaith and EPISO, for example (Wilson and Menzies 1997). Nor has the tradition emerged in Texas for colonia upgrading and improvement to occur through community and state collaboration and partnership, as is the case in most developing countries (Gilbert and Ward 1984; Moser 1989; UNCHS 1996). In Mexico, too, as has been mentioned above, colonia development projects are invariably undertaken in close collaboration with neighborhood communities, a process that was further institutionalized through PRONASOL projects between 1989 and 1994, and which continues today through municipal and state agencies, and through local government.

In light of these many factors which differentially shape the propensity for community participation, it is little wonder that the wherewithal for community solidarity and organization is largely lacking in Texas, whereas it is almost ubiquitous in Mexico. High participation levels in Mexican colonias are a social necessity in order to successfully establish the colonia, and to obtain physical infrastructure. Such active participation by residents enhances the emergence of a genuine sense of community. The quest for legal recognition of land claims, resistance to eviction and displacement, and pressure politics for essential services, all help to account for the significant vertical integration in the colonias of Mexico, which will be discussed in the following sections. In Texas, low levels of participation and high levels of resident passivity and dependence suggest that colonias begin very much as settlements and, lacking strong prospects or support that will enable horizontal and vertical integration to develop, have a difficult time becoming communities.

Social Development in Texas and Mexican Colonias: Evidence from the Border Case Studies

Having spelled out the barriers to and opportunities for the cultivation of the horizontal and vertical integration within settlements that might lead to their being considered communities, I now turn to an evaluation of how these play out in the border case studies that we analyzed, particularly on the Texas side, using the Mexican case largely as a referent. Specifically, I propose to examine horizontal integration in two ways: first, through the levels of community participation achieved, and second, through the nature of local leadership that emerges. My examination of vertical integration will focus upon the role played by supra-local actors, nongovernmental as well as governmental.

Horizontal Integration within Colonias

Levels of Public Participation Found in Colonias   For many years now public participation, or community participation as it is sometimes called, has been widely espoused by international agencies and governments, as well as those on the political left and right—albeit for different reasons (Gilbert and Ward 1984).[2] Moreover, it continues to be the flavor of the decade among international development agencies (UNCHS 1996; Moser 1989, 1996). However, official espousal of support for community participation tends to focus upon participation as an *end in itself* (i.e., as a goal that will have some measurable impact in enhancing the implementation of a project), rather than as a *means to an end*—namely, as a mechanism to empower local populations in order that they be more autonomous, effective, and self-sustaining as communities (Moser 1989).

In Mexico, there has always been a strong tradition of community participation, albeit played out as a two-way co-optation exercise between government and local communities in which both sides have generally benefited (Gilbert and Ward 1985). Although more institutionalized today, through programs such as PRONASOL during President Salinas' mandate, or under state and municipal committee aegis (COPLADE and COPLADEMUN), as is more common under President Zedillo's initiative for a "New Federalism," local (community) participation remains highly significant (Rodríguez 1997). Even in PANista-governed cities such as Ciudad Juárez, where there was some ambivalence regarding federal government (PRI) Solidarity funding, the principle of encouraging community participation in colonias has also been very important (see also Cabrero Mendoza 1995, 1996, for other PANista cities). The result is that in Mexico high levels of colonia participation are the norm—at least if one takes a liberal definition of what constitutes "participation."[3] For the reasons outlined earlier—speed of formation, insecurity of the land capture process, relative political strength, the "rules of the game," and so on—Mexican colonias exhibit high levels of horizontal solidarity and interaction, often precipitated by community participation in local development.

Participation along the Texas side usually occurs only within pockets in the colonia comprising small groups of motivated individuals, occasionally led by a charismatic individual with a few followers. But widespread community participation is rare. The Cameron Park Residents' Council reflects this pattern. This involves a small number of colonia residents led by a dominant leader, Gloria Moreno, who has attracted considerable attention and a loyal following. No programmatic activities receive local support without her approval. Also, some colonias do appear to attract high levels of participation. The small study colonia of Sunny Skies near Brownsville has high participation levels, with nearly all residents involved in improving local infrastructure and general well-being, but even so, participation does not seem to translate into strong horizontal bonds of community. Where it does, it takes much longer in Texas than in Mexico.

Autonomy and Local Leadership   Leadership structures are key contributing factors in elevating a settlement to a community, as well as in shaping the speed and levels of colonia physical improvements (Cornelius 1973; Ward and Chant 1987). In Mexico a wide range of leadership types may be observed, ranging from mafioso-type *caciques*, to local residents democratically elected as representatives, to "positional" leaders whose authority is externally derived from an organization that they represent (Church, political party, NGO, etc. [see Ward 1989b]). It appears that the nature and preponderance of different leadership structures evolve over time, in response, on the one hand, to the macro political environment which shapes state-community relations (Ward and Chant 1987), and on the other, to the physical development needs and "stage" of colonia integration. As the opportunities for *caciques* to exercise a stranglehold over residents diminish (through regularization and greater tenure security, for example), so more democratic and less authoritarian leadership structures are likely to emerge. Once the community has achieved most of its goals, the instrumental reasons for firm leadership and for committed followership diminish, and positional leaders come to the forefront, although usually with a smaller following built around other associative dimensions (politics, religion, sports, unions, etc.).

Another feature of Mexican colonias is that their large size, even in the early formative phase, means that there may be several competing leaders vying for influence and for control of the rich pickings which may be had from organizing land development, plot allocations, quota contributions for informal services, and so on. Such leadership types and dynamics were common during the 1970s and early '80s (Cornelius 1975; Montaño 1976; Ward 1989b). More recently, however, they have become more "structured" as the bureaucracy has become more streamlined, and as local governments have become less tolerant of the exploitative practices of undemocratic leadership. Even though the PRI has continued to seek to strengthen its corporatist alliances with colonias through sectoral organizations such as the CNOP/UNE, their influence has been seriously eroded since the early 1990s. In their place, Solidarity committees were created, often overlaying the PRI's traditional local leadership, as Contreras and Bennett (1994) have demonstrated for northern border cities. The PAN, on the other hand, recognizing that it lacks the corporatist party networks into the colonias, has sought to open its doors to all residents, and to undermine existing (PRI) community-state relationships (Rodríguez and Ward 1992, 1994; Guillén López 1993; Craske 1996). More radical left-wing leaders and groups still remain, such as a few localized CDP colonias in Juárez, and their more widespread counterparts in Durango (Lau 1989; Rodríguez and Ward 1992; Haber 1994; Staudt 1998), but today these are the exception rather than the rule.

In Texas, leadership is also largely informal in nature, but it lacks the diversity, dynamism, and external connectedness of its Mexican counterparts. In some Texas colonias strong leaders may exist and be influential in articulating the needs of their communities to supra-colonia service providers, and they may be successful and win resources and services for their communities. In other cases, power struggles can also be observed between leadership factions, where each claims paramountcy of influence, thereby undermining the much-needed focus upon the settlement's problems. In other cases there is a vacuum, since no effective leadership exists, and colonia residents struggle individually or in small groups to address their infrastructural and social needs. The lack of clear leadership structures in Texas colonias is evident in one survey conducted by researchers in Brownsville, where in four out of the five colonias studied, only 25 percent of respondents declared that there were individuals in the settlement who took on responsibility for organizing activities or tasks. In the fifth colonia, one which had a strong and highly visible leader, 37 percent of *colonos* surveyed confirmed the existence of strong leaders (Rogers et al. 1993, 55). Another survey in El Cenizo revealed leadership to be either allied with the developers, Cecil McDonald and his former wife Martha Cadena, or with leaders from within the settlement, including Gloria Padilla, Juan Hidrógo, and Arturo de la Fuente. In contrast, colonias on Highway 359 near Laredo have been successful in allying themselves around landowner Harold Meier, creating a seven-colonia coalition which petitions for improved services. I shall return to this question of cross-colonia horizontal alliance in a moment.

The existence of strong leadership is a critical component in forging community participation and development in colonias on both sides of the border. In the Mexican colonias we studied, participation levels were generally high in those colonias led by strong and active leaders, and low in those with less-committed leaders. Similarly, the Texas colonias with strong leadership generally exhibited higher levels of community participation. Our Brownsville survey of Sunny Skies and Cameron Park residents reported that attendance is generally much lower for activities in which the community leader does not participate.

Cross-colonia Horizontal Integration and Social Movements

One way to enhance a colonia's influence is to collaborate with other colonias. In Mexico there is generally less incentive to develop a common front with extra-neighborhood residents, in part because the size of the settlement is usually sufficiently large to provide *colonos* with the necessary clout to make their demands heard in city hall. However, there are also important local structural barriers which further reduce the propensity for wider (horizontal) social mobilization to take place. First, there is the resistance of leaders to sharing the spoils and influence of colonia development with their counterparts in other colonias. Generally there is little agreement between such leaders about local development priorities. Moreover, the objective of some "positional"-type leaders is not to develop a strong power base for themselves, but rather to develop a local constituency on behalf of the supra-local organization. Thus, leaders' aims are divergent.

A second barrier to fronts being formed is that these may be threatening to the local state, insofar as their enhanced political power may undermine stability and electoral support. Of course, such power in numbers is one good reason to form a broad front, or *frente*, and there are important examples in Mexico where these have formed successfully and have forced governments to take their demands seriously: the Colonos' Restoration Movement (MRC) in 1970 Mexico City (Gilbert and Ward 1985); "Land and Liberty" in Chihuahua during the 1970s (Montaño 1976); the Urban Social Movements Coordination (CONAMUP) during the late 1970s through the mid-1980s (Ramírez Saíz 1986); the Barrio Assembly in post-1985-earthquake Mexico City (Eckstein 1990); the Popular Defense Committees (CDP) in several northern cities during the last decade (Lau 1989; Haber 1994); and the Popular Independent Organization (OPI), formed in 1987 in Juárez, which continues to represent some 14 colonias and seeks to use the courts to oblige owners to meet their infrastructure responsibilities (Ruf 1995). These are all cases where cross-settlement alliances have been forged to good effect. But while they have sometimes had success, they may just as readily invoke a hostile response from government, which seeks to undermine the vitality of such movements through a number of mechanisms—co-optation, divide and rule, starving settlements of resources, creating parallel structures, bureaucratic routines, etc. In terms of local authorities managing recalcitrant colonias in Mexico, Machiavelli's *Prince* is alive and well. Generally speaking, such cross-colonia or intergroup horizontal solidarity and mobilization are optimum forms of self-defense, but they are neither prime nor fast-track routes to get one's demands met, nor to secure development infrastructure. In this sense it is the government which sets the rules, and increasingly such rules privilege law-abiding, participative, quiescent, and sometimes electorally supportive settlements which "deal" on an individual basis.

Sometimes political parties or influential government organizations such as PRONASOL may promote cross-colonia convocations, but these are guided by the rationale of that wider organization. An example is the regional colonia council in Matamoros, which offers a forum for colonia leaders to meet and exchange ideas, albeit under the auspices of the PRI-controlled municipal government. As a result, intercolonia organization is closely aligned with the interests of local and, ultimately, national leaders. Similarly, in Nuevo Laredo, intercolonia interaction occurred only within the realm of PRONASOL, and hence it was directed and controlled by governmental authorities.

In Texas, the smaller local constituency of colonias and the political neglect to which they have been subject have made horizontal integration an imperative. However, the initiative has not come from grassroots colonia leaders but from external activist organizations. As in Mexico, these are NGOs. The first NGO to develop around colonia issues was Colonias del Valle, Inc., founded in late 1967 as a response to Hurricane Beulah, which caused widespread flooding and property damage in the Lower Rio Grande Valley colonias (Wilson and Menzies 1997, 235). But it was not until the early 1980s that NGOs really began to kick in and offer more effective leadership. These NGOs arose around the activities of the Texas Industrial Areas Foundation (IAF), whose organizers helped to meld what were to become three important regional religious organizations: Valley Interfaith, embracing a large number of Catholic parishes in the Lower Rio Grande Valley; the El Paso Interreligious Sponsoring Organization (EPISO); and the so-called Border Organization, in the Eagle Pass–Del Rio area, which began to gel around IAF organizer Sister Maribeth Larkin in 1986–1987. Two features set these organizations apart from their Mexican counterparts. First, the fact that they represent a number of colonias, offering cross-settlement organization; and second, their origins as religious organizations.[4]

Cross-colonia organizations, such as Valley Interfaith in Brownsville and EPISO in El Paso, have been influential in training local leaders in political and communications skills and ultimately have come to have considerable influence upon Texas state leaders and the legislature (Bath et al. 1994; Staudt 1998). But they have also been criticized for increasing the dependency of local leaders upon the organizations and for using leaders for their own political ends (Wilson and Menzies 1997, 241). In Sparks colonia, EPISO has worked with *colonos* to secure water and other basic services for the community. Yet EPISO's involvement has also created a split among residents, some of whom resent the organization, seeing it as paternalistic. Opponents of EPISO in the community would prefer to be independent of the organization, while supporters (generally older residents who speak English less well) believe affiliation with EPISO strengthens community efforts to organize.

Lower Valley colonias appear to have more social contact with residents of other colonias, in contrast to residents of the Laredo and (especially) El Paso areas, where it appears that colonias in the same region have little contact with each other. These differences may relate to the goals and the nature of the principal organizations (Valley Interfaith and EPISO), but it may also reflect the work environments in the two regions. Many El Paso colonia residents work in the informal sector of services and sales, while in the Lower Valley important sectors providing employment are agriculture and low-cost services. Probably significant, too, is the physical distance between colonias: El Paso and Laredo colonias tend to be more isolated, and are sometimes located several miles from any other development, already limiting the potential for intercolonia interaction.

There are exceptions to the rule in Texas. In 1994, several colonia leaders formed a coalition made up of colonias located just off Highway 359 in Laredo, Texas. This organization was supported by money won in a settlement against land developer Cecil McDonald. With this money, colonia residents and landowner Harold Meier formed a cooperative to install water pipelines. Together with Texas Rural Legal Aid, Meier and his associates formed the Unión de Colonias Olvidadas, or the Union of Forgotten Colonias. The Union has a representative governing council, with two elected representatives from each of the nine associated colonias off Highway 359 coming together on a regular basis to discuss issues of common interest. The longevity and ultimate success of the pioneering regional colonia organization are yet to be determined. In addition to the Union, two colonias south of Laredo, El Cenizo and Río Bravo, have had recent success in creating a coordinating body in response to the bankruptcy of Cecil McDonald, the developer of the two colonias. Both El Cenizo and Río Bravo are soliciting aid in social welfare and infrastructural improvement, and the key leaders, Gloria Padilla and Rita Urbide, were introduced to one another through Texas Rural Legal Aid. However, in these two cases it remains unclear whether this capacity to organize a common front among clusters of colonias has come about because of the need to agree upon how to divide the spoils from Cecil McDonald's defeat, or from the fact that he can no longer exercise informal influence in the settlements that he promoted and developed.

Vertical Integration between Colonias and Supra-local Organizations

In Chapter 5 I will focus upon the extent to which external social services are effective in overcoming some of the deficiencies and weakness in social infrastructure encountered especially in Texas colonias. Here, however, we look more at the *informal* vertical linkages that colonias forge through their leadership structures with supra-local bodies.

Vertical Leadership Linkages to Government Organizations

Characteristics of leaders vary tremendously on both sides of the border in terms of their independence from political and nongovernmental organizations. In Mexico, the independence of leaders depends to a large degree on the political affiliation of the municipal government. One study of the Solidarity program in the northern border cities of Tijuana, Mexicali, and Nuevo Laredo found that cities led by opposition governments had more diverse types of leadership structures—that is, divergent from the traditional Solidarity committee format—than did cities controlled by the PRI. In PRI cities, federal agencies were more apt to exert control over local colonia leadership structures and initiatives. Additionally, colonia leaders who did not have prior experience in community, political, or union leadership had more autonomy and encouraged greater participation within the community (Contreras and Bennett 1994, 303–304).

This study's research in the Mexican border colonias supports Contreras and Bennett's findings. Colonias in Ciudad Juárez, a PAN-controlled city, appear to have a greater diversity of leadership structures and greater autonomy from federal agencies. Indeed, formal leadership committees have different names (e.g., *comités de vecinos*) and compositions than was the case for the standard Solidarity format. Colonia leaders are much more closely aligned with city and state officials than with federal officials. Ciudad Juárez provides an example of how new community-authority relationships may be forged by "opposition" governments (Barrera Bassols 1996). In contrast, Matamoros as a PRI-controlled city exhibits a high degree of affiliation between the colonia leadership and the federal government, as well as with city and state officials. Nuevo Laredo has leadership patterns similar to those of Matamoros, with local colonia leadership aligned with federal, state, and municipal organizations, but with new leaders free of traditional corporatist ties (Contreras and Bennett 1994, 299). Nueva Era, a Nuevo Laredo colonia whose *patrón* was the PARM party, appeared to be unsuccessful in securing Solidarity funding because it was not affiliated with PRI-driven municipal, state, and federal organizations. In contrast, a PRI-sponsored municipal program, Colonias en Acción, offered to augment assistance provided through Solidarity.

Political careers, too, can be forged around state-community relations and Solidarity funding: in 1995 the former local director of Solidarity, Mónica García, successfully ran as PRI candidate for the mayorship of Nuevo Laredo, and before her term was ended she was elected to the federal Congress as representative for Tamaulipas in July 1997.

In Texas, municipal entities are most directly impacted by the colonia situation, and planning departments in the cities of El Paso, Laredo, and Brownsville are designing strategies to deal with unincorporated settlements. Because of the constant interaction of colonia citizens and urban dwellers, public health departments are attempting to control health problems that could pose a risk to the region at large. School systems are another municipal entity capable of reaching most families in the colonia. In interviews with *colonos*, a principal priority for them was providing their children with improved educational, social, and employment opportunities, and efforts within the school system are already underway to provide aid directly to colonia residents, through such means as Parent-Teacher Associations (PTAs) and other extracurricular programs. In addition, local universities have provided health and other programs for colonia citizens at a reduced fee or free of charge.

It is evident, however, that resources remain spread across a broad range of governmental and nongovernmental entities. Unlike Mexico, Texas still needs to develop a cohesive policy which provides "big-picture" development, and increases the opportunities for both horizontal and vertical integration. Channels for interaction between the colonias and the state are limited. For example, funds allocated to assist colonias from 1983 to 1993 through the TDHCA Texas Community Development Program (TCDP) amounted to just over $4 million. Significantly, "community development," as classified by the TCDP, included the construction of community centers, water lines, and sewers; paving; weatherization; and planning studies—i.e., hard physical infrastructure components rather than actions which would enhance the development of informal social infrastructure. Community centers (analyzed in the following chapter), which would, it was hoped, enhance social infrastructure and help to create self-sufficient *communities*, received only 15 percent of the funds allocated. Texas A&M's Center for Housing and Urban Development has constructed several community centers in the colonias, but recent surveys have found that these community centers are not fostering community interaction as much as they are serving as distribution points for social services—a point to which I shall return in Chapter 5.

Vertical Linkages to Nongovernment Organizations   Connections with government authorities and agencies are not the only form of external (vertical) linkage that settlements seek to develop through their leaders. As we have already seen, NGOs such as EPISO and Valley Interfaith have been very important in Texas in building integrative capacity across colonias. Generally speaking, the volume of NGO activity is much greater than in Mexico, because government antipathy has limited colonias' capacity for development (in the past), or has left them little effective space in which to develop (as is the case at present). NGO expansion is inversely related to the extent to which public agencies meet colonia needs, hence their greater profile in Texas. Some of these NGOs are cross-border: for example, Mano a Mano (a March of Dimes–funded cross-border organization), gives prenatal counseling to pregnant women in Matamoros and Brownsville, while another organization provides services to victims of domestic abuse. The Mexican Federation (FEMAP) began in Ciudad Juárez under the direction of Guadalupe de la Vega, and now has branches throughout Mexico (Staudt 1998).

Colonias in Texas are host to a wide variety of small and large NGOs offering many different types of services. In Brownsville, prominent NGOs are the United Way, Valley Interfaith, the Brownsville Adult Literacy Center, Mano a Mano, and Friendship of Women. Gateway Health, Mercy Hospital, and Texas Rural Legal Aid are prominent NGOs serving the colonias in Laredo. In El Paso, EPISO, La Mujer Obrera, Homestead MUD, and the Kellogg Community Partnership also offer services to *colonos*. Primarily, these NGOs provide short-term supports to the long-term problems of disenfranchisement, marginalization, and lack of political voice. Yet the frequent eruption of service needs in the Texas colonias has inspired some NGOs, most notably Valley Interfaith and EPISO, to address the longer-term problems by attempting to organize leaders and communities in the colonias. The Gateway Health program in Laredo has now trained *colonos* to disseminate information on health issues and provide community-wide initiatives on improving community health. While such programs have had mixed results, efforts to organize colonias in these ways are a good approach to generating self-sufficiency and a sense of community. Successful organization can result in the empowerment of colonia communities to command political attention and meet their service needs in a comprehensive fashion, rather than the piecemeal one which now predominates.

Conclusions and Policy Recommendations

As we have observed in this chapter, informal social infrastructure patterns in colonias vary greatly from one side of the border to the other. One marked difference between the two countries appears in the degree to which *colonos* are able to interact both horizontally and vertically in order to meet their needs. Briefly, this may be characterized as "*mobilizing* to get" in Mexico, while in Texas it is "*being* mobilized in order to get." In Mexico, colonias are led from the outset, and these leaders petition and harass public agencies for services. Public officials tacitly acknowledge the legitimacy of these leaders and their constituents by providing a range of services which begin to meet colonia infrastructural needs. Due to high levels of interaction between *colonos* and public agencies, there is less opportunity or need for non-governmental organizations to emerge in Mexican colonias; the few NGOs working in Mexican colonias are usually small and narrowly targeted, and tend to be associated with areas of activity that the government feels unable or unwilling to perform (reproductive rights, protection for battered wives, religious functions, etc.).

In Texas, colonia residents and their leaders enjoy little legitimacy in the eyes of public officials. Sometimes, too, colonia leaders fail to command significant support from their communities. With no clear representational structures in place, democratic representation can give way to intracolonia rivalries or, more usually, to a leadership vacuum, weakening the potential of *colonos* to advance their case for recognition, incorporation, and the provision of services. NGOs have responded to the lack of political representation in colonias by seeking to create and enhance colonia capacity for self-organization.

The greatest variable shaping *colonos'* political access is legitimacy: the high degree of legitimacy accorded *colonos* in Mexico and their significance within the electorate result in political responsiveness, while the political underrepresentation and social marginalization of colonias in Texas yield their political neglect. The challenge for colonias on both sides of the border is twofold: to establish and to maintain their legitimacy. In Mexico, while colonias very quickly acquire legitimacy by virtue of their existence, and by virtue of the large number of citizen-voters living within these settlements, the principal problem is one of *sustaining* their community structure, and avoiding social and participatory atrophy. Generally, social interaction and horizontal integration drop off as colonias mature and gain basic services. The resulting contraction of social infrastructure lessens the potential of the colonia for long-term empowerment.

In contrast, colonias in Texas have never enjoyed anything like the same legitimacy. While many factors contribute to the marginalization of these colonias, the root of the problem lies in social perceptions of poverty and illegality. While colonias cannot easily change such deeply embedded social perceptions, they can command greater attention from government agencies through concerted efforts at intra- and intercolonia interaction. Greater horizontal integration, manifested by vociferous community groups and adept leaders, offers the prospect of a dramatic increase in the vertical integration of colonias, as public officials respond to the growing voice of well-organized colonia citizens.

Unlike their Mexican counterparts, which quickly develop community activism and integration only to have to find ways to sustain them, Texas colonias must seek to establish the social infrastructure of a community through effective horizontal integration. In both countries, horizontal integration may be achieved through three channels: community participation, independent and responsive leaders, and intercolonia interaction. Specific recommendations for improvement are outlined in the matrix displayed as Table 16. This seeks to identify the arenas of high-priority action that are desirable in Texas and Mexico in order to forge self-sustaining horizontal and vertical integration for colonias. Recommendations for Mexican colonias focus on the maintenance of social infrastructure within a formal system of organization and participation. Those for the colonias of Texas stress the development of formal channels of participation within and outside of colonias. The bottom line, however, is the building of well-integrated communities, which will shift policy agendas from short-term service provision to long-term attention to the deeper needs of colonias on both sides of the border. A quick glance at the matrix in Table 16 shows that there is greater urgency in Texas (i.e., more high-priority items).

Table 16. Redistribution of Power through Horizontal and Vertical Integration

	Texas	Mexico
A. Horizontal		
1. Increased community participation		
Voter registration campaigns	High	Low
Mutual aid projects	High	High
Community "focus" groups	High	Low
Social interaction—sporting tournaments, parties	High	Low
2. More responsive leadership		
Regular voting for community leaders	High	High
Formalize representative structure	High	Low
Encourage new leadership from within colonia	High	High
3. Intercolonia interaction		
Independent regional colonia councils	High	Low
Multiple colonia use of regional community centers	High	Low
B. Vertical		
1. Community development initiatives from within		
Information dissemination	High	High
2. Independent community leadership		
Solidarity to become nonpartisan	Low	High
Weaken the role of developer	High	Low
3. Institutionalize vertical relationships to create legitimacy		
Organize as a nonprofit	High	Low
Bypass local to state and federal	High	Low
Lobby local politicians and actors	High	High
Coordination/rationalization of agencies and policies	High	Low
4. Nongovernmental organizations		
Coordinate priorities with residents' councils	High	High
Empowerment training—focus on developing the community	High	Low
Coordination/rationalization of NGOs with government	High	Low

"High" and "Low" refer to high and low priority.

FOSTERING HORIZONTAL INTEGRATION IN TEXAS COLONIAS

At the horizontal level three broad areas of action are required. First, it is necessary to foster greater community participation. Adopting actions that will encourage voter registration and therefore political participation in elections legitimizes the ideals of citizenship and participatory democracy. Also important here are activities that will bring residents together in participatory activities, whether these are decision making focus groups or town-hall-type meetings, mutual aid development projects, or associational activities such as sports events, fiestas, etc. The latter are especially important in sustaining a sense of community, particularly, as in Mexico, once the urgency of immediate colonia needs has attenuated, and the proportion of low-stakeholders such as renters and nonowners grows. While the presence of these last two groups is less of an issue in Texas, promoting social and recreational activities might, nevertheless, be the most effective way to foster a genuine community spirit. A colonia's failure to achieve short- and medium-term developmental goals (services and the like) is likely to demoralize households very fast, and cause an incipient community spirit to implode. Lightweight promotional social activities are invariably low budget for local governments, and can legitimately be tied to some county- or city-desired goal (information promotion about voter registration, AIDS, council activities, etc.) if they need to be justified.[5] While I would usually be the first to criticize "bread-and-festival" type responses in Mexico (where their promotion is placatory and politically disingenuous), in Texas they may be justified and do a lot of good if conceived in terms of fostering community spirit, and provided that the actual event is acceptable and supported locally. If it isn't, no one will participate.

A second important arena of horizontal integration is the existence of responsive and responsible leadership. Exploitative *cacique*-type authoritarian leaders are rarely the answer. Rather, the task is to reinforce democratic structures of leadership that will empower and legitimate leaders to act on the residents' behalf. This requires regular, transparent elections of leaders and formal (but simple and unbureaucratic) community representatives, along with the recruitment of new leadership and participation. This implies two things: (1) That structures be simple, with a minimal hierarchy among participants. Collective leadership may not be an ideal, but it generally works best in low-income environments. (2) That there be some tangible progress; otherwise community activity will quickly implode.

Finally, a sense of community may be promoted by seeking to relate to the wider community—to other colonias and worker groups. Not only can this offer greater strength and political voice in numbers (as relations with EPISO demonstrate), but it may help to provide a sense of progress and commitment even when actual conditions within one's own colonia show little perceptible change. There are drawbacks, however, if the agenda and goals of supra-local cross-colonia organizations come to dominate colonia agendas. Recommendations here are to build independent (nonpartisan) regional colonia councils which also have an open and transparent democratic structure. Most successful cross-colonia organizations in Mexico have only been successful if they have not been appropriated by any one political party, but remain strictly civic structures. However, the less partisan nature of Texas colonias makes this less of a problem. Well-located regional colonia community centers can do much to bring together residents from several colonias, but they will only work so long as they are not appropriated by the single colonia in which they are located (see Chapter 5).

Fostering Vertical Integration in Texas Colonias

Here there are four principal arenas of policy formation designed to enhance vertical linkages between colonias and external agencies and authorities (see Table 16). The first comprises community-initiated actions that will foster external links. An important tool here is to develop accurate and simple information dissemination among community members about those external bodies: their role, effectiveness, key contact persons, etc. Nor should leaders, on the basis of unwarranted assumptions, denigrate those residents who do not participate as being apathetic and uninterested. It may be that they are interested, but for whatever reason do not wish or are presently unable to actively participate. Keeping them informed by newsletter, handbills, and so on is an important leadership function that may pay off in the long term.

Second, vertical linkages will also be fostered if the leadership is perceived to be independent and honest. Independence here usually requires the setting aside of partisan and religious affiliation, at least insofar as the conduct of community affairs is concerned. Nor do strong perceptions that leaders have vested interests foster good community development, since these will detract from community-oriented actions in favor of those which are (or are perceived to be) self-serving. Developers, for example, should not be part of the community leadership structure—no matter how well-meaning. Sooner or later a conflict of interests will inevitably arise.

Third, and perhaps most important of all, are those efforts and actions which serve to institutionalize external linkages and which, at the same time, serve to enhance the legitimacy of the colonia in the eyes of those whose support is sought. Organizing and constituting the community as a nonprofit may help lever resources and respectability. In this respect, colonia interests may be advanced by targeting and lobbying local politicians and powerful actors and, where appropriate, bypassing them in favor of state and federal agencies who are empowered and/or have jurisdiction to act. In the past, colonia communities have often been passive and waited upon external actors to approach them, rather than go on the offensive and shake the bushes (local and distant). This is where cross-colonia interaction (discussed above) and mobilization can prove especially helpful. For the government's part, much needs to be done at an intergovernmental level in order to better coordinate and rationalize policies and the actions of agencies. Many of these bottlenecks were documented in previous chapters, but in this context much needs to be done to enhance the flow of information to colonia communities and to expedite processing of colonia requests and demands. Mexico's *ventanilla única* system, whereby one agency or office receives documentary requests and paperwork, and then circulates it to the relevant authority or agencies for processing, has done much to reduce the social costs associated with passing *colonos* from agency to agency.

Finally, the role of nongovernment organizations should be fostered, particularly insofar as they may empower community organizations and citizens. NGOs can act as catalysts to assist colonia committees in prioritizing and preparing their program demands. They can provide valuable guidance and empowerment training for leaders, and where necessary, they can act as intermediaries between communities and external authorities. The latter, however, should not be an objective: rather, their focus should be to encourage the colonia leadership to deal directly, or in concert with leaders of other colonias.

NGOs become counterproductive when they become too proprietary toward any particular colonia or leader. This leads to factionalism and competition, and reduces the likelihood of community formation.

In short, cultivating the transition of colonias as settlements into colonias as communities in Texas will go a long way toward improving the quality of life of colonia populations. Similarly, by creating more cohesive and legitimate structures, colonia communities are likely to be more successful in pressing their demands upon external power brokers and agencies. But vertical interaction is a two-way street, and supra-local actors will also take several steps forward if they begin to see colonia communities as local development partners, rather than as possible settlement recipients of the scarce resources that they command.

Five

Social Services to Colonias: Shifting the Focus toward Means Rather than Ends

The Underprioritization of Social Services

In analyzing formal social service provision in the colonias on both sides of the Texas-Mexico border, it is possible to identify two predominant styles of provision. The first style is top-down and responds to an agenda that is set outside of the community being served. The second is a bottom-up approach, in which the community has some opportunity to define its own needs and to work in collaboration with service providers to see that these needs are met. In this chapter the aim is to explore the ways in which social infrastructure—principally health, education, police, and fire services—is provided in the six border cities that were studied.

Although I analyzed physical infrastructure provision separately in Chapter 3, it is misleading to think of social service provision as independent of, or even sequential to, physical services (Gabriel 1991). Only a minimum level of physical infrastructure—vehicular access to the settlement, for example—is required before social services can begin to have an impact. Yet invariably the gamut of social services are promoted sequentially and are mostly targeted to arrive *after* physical infrastructure. In short, social services are underprioritized, and there are several reasons why this is the case. First, an absolute lack of physical services such as water, drainage, and power lines is much more shocking to the eye: it is tangible evidence of ongoing deprivation and neglect. However, a lack of social services such as health care, fire service, and policing—which may be seen to be "consumed" ephemerally—is much less tangible. The demand for education services is much more ubiquitous, but even here, as in the case of other social services, to the outside observer the visible absence of a clinic, fire station, or a school cannot be taken to imply that no service exists—it may be down the road or in a neighboring settlement, or pupils may be bused across the city. Thus, the absence of social services appears to be less *absolute* than are deficits in physical infrastructure.

A second reason for the lower-key role of social services is that residents themselves prioritize much more highly physical infrastructure, which they almost uniformly consider to be more urgent. In part, of course, this prioritization is itself a "construction" of what residents know and perceive the state and local companies to be most likely and willing to provide; but few would quarrel with residents' demands for water and power first, and for doctors, and even for schools, second. Third, once a political commitment toward colonias begins to come on line (as it did in Texas in the late 1980s), it is administratively easier to justify direct investment in physical elements, since these are usually one-time capital costs. Once they're installed and the "lumpy" up-front costs are covered, they become self-financing through consumption and standing charges and require only maintenance: they do not carry the extensive *recurrent* costs of personnel, salaries, and equipment. Consequently, the ongoing political commitment is much greater for social services, and these are almost always provided (and financed) by local county and city jurisdictions—usually from the public purse. Tied to this is a fourth factor, the differential nature of funding sources for physical and social infrastructure. As I showed in Chapter 3, in Texas the impetus for physical infrastructure provision to colonias came from state legislative action which made Texas eligible to leverage funding from the federal government and to complement this with state funding and bond issues. Social infrastructure, on the other hand, is much more likely to be funded through *local* fiscal resources. To the extent that many cities confront a severe fiscal crisis, and unincorporated colonias are a cost that would greatly add to the burden, there is little prospect or incentive for local (city and county) social services to be extended to them. Thus, subsidized federal programs, charities, NGOs, volunteerism, and the sweat equity of the residents themselves must pick up the slack.

Although in Mexico the same broad funding dilemmas apply (i.e., the share of funding and its central versus local source), the colonias are less severely disadvantaged than their Texas counterparts because of the stronger and more ubiquitous penetration of federal and state government social programs to the municipal and settlement level. Also, there is no jurisdictional ambiguity: whether it can afford to or not, the municipality is mandated to provide or coordinate most physical and social infrastructure. Moreover, most municipalities today are being encouraged to strengthen their fiscal base, particularly through the local tax-generated component (Rodríguez 1997; SEDESOL 1996), so part of the price of bringing colonia residents into the city tax base is the quid pro quo that cities must meet their physical and social responsibilities more effectively.

Finally, there is the fifth factor: politics. Both residents and politicians have greater confidence in physical inputs, which, once negotiated and installed, cannot readily be removed—they are less fungible than are, say, visits of social workers or medical staff, or even a community center, which, while difficult to physically remove, may fall into disuse if local authorities and private service providers fail to maintain usage. This was especially important in Mexico in the past, where clientelistic mobilization of colonia populations around physical infrastructure and land titles in exchange for political and electoral support was the norm (Montaño 1976; Ward 1986). Moreover, physical infrastructure and large-scale urban projects offer greater potential for enhancing reputations through being identified with a particular politician or administration—a feature sometimes called *"plazismo"* in Mexico. Clientelism and *plazismo* are less prevalent today, as city authorities recognize the desirability for more coordinated integration of colonia populations and more effective responsiveness to their needs (Ward 1989b, 1998a). Today, votes, much more than patronage, win city and state elections. In Texas, with only a few exceptions, politicians see little to be gained from cultivating colonia populations, although voter registration drives and coordination by coalitions such as EPISO have made some local politicians more sensitive to colonia demands (Wilson and Menzies 1997).

However, this underprioritization of social infrastructure is problematic. In Mexico, for example, local government failure to provide for ongoing (recurrent) costs may lead to the creation of "white elephant" capital-intensive projects, whose beneficiaries are ill-equipped to take advantage of them. The classic example, not uncommon in Mexico, particularly in the past when *plazismo* was more prevalent, is the community center facility or covered market which fails to function because there are no funds for staff and service providers, or because there is no effective demand. Barrio centers lie idle or under-used. Recently, too, PRONASOL was roundly criticized for building open-air basketball courts in many rural villages in the south of the country, although this was often a low-budget project that many villagers actively sought (Hughes 1994, but cf. Rodríguez 1997; Fox and Aranda 1996).

It seems desirable that physical and social infrastructure be linked in a more integrated and progressive manner, especially in Texas where the structural incentives to de-link them (outlined above) are especially strong. The point is that by investing in human and social "capital," thereby raising human potential, regions and communities will be better equipped to assist and participate in the development process as a means to an end, rather than waiting on the ends to arrive from on high by themselves.

The Process of Social Service Provision

Both the means and the ends of social service provision are important. Of course, the end product, the service being delivered, is of central concern. However, the mode of provision is pivotal to the impact of the service. Successful provision of a social service requires that the needs and perspectives of the recipients be considered. When the agenda for social service provision is set "top-down" without recipient input, there is likely to be a major mismatch between policy and need.

Social service provision should be seen as a dynamic process of exchange between providers and recipients, and as a continuous, mutually reinforcing process. The traditional view prevalent in both Mexico and Texas, which emphasizes the *ends* of social service provision, fails to take advantage of the learning and empowerment possibilities inherent in the process itself. Educational services, for example, should not only be measured in terms of the number of school rooms provided. Rather, receiving an education is a means of self-actualization for the recipients, leading to the creation of human capital. Shifting health care concerns to cover *both* preventive and curative functions similarly focuses local populations' attention upon means rather than ends and makes them part of the health care process. The manner and conceptualization of social service provision are crucial, therefore.

Obtaining and incorporating input from residents can be difficult. For them to communicate their priorities and preferences, a minimum level of political representation, organization, and leadership is needed (Lamporte 1992). As we saw in the previous chapter, there are marked differences between Mexico and Texas over the propensity to develop a significant "density" of horizontal social organization that is commensurate with a purposeful sense of community. Also, the degree to which service providers and policymakers are receptive to residents often leaves much to be desired. Their attitude may be patronizing, and they often think that, as trained professionals, they know best. They may be inflexible, particularly in Texas, where there is less room for maneuver in decision making and for dodging bureaucratic rules, and where the threat of litigation is omnipresent.

Factors Influencing Social Service Provision

Previous chapters have rehearsed many of the principal factors which lead to the differences observed in land development policy, physical service provision, and community organization. Not surprisingly, social services are subject to similar constraints. First, the geography and settlement structure mean that Texas colonias are often far from urban centers, lying outside a city's jurisdiction. For example, when Laredo fire officials refused to send equipment to Río Bravo colonia, the city manager responded to criticism by stating that Laredo was "not legally or morally responsible to provide services for free" (*San Antonio Express News*, February 6, 1993). For residents of Cameron County, the nearest major hospital facility is in Corpus Christi. Moreover, responsibility for the provision of social services (state, city, or county) depends upon the particular service provided, and given the weaker or nonexistent leadership structures (vis-à-vis Mexico) in Texas colonias, residents are less likely to receive effective guidance toward the responsible government entity.

Nor do Texas colonias have significant voting power and political clout, located as they often are in the limited-power jurisdictions of counties. In Mexico, the opposite is true: settlements are larger; they are more densely populated; they have greater voting influence; they are not located in a jurisdictional no man's land; and as a predominant form of housing, they have much greater moral legitimacy, even though their origins are often illegal.

DISTORTIONS IN THE CHANNELS
OF SOCIAL SERVICE PROVISION

The dominant model of social service provision all too often re-
sembles Figure 8. Here, social service provision is depicted as a circular, top-down flow. "Policy" is rather authoritarian and is directed
at addressing "Need," but the implementation of social service policy
is shown as being diverted by deficient policy design; by inappropriate
or insensitive attitudes and perceptions of service providers; and by
severe resource constraints. In this version of the model "Need" is
likely to sharply inform policy through feedback loops, but the effectiveness of such feedback is weakened by a lack of colonia voice and
power; an inadequate medium or forum for dialogue; and a failure to
listen on the part of policymakers.

Policy design may be inadequate from the start, or may prove to be
inadequate due to problems of implementation. Deficient policy design may be the direct result of a lack of colonia input, with policymakers being too far removed from colonias to correctly assess their
needs. For example, Texas' policy is to provide an education to every
school-age resident of the state, but not all colonias can be accessed by
school buses, a fact which is frequently overlooked or ignored.

Perceptions or biases on the part of service providers can significantly impact policy implementation. A service provider in Webb
County, for example, complained that colonia residents simply were
not interested in self-help programs, and mentioned "off the record"
that in his view residents mainly wanted handouts, and that they were
not very hardworking. He was insensitive to the fact that low participation rates might be an outcome of many other factors. In Mexico,
too, while such insensitivity is not unknown, policy diversion may
occur by virtue of the competitiveness of service providers. Sometimes, too, one department is particularly powerful, and for political
reasons (partisan or otherwise), may obstruct the intervention of the
responsible service provider (Ward 1986).

Resource constraints are a major impediment on both sides of the
border, although they might reasonably be expected to apply more in
Mexico than in one of the richest states of the world. In Texas, as elsewhere in the United States, service providers are required to submit
projected budgets and growth plans in order to receive funding, but
they often find that they have underestimated these costs or the rate of
population growth, leading to shortfalls and inadequate service provi-

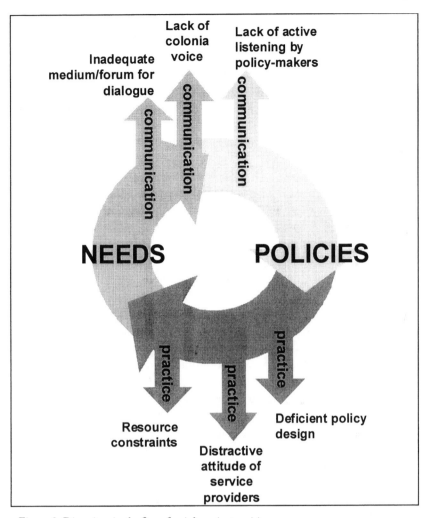

Figure 8. Diversions in the flow of social service provision.

sion. In the case of school districts on the Texas side, while many have been able to raise substantial sums for new buildings, they have quickly discovered that they cannot keep pace with population growth.

Public service providers in Mexico also complain of a lack of funds. A lack of resources prevents one social service agency, the Desarrollo Integral de la Familia (DIF), from being able to fulfill its mandate of providing much-needed medical services and nutritional assistance to young children, commented Leticia Sánchez de Sampayo, community development coordinator in Matamoros. A school principal (Sr. Soto Ugalde) in the same city expressed his intense frustration over the restrictive effects of limited funds upon the quality of teaching materials he was able to provide. And the local branch of the federal adult education agency INEA in Matamoros reported a long and increasing waiting list for its services, but lacks the funding to expand in order to meet those needs.

The communication flow between those in need and those able to shape policy is particularly weak or distorted on the Texas side of the border. As has already been observed, the lack of colonia voice arises from many factors: the low level of effective representation, colonia isolation and lack of horizontal and vertical integration, their relative political weakness. Many residents of Texas colonias see the commissioners court and city hall as places far removed from their communities (as indeed they are), but they also view them as intimidating and unconcerned with their needs. Residents rarely view official government office buildings as places where they can voice their concerns. Often, too, they are suspicious, cynically assuming a hidden agenda when surveyors come to them and viewing such actions as intrusive. In these circumstances there is an urgent need for effective and appropriate venues in which two-way communication can occur (Ward and Chant 1987). Colonia residents need venues for communicating that are neither political in nature nor threatening or overly solicitous in their design and practice (Friedmann 1992).

Policy will not be informed by need unless policymakers are willing and able to listen actively to colonia residents. In some respects colonia residents in Texas are thrice-removed from the attentive ears of policymakers. First, coming from the border they have traditionally been ignored by state and federal governments; second, they are often perceived to be illegal residents, unworthy of and ineligible for government attention and social services; and third, their physical marginality and relative invisibility allow policymakers to place them on the back burner, attending to their social service needs only insofar as their needs are in common with the wider working population of Texas.

In Mexico, policymakers generally are more attentive to colonia needs—whether for partisan-political or developmental reasons has varied over time. Generally speaking, policymakers have developed more social policies that are intrinsically better at meeting colonia needs, as well as improving the institutional capacity to implement those policies, both procedurally and locationally (Ward 1993). Service providers in PANista cities like Ciudad Juárez and León (Guanajuato) have sought to open access and communication with municipal officials by organizing a weekly "fair" (*tianguis*) in city hall at which senior department officials may meet with residents. Much remains to be done, however, and despite these encouraging steps in the direction of greater public participation, servicing programs remain largely top-down, but at least they are slowly being separated from overtly partisan considerations.

Social Service Provision in Mexico and Texas

EDUCATION IN MEXICO

Education in Mexico is an example of a social service that suffers from deficiencies in policy design, even though policymakers place a high priority on expanding educational services. By law every Mexican has the right to receive basic education across twelve grades, consisting of three years of preschool, of which only one is obligatory, six years of primary, and three years of secondary education. In Mexico the targets on *quantity* of school provision have generally been reached, but the *quality* of education has not been addressed satisfactorily (Martin 1994). The main success exhibited by the current policy has been the high rate of primary school enrollment. In Matamoros, for example, approximately 90 percent of all children between the ages of six and fourteen were enrolled in school at the time of the 1990 census (INEGI 1990). High rates of enrollment by children from the colonias are facilitated by the existence of primary schools within the colonias. Even irregular settlements either have their own schools or have access to schools in neighboring colonias. There is no general policy of busing children to schools in Mexico, as is the case in the United States. While resource limitations do reduce the quality of the physical facilities and educational materials, they are not the principal problem.

However, inadequate policy design means that too low a percentage of children from the colonias advances to secondary and postsecondary education. In Matamoros, only 52 percent of students over age fifteen are attending postprimary school. The forces behind lower rates of secondary school attendance are complex and not easy to as-sess. The most important factor is no doubt the poverty of families, which forces many children to work to augment family income. This pressure accounts for the majority of school dropouts (Martin 1994; Nord 1994). Education in Mexico began to be decentralized in the later 1980s, and under President Zedillo's policy of New Federalism the operational side of all primary and secondary education in Mexico has been passed to state governments (Pardo 1996, 1998).

EDUCATION IN TEXAS

The goal of school funding and education provision in Texas is both simple and ambitious: to provide each child, regardless of immigration status, with a basic education. School districts receive the majority of their funds from local property taxes, but their main educational di-rectives are set forth by the Texas Education Agency (TEA). This bi-level policy formulation by local school districts and the TEA contrib-utes to some of the shortfalls in educational services experienced by colonia residents. The problem is that school districts cannot continue to provide quality educational services in the face of rapidly expand-ing school-age populations. The United Independent School District, serving Laredo and Webb County colonias, must build nine schools in the next three years alone in order to keep up with population growth. The political and fiscal obstacles to school funding make this process difficult at best.

As it stands now, the majority of colonia children are bused to school, with more colonia-based schools planned for the future. Since property values and hence property taxes are relatively low in the co-lonias, funding the construction of schools in the colonias can be a controversial and socially divisive local issue. The TEA and the State Board of Education are primarily regulatory agencies, not funding sources, and heated debates have occurred at the local level about intracity differences in educational services. The Mexican-American Legal Defense Fund (MALDEF) lawsuit against the State of Texas for discriminatory funding practices in border communities provides evi-dence of the frustration of many border residents. Again, colonia res-idents are often geographically isolated from the primary sites of ser-vice provision, and must be bused to distant schools or attend classes in temporary trailers (as in the case of the Brownsville Independent

34. Elementary school at the entrance to El Cenizo (Webb County [Laredo]).

School District). This is not to suggest that some colonias do not have schools located within them. The Montana Vista colonia in the eastern ETJ of El Paso County has a modern school which serves a cluster of colonias north and south of Highway 180, while Río Bravo has three schools (at all levels) and El Cenizo has an elementary school at its entrance (Photo 34). Occasionally, too, the sequencing alluded to earlier, whereby social services follow a late second to physical infrastructure, may be reversed by the decision to build a school. In the case of Montana Vista, the location of new gas collector tanks a mile away from the school, and the extension of underground lines to the facility, meant that households adjacent to the line could opt to hook up—as many have done (Photo 35).

The attitudes and perceptions of the direct service providers—the teachers—can also present problems. Locating qualified individuals to teach in the colonias can be difficult. The situation is so pronounced that some school districts along the border recruit prospective teachers from the Midwest, advertising competitive beginning salaries and alternative certification programs. As one school district administrator whom we interviewed (Ms. Mary Morín) noted, it is often hard to bridge the cultural gap between the imported teachers and low-income children, some of whom may be recent immigrants.

Present resource constraints and the shortage of direct service pro-

35. *Although rare, gas supply to public utilities (such as a school) allows adjacent homes to hook up, as here in Montana Vista (El Paso County). The trench is to connect the home to the supply meter at the front of the lot.*

viders therefore make it difficult, if not impossible, for Texas' border school districts to fulfill the mandate that the state provide a basic education to all its children.

HEALTH SERVICES IN MEXICO

The health care system in Mexico is an example of top-down agenda-setting, resulting in deficiencies in policy design. Health care has had a relatively high priority among social services in Mexico since the Mexican Revolution. The primary weakness of the state system lies in its being firmly wedded to curative medicine, and in its reluctance to adopt a strong commitment to preventive medical care, which the World Health Organization views as the most effective way to address the issue of good health. The Mexican system, even more than that of the United States, largely emphasizes curative medicine. While Mexico has made dramatic advances in inoculation rates since the early 1990s, major problems persist: inadequate prenatal care, excessive levels of environmental contaminants, and high rates of tuberculosis and hepatitis A (Hatcher et al. 1995). These types of health problems disproportionately affect residents of *colonias populares*.

Deficiencies in public policy related to the provision of health services in the colonias have even more significant impacts due to the high proportion of coverage provided by the state. Rough estimates of the split between public and private spending on health care in Mexico place the public sector in charge of more than half (56 percent) of the total funding (Cruz et al. 1994). Public health care is organized in a top-down fashion, and is provided primarily by federal entities, including the Health Secretary (SS), which covers approximately 28 million, or 33 percent of the total population; the blue-collar workers' social security system (IMSS) and its extension IMSS-Solidaridad (formerly IMSS-COPLAMAR), covering approximately 36 million (40 percent); and the social security system for public employees (ISSSTE), which embraces around 9 million, or 10 percent of the total population (Bloom 1994, 11). In fact, the SS's mandate for one-third of the population is not as large as it first appears since most middle-income groups will go private,[1] and the SS offers a backup system for the poor who do not have access to the two social security agencies. In addition, the federal family assistance agency provides limited medical services and nutritional assistance for the poorest sector of the population. Since 1983 there has been a concerted effort toward the decentralization of health care in Mexico, and although the transfer of full responsibility to the states was slow until the late 1980s, it has since quickened markedly as part of the Salinas administration's initiatives, and more recently still as a result of the New Federalism (González Block 1991; González Block et al. 1989; Bloom 1994).

Those without private medical insurance or access to services can use both private facilities and public facilities operated by the SS, the IMSS-Solidaridad, and state-level agencies. Low-income citizens, and even some in the insured population in IMSS, frequently make use of local (in-colonia) private medical consulting rooms provided by recently qualified or trainee doctors fulfilling their one-year social service requirement (Ward 1986). In addition, the private Red Cross and Green Cross of Mexico offer some emergency care services for the uninsured. While in theory medical care is available to all, Mexico's system still exhibits a large divide between the covered population and the uncovered population.

HEALTH SERVICES IN THE TEXAS COLONIAS

Health services in the Texas colonias have been geared to preventive programs such as immunization clinics and physical exams. The federally funded Gateway Community Health Centers and the Women, Infants, and Children Program (WIC) target migrant workers, mothers, and children. However, while the relatively low-cost vaccinations and health exams have been successful, a more widespread and urgent need along the border has not been adequately addressed—namely, the lack of doctors and hospitals. The doctor/resident ratio in the border region has been estimated to be 1:984, and underserved communities such as Laredo may have a ratio of 1:1,500. These ratios compare unfavorably with the World Health Organization's recommendation of 1 doctor for every 600 persons. While the Texas border region is one of high rates of population growth, the dearth of physicians, even in cities, makes colonia residents even further removed from access to primary and curative health care.

The federally funded WIC programs have received widespread praise for the services provided to low-income families. Certainly WIC programs are very familiar to colonia residents for the variety and consistency of the services they provide. "El Wik," as many residents refer to it, not only runs immunization campaigns and health assessments but also provides food vouchers for qualifying residents. One WIC office along the border collaborated with Southwestern Bell to secure less expensive phone hookups for colonia residents. However, WIC programs cannot substitute for the care of a nearby and affordable hospital or doctor.

Private hospitals which have offered services to indigent residents have estimated their losses at $166 million in uncompensated service provision. This means that few hospitals continue to accept uncovered, low-income patients. Colonia residents are therefore often referred to hospitals which are many hours away. The federally funded and locally operated community health centers provide the closest thing to hospital care available to many residents, both literally and figuratively. Yet even these centers may be many miles away for colonia residents. Community health centers are attempting to fill the gap caused by the lack of physicians along the border by recruiting medical practitioners from the National Health Service Corps.

The lack of health services along the border is further aggravated by the poor environmental and living conditions, such as the absence of potable water and sewage infrastructure. City and county officials link poor environmental conditions to high incidences of gastrointestinal illnesses, skin diseases, and anencephalic babies. High rates of premature births and underweight infants are an outcome of the lack of prenatal care for mothers.

Health care and treatment appear to be one of the principal "spillover" arenas that I referred to in the Introduction. Many Texas colonia households, and city residents generally, appear to cross over into Mexico to take advantage of the cheaper private medical and dental services (Vogel 1995). Moreover, the pharmaceutical industry in Mexico offers goods without prescription and at a dramatically lower cost (around one-fifth) than in the United States, and as is the case in Mexico, many low-income people on the U.S. side self-prescribe or take the advice of a local pharmacist in Mexico (Ward 1986). Citing Vogel (1995), Staudt notes that one month's supply of Zantac costs $19 in Juárez compared with $85 in El Paso. Staudt (1998, 74) further argues that:

> Although El Paso County funds public health clinics for low-income residents, hours are irregular and waiting time considerable. People take health care into their own hands through cross-border consumption. Yet this relatively free trade in drugs has medical consequences, such as the overuse of antibiotics.

Fire and Police Protection in Texas and Mexico

On both sides of the border, police coverage in the colonias is markedly higher than fire service coverage. Residents of both Texas and Mexico report that public safety is a principal concern. The border region generates a great deal of illegal activity, and there is the fear that this will spill over and threaten the safety of colonia residents. In Mexico, the high priority given to street lighting discussed in Chapter 3 is a reflection of these public safety concerns.

Fire protection in the colonias has historically been inadequate in both Texas and Mexico. Many colonias do not have access to fire services, as was described earlier in the case of Río Bravo not being eligible to use Laredo's fire services. Elsewhere, counties will lease fire service facilities from nearby cities (El Paso, for example). However, traditional fire trucks may be useless in most colonias, which have

36. Neighborhood mailboxes in Montana Vista (El Paso County), with trailer homes and fire hydrant in the distant background.

no fire hydrants, and may not even have any water. The extension of water to some colonias in the past two years has meant that fire hydrants can now be located strategically to provide water for fire fighting (Photo 36). In Ciudad Juárez, the city has recently purchased its first two water tanker fire trucks for use specifically in areas of the city where there is no ready access to a main supply.

Compounding the inadequacy of police and fire services is the absence of emergency telephone services, especially in Mexico. Many colonia residents have no way to call for assistance in an emergency—few have access to a telephone. In Juárez, the city has provided some two-way radios to the presidents of the *comités de vecinos*, which has met with some success.

Policy Prescriptions: Redirecting the Flow

Figure 9 presents a model in which the imperfections of social service provision identified earlier are redressed. In this graphic, Policy and Need are pictured and understood to be on an equal plane, side by side. Service provision is still shown as a dynamic, circular process, but without any diversionary arrows. This figure, therefore, represents the ideal mode of service provision, a collaborative effort in which practice and communication are interwoven. Policy and Need

Figure 9. Redirecting the flow: practice as communication.

have reflexive qualities, one necessarily informing the other, unfiltered and undiverted by biases or constraints. As the self-contained circle indicates, practice as communication creates the nexus between Policy and Need.

Rethinking Practice as Communication Much has been written about education and empowerment going hand in hand, particularly in the field of liberation theology. In relation to social service provision, the act of providing is not an end in itself, but rather a means of self-actualization, a way of independently improving one's condition (Moser 1989, 1996). The manner in which services are provided determines not only the quality of the services themselves, but also the degree of dependence of the recipient on the provider. If an individual sees a service as a handout, delivered in a top-down manner, then the recipient is inclined to exploit the service to the extent that s/he bene-fits, without commitment (Skinner 1983). If, on the other hand, there is a reciprocal exchange of ideas and actions, then the recipient's in-volvement and "stake" enhance the potential sustainability of the ser-vice activity.

Specific Policy Recommendations

THE POLICY IMPLICATIONS FOR SOCIAL SERVICES IN MEXICO

Education   In looking at education in Mexico, it became apparent that there exist mismatches between the number of students and the number of classrooms in some areas. While city master plans refer to an abundance of classrooms, some students from colonias are not able to attend school. The solution is to better balance capacity with need. This might be achieved through a busing system to take students from outlying colonias to the areas of town where underutilized schools are located, although there has never been any tradition of this in Mexico as there is in the United States (where its origins were in the move-ment toward racial and ethnic integration). This is especially true for high school students, since there is a virtual absence of *secundarios* in any but the oldest colonias. Additional primary schools may still have to be constructed in some colonias, and these can be semipermanent rather than brick-built structures (Photo 37).

Another source of school resources would be to ask local busi-nesses, primarily the *maquilas*, to make donations of resources and ma-terials. In Ciudad Juárez, *maquilas* have donated wooden pallets, which have been used to construct "classrooms," but more substantial mate-rials and resources should be sought in a systematic manner.

The design of education policy in Mexico does not adequately ad-dress the conflict faced by older children who need to work in order to contribute to household survival. Any policy which seeks to in-crease secondary and postsecondary enrollment rates needs to take this factor into account. Again, one way to address this situation would be to incorporate the business community into the development of an apprenticeship program which would allow some area adolescents the chance to work while continuing with their learning. This form of

37. Primary school in Paso del Norte colonia, Ciudad Juárez.

investing in human capital would also pay dividends in improving labor quality in the workplace. Regular school hours could also be made more flexible, so that children can continue to attend at night, after work. Costa Rica has such a program for its working high school population that is very successful.

Students from families of limited means may need extra incentives to go on to secondary and postsecondary education. Both financial and logistical assistance may be required for those who want to attend school in Mexico. Adult learners who have gone back to school comprise another group which should receive government assistance, and strengthening the INEA program would help in this respect.

One major area of collaboration between Texas and Mexico has been the former making places in border institutions available to qualified students from Mexican border cities at in-state tuition rates (i.e., as though they were Texas residents). This dramatically reduces (by two-thirds) the costs of a Mexican student's fees, although the cross-border tuition differential remains large since in Mexico university education in state schools is virtually free. Nevertheless, it is a laudable program which fosters cross-border cooperation.

Health in Mexico   Changes in health policy in Mexico should focus on several different issues, including financial and technical constraints. In order to reduce the current high levels of infant mortality and infectious diseases, further public investment must be made. Resources, however, are not the only problem. A policy shift toward preventive medicine and care is desirable, together with greater public education in the areas of sanitation and nutrition.

There is a continuing need to build more small clinics within the colonias. While the initial investment required is high, user fees might cover at least part of the costs. Community contributions, particularly in the form of labor, could also be substantial, as was observed in the colonia of Puerto la Paz in Ciudad Juárez. *Maquilas* and other area businesses might also assist with materials and in-kind contributions.

An emphasis on preventive health care gives the largest return for the scarce resources. This focus must also incorporate citizen participation and public education. Public information campaigns using television advertisements, radio announcements, school programs, and churches are important means of community outreach to cover topics such as domestic violence, family planning, HIV and AIDS, the links between environment and disease, etc.

Health issues in the border region, like the environmental issues with which they are so closely interconnected, are an international problem, and there needs to be increased binational cooperation in health issues, especially in the areas of preventive health care and education. Binational health associations and improved technology transfer are two aspects of cooperation which should receive increased attention and promotion.

Police and Fire Protection in Mexico   In the area of police and fire protection in Mexican colonias, there is a need to improve access to emergency calling. Call boxes or two-way radios could be installed within colonias that do not have phone service. Police and fire fighters also need to be properly equipped to deal with conditions in the colonias. Some areas of the colonias are not easily accessible to large trucks due to the poor condition of the roads. In the case of fire services, there is an absence of fire hydrants, which means that auxiliary water tanker lorries are essential. Involving the community more in police and fire services would also raise the quality of the services. Relations between the police and colonia residents are sometimes harmed by the perception that patrols are not for the *colonos'* safety, but to keep

38. Social Services Module on west side of Ciudad Juárez. At the rear is an IMSS Unidad de Asistencia Familiar, and alongside is a series of other government social service program offices. The local police precinct is at the near end of the module (not visible in photo).

them in check. Community outreach efforts and improved communications, as part of a self-policing program, might help to mitigate these misconceptions and raise levels of public safety simultaneously. Fire protection efforts would benefit from a program to provide fire extinguishers and smoke detectors at low or negligible cost to colonia residents.

Given the higher population densities in Mexico, this range of social services can usefully be clustered in an area to serve several settlements. For example, the IMSS clinic on the far west side of Juárez has a series of service providers alongside, as well as a municipal police precinct (Photo 38).

The Policy Implications for Social Services in Texas

Education   The educational system in the state of Texas is currently facing a number of challenges, some of which are magnified in the school districts that serve colonias. The primary problem is a lack of funding. It would be easy to come forward with a recommendation to build schools throughout the colonias, but this cannot be pursued in the near future by the school districts under current policy. One possibility would be to modify (i.e., lower) current TEA standards for the construction of new (primary or preschool) facilities in the colonias. An advantage of this proposal is that it would create an opportunity for increased participation by the community in the construction of their schools. This participation would reduce costs while increasing the sense of "ownership" of the facilities felt by residents.

There is currently a deficit of educators in the border region, and addressing this problem should have top priority, even over facility expansion. Spending more energy and resources on recruiting and attracting qualified teachers is a short-term solution, however. Teacher training programs and incentives for residents to teach in the colonias, similar to those proposed for the health professions below, would be critical aspects of a long-term strategy.

Health Care   As noted previously, the provision of health care in the colonias is hampered by the shortage of health care personnel and facilities, as well as by poor environmental conditions. Jurisdictional conflicts complicate the picture further. Any attempt at developing an effective health care policy will require finding medical personnel who are willing to work in the colonias. The most immediate way to accomplish this would be to increase opportunities for colonia residents to receive training in the allied health professions. The Partners for Improved Nutrition in Health (PINAH) has had some success in training local leaders in the areas of prevention and treatment. A similar program could be created for extension to the colonias. Local community colleges and universities could be encouraged to recruit colonia residents for a two-year medical assistant program, and give them financial incentives to work in the colonias in the form of tuition waivers or assistance. Doctors are in extremely short supply in the border region, and one possible solution would be to recruit through the Doctors without Borders program. Other pressing needs include twenty-four-hour clinics and bilingual 911 service.

It is essential to stress the connection between health and environmental issues. It is hoped that resources allocated through the North American Development Bank to the Border Environmental Cooperation Commission (BECC) will enhance its programs, although the NAD Bank to date has had virtually no success in providing loans to support BECC programs, whose executive officers have generally chosen to find alternative and less encumbering sources of loan support.

Both Mexico and the United States must take responsibility for the institutional incapacity of the NAD Bank to be made operational, and the simple fact of overcoming these barriers would have a significant effect in improving environmental conditions along the border.

Health care provision is also hindered by the multiplicity of responsible jurisdictions. Both cities and counties have health boards and departments. Pooling the resources of the two could lead to improved service for the colonias. On the Texas side, the same need exists to increase cross-border cooperation and communication. The Pan American Health Organization and its affiliate, the U.S. Border Health Association, were formed to track United States–Mexico health statistics and promote maternal and child health care. This information should be disseminated more widely to regional and local health care providers who service the colonias, as well as to the residents themselves. A health outreach network might distribute this information using direct mail, school fliers, and the media, and WHO-type community-based data collection exercises might also serve as a means of gathering information about health problems and environmental hazards (World Health Organization 1988).

Police and Fire Services   There are a small number of reforms that can be implemented in the area of public security in Texas that utilize community participation. The isolated nature of the colonias increases the vulnerability of the residents. One means of addressing this situation would be to promote community policing through the Neighborhood Watch Program. Another recommendation would be to establish county sheriff substations in closer proximity to the colonias. A helpful policy would also be county or city support for street lighting, which is provided by the municipality in Mexico, but is almost nonexistent in Texas colonias.

In the case of fire services, county governments should be encouraged to "lease" fire services from neighboring cities, and the practice has widened in recent years. For example, Montana Vista now gets its fire service from the City of El Paso. Counties might also usefully promote volunteer fire units within the colonias, and assist with training and resources.

Indeed, where they are large enough to do so, colonias may be well served by incorporating themselves as "cities" in order to have greater control over their service provision and definition of codes. The frus-

39. City hall, Río Bravo, with ambulance and fire service vehicles.

40. City hall, El Cenizo, with moribund fire truck and garbage truck (not in photo).

tration and failure experienced by Río Bravo and El Cenizo with respect to Webb County and the City of Laredo prompted them to incorporate themselves as cities (Photos 39 and 40). However, it appears
that the strategy worked better in Río Bravo, where residents also
agreed to modest local tax levies for settlement improvements and ser-

vices. In El Cenizo the garbage and fire services languish for lack of funds and upkeep. Clearly, local leadership and community integration are prerequisites for successful incorporation.

Formal Social Infrastructure: Texas' Second Wave

Increased economic activity on both sides of the border has not led to concomitant improvements in standards of living for colonias, and the lack of social services support adds to the ongoing social costs endured by residents. There are serious shortfalls in the provision of social services such as health, education, and police and fire protection. While additional cash investments are urgently needed, existing resources could be used more effectively. Policy changes, including the adoption of more progressive means of social service provision, would result in colonia residents' needs being addressed more directly and fully.

Once again the principal challenge for Texas appears to be two-fold. First, to adopt a different mindset and to recognize that colonias are legitimate working-class neighborhoods of U.S. citizens who are left largely bereft of access to social services. Part of this challenge is to overcome jurisdictional constraints and exercise imagination about ways of making interjurisdictional providers work collaboratively, even if this involves state and/or county subsidy programs to cities that extend social service coverage to colonias. It makes little sense for a county to duplicate a raft of social services, even if it had the resources to do so. As I highlighted at the outset, the costs of social service provision are ongoing and must usually come from fiscal resources. And callous though it might appear for Laredo's fire officers to turn their backs on Río Bravo colonia, it is not unreasonable for them to do so if there is no way their costs can be recovered from the county.

If interjurisdictional collaboration cannot be achieved, then perhaps social services should be more aggressively organized and provided by the state—possibly alongside the TEA and independent school districts. The educational model of ISDs and cross-state subsidies to provide education is accepted practice in Texas. The creation of a similar structure alongside or even grafted onto the educational system would be designed to provide or coordinate social services more expeditiously and effectively to colonia populations. Legislation since the late 1980s to prevent colonia proliferation was only the first step. Now those populations need both physical and social infrastructure. The provision of physical services is well underway, and provided that the feeder lines are appropriately planned to allow for ongoing hookups, future occupation of plots can be readily serviced. But that is not the end of the story. There is little that can be done (or should be done) to prevent colonia populations from growing substantially as platted areas developed prior to MSRs are occupied, and as already purchased plots are occupied to provide homes for the working poor. Most of the colonias I have studied in Texas still have low density and occupancy rates, often with more than one-half of lots being undeveloped. As these lots are occupied the demand for social services will intensify, and thus far Texas does not appear to be exercising the imagination or commitment, or laying the institutional groundwork, to attend to the second phase of the colonias problem: the development of social infrastructure.

This brings me to the second important challenge—that of emphasizing means rather than ends. Extending social services to colonias will only be successful if it is done in a way that makes the services self-sustaining, breaking dependency upon supra-local agencies. By seeking to work in partnership with colonia communities—whether in policing, preventive health care programs, school construction, or other enterprises—providers will enhance their capacity to deliver social services to a wider population, but they will also begin to create the wherewithal within the population to make many of those programs self-sustaining.

The Role of Community Centers
in Developing Social Infrastructure

To date, to the extent that imagination has been exercised, it has come largely from nongovernment organizations. Legislative support has been important in helping some of these organizations take steps toward enhancing the provision of social infrastructure. At Texas A&M University, as part of its legislative line of funding for colonia research, the CfHUD has established a number of community centers in colonias along the border, including the study colonias of Cameron Park, El Cenizo, Highway 359 East, Montana Vista, and Sparks (Photo 41).[2] These are designed to provide a base from which social service provid-

41. Texas A&M's recently completed community center in Sparks colonia (El Paso County).

ers may operate, and to act as a facilitator for community development, both intramurally, and between neighboring colonias.[3]

One of the agreed tasks of the Policy Research Project was to provide an independent evaluation of two of Texas A&M's first established community centers—in El Cenizo and Cameron Park. The community center in Montana Vista was not fully operational when the project commenced, and therefore it was not included. This component of the overall colonia study examines specifically the manner in which the community centers address and redress the privations in social and physical infrastructure described in this and in previous chapters. The principal objective in the following sections is to examine the patterns of community center *utilization* among residents of the Cameron Park and El Cenizo colonias. The second is an *evaluation* of the community centers by the users.

In the following discussion I explore the results from household surveys which were conducted in Cameron Park and El Cenizo. I begin with a brief history of the genesis of community centers, followed by summary descriptions of the communities themselves. Before turning to the survey results I outline the survey methodology and the questionnaire that was used. It was intended that the household user evaluation would be complemented by an analysis of the opinions of the some eighty service providers working out of the two centers. Regrettably, however, only fifteen of these service providers responded to our mail questionnaire, so that evaluation is otiose. Where appropriate, however, I will refer to their responses during the broader discussion.

RATIONALE FOR THE COMMUNITY CENTERS

The community centers of Cameron Park and El Cenizo were designed primarily to address the above mentioned lack of informal social infrastructure (see also Chapter 4) that typically makes colonias in Texas settlements rather than communities. Furthermore, they were conceived as "anchors" for formal social infrastructure in the form of social service providers. In this sense they were intended to serve as clearinghouses through which colonia residents could readily access much-needed services in areas such as health, education, and housing. Equally important, they were designed to provide places where residents could come together to discuss community strategies for addressing needs, thereby fostering horizontal integration. Texas A&M—the centers' author and architect—envisioned these multipurpose centers as "walk-in centers," which it defined as "community-based centers with a service area limited to a distance approximately equal to what could be walked comfortably in an hour" (Rogers et al. 1993, 5). In effect this meant that they would serve a population within a 2.5-mile radius of the center.

In 1995 each of the centers discussed here had been in operation for more than one year. Capital funds—$920,000 annually—were disbursed on a biennial basis by the Texas Legislature, through the General Revenues Fund, for their construction, facility costs, and economic development work. Funding of recurrent expenditures is provided by Cameron and Webb Counties and covers the salaries of the director and ancillary staff, as well as all operation and maintenance costs and administrative expenditures. The amounts received by each center to cover such expenditures are minimal: according to Cameron Park center director Marbelia Moreno, the center receives $50,000 per annum.

In 1995 the centers each had approximately 3,000 ft² in area and were thought by CfHUD to provide 2,000–3,000 contacts a month to twenty-five to thirty service providers. The services and community activities include the Women, Infants, and Children program (WIC), food stamps,[4] aerobics, general equivalency diploma (GED) classes, English as a Second Language (ESL) classes, Co-prima,[5] and a medical clinic. Because of the previously mentioned budget constraints, the centers rely heavily on volunteers and donations for their continued operation.

HOUSEHOLD COMMUNITY PROFILE

Cameron Park   As we observed in Chapter 1, this colonia is located five miles northeast of *downtown* Brownsville, and is considered to be the oldest colonia in Texas, the first residents having arrived approximately thirty-five years ago. Officially, 5,000 mostly Hispanic residents reside on 1,624 lots in this community.[6] The per capita income is below $8,000 per annum, compared with $13,000 for Texas and $14,000 for the United States (*United States Census* 1990).[7] Cameron Park suffers not only from the social, employment, and educational privations that affect all low-income communities, but also from the infrastructural deprivations and isolation associated with border settlements in particular. Housing conditions vary considerably within the colonia, probably in association with income level and length of residence in the colonia.

El Cenizo   This colonia is located approximately twenty miles southeast of Laredo and comprises 920 lots, of which 575 are occupied (LBJ 1997, 2:128). The Rio Grande–Río Bravo forms the western boundary of El Cenizo. The colonia is relatively young—having begun around 1984—with most residents having arrived in the early 1990s. Consequently, one sees far less consolidation and fewer resources than in the more established Cameron Park colonia. El Cenizo has gained some public notoriety, in part due to the indictment of its principal developer, Cecil McDonald, for violation of state laws regarding colonia development. Home ownership is in the process of being transferred to residents. Many of this incorporated colonia's 3,500 residents, along with those of nearby Río Bravo colonia, are of Mexican descent or origin, and arrived at the colonia as immigrants or as out-migrants from Laredo's affordable-housing squeeze. Adult unemployment is high (between 20 and 40 percent), and most employment is in the semiskilled, service, agricultural, and construction sectors (Rogers et al. 1993, v). Per capita income is among the lowest in the state of Texas, at $3,000 per annum, and relative to many other colonias that we examined, El Cenizo suffers from particularly inadequate social and physical infrastructure.

Survey Methodology

As stated earlier, the purpose of the survey was to assess, through household surveys, the community centers' utilization and effectiveness in responding to community needs. Fieldwork was carried out by two teams of graduate students on the weekends of April 8–10, April 22–25, and April 29–May 1, 1995. Because women tend to spend more time within the community, and because traditional gender roles define them as families' primary caretakers, it was expected that they would have greatest interaction with the community centers, and we decided to target them in our interviews. Thus, surveys were directed toward female heads of household, and additional questions were asked of them about their spouses' and family members' interaction with the centers.

The survey consisted of five broad sections: (1) a minidemographic profile; (2) a section for respondents who were not users of the center; (3) a section for service users;[8] (4) a center profile; and (5) a section on Texas A&M's perceived involvement (i.e., were people aware of the university's role in establishing the center?). The surveys were written in both English and Spanish, but typically were administered in Spanish. Interviewers conducted the surveys in pairs. Survey responses were subsequently coded and statistically analyzed using SPSS.

The target population was colonia households, and the sampling frame was derived from plat maps obtained from local planning offices. The plat maps were quite thorough—listing residences by both block and lot. The exact sample frame and survey trajectory varied according to locale. In Cameron Park, fifty-two interviews were conducted randomly on two consecutive weekends in April. According to its plat map, Cameron Park contains approximately sixty blocks. Thus, in an effort to reach the broadest possible cross-section of colonia residents, interviewers attempted to survey one household from each block. The middle lot on the south side of each block was arbitrarily

decided upon. In the event of nonavailability or noncompliance of respondents, interviewers moved one lot east from the designated lot
until a participating household could be found.

The El Cenizo surveys were carried out by five graduate student
interviewers during the weekend of April 8–10. Forty interviews were
conducted randomly but on a basis which ensured that as much of the
physical extent of the colonia as possible was covered.

For both colonias, contact rates were high, due probably to the
fact that surveys were conducted over the course of a weekend, when
residents tended to be at home. Response rates were also extremely
high—over 70 percent for El Cenizo and close to 90 percent for Cameron Park. Such a high response rate was not a surprise: Hispanic
working-class culture values hospitality and politeness. Thus, colonia
residents were more willing to talk with interviewers than would possibly be the case in other neighborhoods throughout the United States
(see also Rogers et al. 1993).

Survey Results: Cameron Park and El Cenizo

Demographic Profile   To use a simple analogy, Cameron Park and
El Cenizo may be likened to adult and child. Cameron Park is a
"mature" colonia, as evidenced in its residency patterns. A substantial
number of respondents—44 percent—have lived in Cameron Park
for over ten years, and as expected, almost all of them (78 percent)
own their homes (i.e., rather than being renters). A similar proportion
of households comprise a married couple, with the modal group having between 2 and 5 children (54 percent). Of the 52 women interviewed, almost half (46 percent) reported using the community center,
while the rest do so sporadically as to constitute nonuse.[9] Of the
46 women who have children, only 6 (13 percent) replied that their
children use the center independently of them. Utilization is lowest
among male heads of household at 8 percent. Overall, approximately
the same proportion of households in the two settlements use the community center (51 percent in El Cenizo compared with the 46 percent
for Cameron Park reported above).

Although Cameron Park and El Cenizo share a very similar demographic profile, El Cenizo's home ownership and length of residence
patterns are indicative of a younger settlement and population. A
slightly smaller proportion of families—69 percent—own their own

homes. The number who are married is quite high, at 64 percent, and almost all of the women interviewed have children, again with the majority (59 percent) having between 2 and 5 children.

Center Utilization and Nonutilization   As mentioned above, approximately half of the women householders interviewed made regular use of the community center. Community center utilization among all groups is somewhat higher in El Cenizo than in Cameron Park (square brackets = Cameron Park scores), with survey results revealing that 51 [46] percent, 33 [8] percent, and 18 [13] percent of all women, men, and children, respectively, use the community center.[10] The slightly higher utilization is most likely an outcome of El Cenizo's greater overall community need, as revealed by per capita income data, and by the relative newness of the community. Although the overall number of renters living in the settlements was low, a much smaller proportion of those living in Cameron Park (21 percent) than in El Cenizo (42 percent) reported that they made use of the community center. Again, this probably reflects the relative youth of El Cenizo and its more isolated position vis-à-vis Laredo, making dependence upon the community center that much more imperative. This location factor may also be the reason for a much lower percentage of Cameron Park men who were reported to be making use of the community center—a figure that increases almost fivefold (to 33 percent) for El Cenizo. Unfortunately, it is not clear if the difference is a result of differences in the interviewing teams in recording responses,[11] or genuinely reflects the reported feelings of men in Cameron Park that the services are geared toward women. Both center officials and household respondents stated that men tended to be interested in using the centers for services typically related to their roles—for example, the regularization of ownership papers, the acquisition of infrastructure permits, legalization matters, canine rabies vaccines, etc., but that more often than not these are not important "provider" services offered through the community centers. Despite this reported noninvolvement, however, it became apparent, through interviews with community center directors and colonia residents themselves, that male involvement is almost certainly more pronounced than these survey results illustrate. In the El Cenizo community center, for example, many men serve as volunteer teachers and janitors, while in both community centers, men are well represented at the monthly meetings (*juntas*).

Table 17. The Reasons for Community Center Nonuse

Reason	Cameron Park (n = 28) (%)	El Cenizo (n = 19) (%)
Time constraints	8	43
No interest	5	4
Mismatch between needs and services	27	9
Personality conflicts with center personnel	3	0
Services provided elsewhere	14	13
Poor quality of services	0	0
No need of such services	11	9
Other*	32	22
Total	100	100

Above percentages measure frequencies of responses given. Respondents could give more than one answer per question. Total responses: Cameron Park = 37, El Cenizo = 23.
*Included such reasons as childcare difficulties, lack of knowledge of services on offer, illness, etc.

As we have seen, roughly one-half of the households interviewed in the two colonias appear to have made little or no use of the community centers. Given the level of investment made in the centers, and the important outreach and catalyst role that they are expected to fulfill, such a high level is disappointing. Our survey sought to identify the reasons why this might be the case, and it appears that important differences may be discerned between the two colonias (Table 17).

In El Cenizo, many respondents cited time constraints and conflicts (in terms of their schedule in relation to center hours of operation) as the principal reasons for nonuse. In spite of the fact that the center is open most evenings to accommodate those who work during the day, the distance between Laredo and El Cenizo appears to preclude many from attending evening classes, particularly if public transportation is used. Moreover, staffing limitations and fiscal constraints in both community centers preclude the centers being opened on weekends, when residents would most likely be free to access services. Such a problem could be overcome by having community volunteers run the centers on weekends, but volunteer rates appear to be quite low in both communities. In Cameron Park, a larger proportion of residents were critical of the mismatch of needs to service offerings through the center. For example, nonuser respondents mentioned wanting garbage collection, recycling containers, pavement, drainage, and water—services obviously beyond the scope of the community centers. Further, many Cameron Park residents reported being unaware of the services offered, citing the lack of a telephone and frequent absence from the home as impediments to receiving such information.

In both communities there is a miscellany of reasons included under the "other" category, most of which related to a perceived lack of support services for community residents. Many nonusers expressed a desire to receive services through the centers, but cited as impediments to doing so a lack of childcare in particular, and poor information about center offerings in general. In El Cenizo, several residents felt that a lack of advertising on the part of service providers was a deliberate attempt to freeze them out of much-needed, but scarce, services. Clearly, remedies to correct such perceptions are required if center utilization is to increase.

In addition to identifying the relationship between household needs and community center services, these reasons for nonuse paint a larger picture of the socioeconomic conditions prevalent in the two colonias. Because Cameron Park is older in terms of both history and demographics, it appears that fewer families have young children, and thus fewer families are likely to be potential or actual service recipients. In addition, Cameron Park's higher per capita income suggests that it has a larger proportion of its population in the work force, and its need and eligibility may be lower. Thus, in addition to receiving a wage and pension, which would disqualify some from service receipt, some residents are presumably receiving other amenities and benefits (e.g., health insurance) through formal employment or Social Security. Moreover, Cameron Park's proximity to Brownsville means that residents can more easily avail themselves of alternative service providers than can the residents of El Cenizo, which is much farther from Laredo.

In spite of their nonuse, however, a significant number of nonusers—46 percent in Cameron Park and 68 percent in El Cenizo—knew someone who uses the center and is satisfied with the services provided. Moreover, nonusers were rarely negative about the centers, but rather considered them to be available to all people who wished to use the services, and their staffs amenable to suggestions. Overall, almost all of Cameron Park and El Cenizo nonrecipients felt that the centers were a benefit to the community.

The Nature of Usage

Sought-after Services As Table 18 indicates, services sought from the centers vary by colonia. In Cameron Park, social services (particularly WIC and food stamps) and health services (family planning, Co-Prima, and the clinic) were easily the most cited sought-after services, comprising together nearly two-thirds of all visits to the community center.

While El Cenizo's pattern of community center utilization is broadly similar, concentrating upon health services first and foremost (almost one-half of sought-after services, see Table 18), there is a wider range of services that are regularly used. Those appearing in the "other" category (namely, miscellaneous services such as legalization "clinics," *juntas*, etc.) account for a further quarter of community center visits, and the aerobics group (recreation) has stimulated some followership and participation. In both colonias, however, centers appear to have done little to serve as foci for recreation, social events, and

Table 18. Most Frequently Sought Services from the Surveyed Texas A&M Community Centers

Service	Cameron Park (n = 24) (%)	El Cenizo (n = 20) (%)
GED	10	0
Health	31	48
Social services	33	13
Recreation	0	13
Social events	3	0
General education	8	0
Other*	15	26
Total	100	100

Above percentages represent frequencies of response. Respondents could give more than one answer.
*Includes infrastructure provision, bow making, *juntas*.

educational activities—i.e., social activities that might help to forge a greater sense of community spirit. Rather, the centers appear to be more geared toward vertical integration—health and social services, for example—and to acting as a conduit toward the supra-local. It appears that, to date, services that provide an economic benefit (in the form of medicine, milk, food stamps, etc.), and require little participation and interaction, are the most popular. Indeed, the role most frequently assumed by respondents vis-à-vis the community center is that of consumer rather than participator.

Frequency of Use   Because the majority of respondents in both colonias seek out nonrecurrent or fixed services (the clinic, for example), the frequency of utilization is low. Over 90 percent of all respondents in both colonias reported using the center less than once a week. Such relatively infrequent utilization is inevitable if centers do not fulfill roles which enhance horizontal integration—social, recreational, and community activities. Residents do not see the centers as gathering places for the community; but rather they view them as providers of goods and services. Thus, their usage is *individualized* rather than socialized.

Perceptions of the Community Centers   A significant number of questions in this section dealt with respondents' perceptions of their neighbors' use of the community centers. Especially in Cameron Park, some 48 percent felt that their neighbors used the community center more than they themselves. A significant number in both settlements—32 percent in Cameron Park and 24 percent in El Cenizo—knew or were willing to hazard a guess about their neighbors' use of the centers. Most felt that their neighbors' use of the centers was probably greater than their own, but few could specify for what services. This suggests that while most residents view the center positively in general terms, their own commitment and take-up of specific services is rather limited, and is rarely for "social" purposes. Indeed, in El Cenizo residents often referred to the center as *la clínica* (the clinic), confirming our suspicion that it was viewed primarily as a service provider, not as a community center.

Propinquity and Usage   Proximity to the community center seemed to be a slightly more important predictor of utilization in El Cenizo than in Cameron Park. Fifty-seven percent of all respondents in El Cenizo—versus 48 percent in Cameron Park—said that more proximate households were more likely to use the center. In terms of the actual households themselves, utilization does indeed appear to be influenced by residential location within El Cenizo, inasmuch as increased household distance from the community center results in decreased utilization. Many of these nonusers live on the periphery of El Cenizo and listed the summer heat, distance, and lack of transportation as impediments to community center use. Thus, Texas A&M's idea of "walking centers" may be ill-founded if at certain times of the year people are reluctant to walk in the first place. In Cameron Park, distance "decay" of home to center did not appear to shape propensity to use the center. Those living next to the center were as likely *not* to use it as those living at the farthest point of the community. It would be interesting to know how most center users got themselves to the centers—on foot or by car. Unfortunately, the originating concept of these as "walking" centers prompted us not to ask this question.

Notwithstanding the apparent significance of proximity to usage in El Cenizo, 41 percent of households interviewed in the colonia reported that people from outside the community use the center, while in Cameron Park the proportion of outsiders reported to use it was much lower (17 percent). This can probably be explained by geography. El Cenizo is smaller and contiguous with the community of Río Bravo, and it makes sense that Río Bravo's residents would avail themselves of the services offered at the El Cenizo community center.[12] Cameron Park, on the other hand, is much larger and is not adjacent to any other settlement.

Gender and Usage Within the communities themselves, women form the overwhelming bulk of the centers' clientele, although the exact percentage varies by community. Seventy-one percent of El Cenizo respondents viewed women as the primary users of center services—as opposed to 96 percent in Cameron Park. Two primary reasons were cited for why this was so. The first was that center offerings were directed toward women; the second was that women, by virtue of being at home with their children, could more readily access the center.

Such a trend unearths both a public relations and a marketing issue, and has implications for further utilization of the centers by both men and women. In the public relations domain, colonia president Gloria Moreno appears to be a significant factor. A majority of the female service recipients interviewed in Cameron Park had been personally lobbied by her to get involved. Such networking explains why a greater number of older female users are found in Cameron Park than in El Cenizo. However, the perception exists among many that

she has not focused sufficiently on the task of promoting male participation, which was why so many have stayed away.

Related to this public relations issue is a second, somewhat tangen-
tial, issue of the nature of demand, although the causal relationship—
is demand created by preferentially directing programs at women, or
does the predominantly female clientele shape supply?—is far from
clear. Despite the contentions and perceptions of female-oriented services, in truth, the majority of programs offered at both centers are
aimed at both men and women. In our view the higher level of female
participation is due more to traditional caretaker roles within the
family, and in the case of Cameron Park, to the promotional role
played by one particular resident. Indeed, in terms of sustained community outreach, the Cameron Park community center has enjoyed
much greater success than has the community center in El Cenizo due
in large part to the efforts of Gloria Moreno, who is the best-known
community center affiliate. Were it not for her sustained involvement
and proselytization in the Cameron Park center, the colonia's age, together with the lower level of need, would probably have led to far
lower success of the center's activities and, by now, to a higher degree
of atrophy in resident participation.

In spite of the fact that the overwhelming majority of respondents
viewed women as the primary consumers of center services, a smaller
majority—58 percent in El Cenizo and 66 percent in Cameron Park—
also stated that women occupy the principal positions or roles as service providers. The type of service accessed by the respondent is likely
to affect whether she is attended by a male or female service provider.
For example, if the respondent's particular use of the center is for the
WIC program, she is more likely to encounter women in the roles of
both consumers and providers. In contrast, if these respondents attend
only ESL classes, they are more likely to encounter a male teacher,
since in January of 1995, the ESL instructor in the El Cenizo community center was male. Also, even in traditional female professions
in the United States, such as education and social work, males continue to occupy a disproportionate number of leadership positions.

The centers were designed to serve all populations, and appear to
have succeeded in this task with three notable exceptions. First, the
lower level of male take-up of services offered discussed above. Second, the perception that the majority of users are adults—specifically,
women with small children. The third exception is that the centers

offer little or nothing for the elderly, although demand would appear to be limited.

Information Dissemination The centers appear to differ in the ways in which each seeks to disseminate information. Whereas 31 percent of El Cenizo's respondents said they first learned about the community center via community center advertising, 56 percent of Cameron Park respondents said they first learned about the center through its own outreach efforts. Just over one-quarter in El Cenizo first heard about the center by word of mouth.

While most residents felt reasonably well informed, some continued to express their concern and dissatisfaction with the frequency and methods of center advertising. Such dissatisfaction was especially prevalent among those who resided farther away from the centers. These individuals often felt that no efforts were made to contact them, and they therefore felt less comfortable in soliciting services. In fact, service providers do attempt to contact residents through a variety of methods—fliers, the monthly community center calendar, and radio. However, manpower and financial constraints preclude the extensive face-to-face outreach that community members appear to want.

Satisfaction Ratings These advertising difficulties notwithstanding, satisfaction with the community centers is generally high. Table 19 provides in detail satisfaction levels with center facilities, services, and employees. Generally, satisfaction with the centers is high, particularly in the case of Cameron Park, where facilities, services, and employees were given ratings of "good" or "very good" in almost all cases, with only one respondent really being negative about the Cameron Park community center. Three-quarters of those interviewed knew a community center worker (usually Gloria Moreno).

Overall approval rates are more variable in El Cenizo, although general satisfaction with the community center remains high. Sixty-nine percent, 56 percent, and 64 percent, respectively, rated the facilities, services, and employees as either "good" or "very good." There was lower approval for employees due to a perception that some community center workers use service provision as patronage and give preferential treatment to friends or family. Part of the reason for this perception may have to do with the fact that only a small number (17 percent) felt that they knew any of the center workers. Trust and familiarity with individual service providers, such as that embodied in a personal respect for community leader Gloria Moreno in Cameron

Table 19. Texas A&M University Community Center User Ratings for Facility, Services, and Employees[1]

	Facilities (%)	Services (%)	Employees (%)
El Cenizo			
Very good	30	14	14
Good	39	41	50
Satisfactory	26	36	21
Bad	3	5	7
Total[2]	98	96	92
Cameron Park			
Very good	92	68	92
Good	4	28	4
Bad	4	4	4
Total	100	100	100

[1] Categories of responses differ because of a variation between El Cenizo and Cameron Park survey forms.
[2] Does not equal 100% because of missing data.

Park, may have an important qualitative effect upon the way in which the centers are perceived and rated by residents.

Proposed Improvements   Most residents felt that the centers had benefited the community and had difficulty in identifying where improvement was needed or might be undertaken. Suggestions fell generally into three areas:

• Larger space: Many felt the centers were far too small to accommodate all of the activities going on. In particular, an extension area for a community day care center was felt to be an urgent need.
• Improved advertising: Community members wanted more personalized outreach, especially those living farther away from the centers.
• Provision of infrastructure and services: Most residents stated that above all else, the community needed adequate water supply, drainage, roads, and garbage collection. Of course, these are not strictly the remit of the social service providers located in the centers.

Awareness of the Role of Texas A&M University Finally, most residents in both colonias were unaware of Texas A&M's leadership role in establishing the community centers.[13] Only 32 percent of Cameron Park's respondents and 26 percent of El Cenizo's knew that A&M had any involvement at all with the centers. Nor were most of them able to explain the university's connection to the centers except that they had seen the A&M name on the sign outside. This may not be considered important—indeed, there may be good reasons why CfHUD would want it not to be widely known. If so, this is a major difference with Mexican institutions, which would always expect to take full credit for their involvement.

Conclusions: The Balance Sheet on Community Centers and Social Service Provision

In summary, this survey has demonstrated the following:

- Most individuals appear not to make use of the community centers, and those that do are relatively infrequent users of one service. Reasons for nonuse vary, but appear to fall into three categories: time constraints, a mismatch between what the resident needs and what the center offers, and a combination of miscellaneous constraints (childcare, transportation, lack of advertising). However, even among these nonusers, there is a belief that the center benefits the overall community, as well as those that do take specific advantage of the center offerings.
- The typical nonuser of the community center is a male head of household or child older than five. It appears that nonuse is linked to levels of consolidation and length of residence in the community, although the relationship is not always strong or unidirectional. Nonuse is common in neighborhoods where social cohesion and horizontal integration appear to be especially low.
- Overall satisfaction with the community centers appears to be quite high. The perception and reality are that the centers have allowed people to access much-needed services (health, WIC, food stamps), and occasionally other activities such as aerobics and bow making. Community members seem genuinely grateful for the center's presence and efforts.
- A general profile emerges of the following typical service recipient: female, married, with two to five children, and a home owner who

has lived in the community between two and five years. This recipient uses the center less than once a month, almost exclusively
for the clinic or some form of social service receipt (usually WIC).
She knows some of the workers and thinks that the center, its facilities, and its workers are good. But her only contact with the
center is as a recipient of services.

- Given that they did not form the bulk of the centers' clientele, men
  would appear to be overrepresented as service *providers*.

- Respondents were more likely to use the centers if they received
  news about activities directly from the centers themselves. At present, firsthand (direct) information is more likely to raise engage-
  ment than word of mouth. Those who lived farther away from the
  centers felt they were being ignored in terms of advertising.

- Residents expressed some need for improvements in the following
  three areas: center facilities (which are felt to be too small); better
  advertising (evenly disseminated throughout the community); and
  the need for the centers to somehow serve as the conduits for provision of water and sewerage.

Texas A&M has been successful in establishing community centers
which provide an important locus for service providers. Satisfaction is
high, and most residents welcome the establishment of the center in
their settlement even if they don't make use of it. Transportation to
the centers remains a problem, especially in the summer heat, and the
concept of these being centers to which people would be willing to
walk from within a 2.5-mile radius may have been flawed. It would
appear that regular walk-in users will come from much closer, while
others will wait until they can arrange a ride. More needs to be done
on getting information out to would-be users, and opening on weekends—at least on Saturday mornings—seems likely to raise user-
ship, particularly among those workers for whom early evenings are
difficult.

However, despite Texas A&M's correctly identified goal that these
centers should be vehicles for horizontal integration of the community, this has not occurred. The majority of community residents view
the centers, not as the basis around which common class or neighborhood bonds might be forged, but as places where they come to procure
a service, and then leave. Thus, the levels of horizontal integration
generated by center usage are low, while levels of vertical integration
are heightened.

Significantly, neither the residents nor the center employees appear to consider social and recreational activities a priority within the center's remit. In my view, urgent consideration should be given to emphasizing and prioritizing such activities, since this would strengthen community horizontal interaction anchored on the center facility. A good place to start would be with the regular *junta* meetings, which many people attend, even though it would appear they do not view such meetings as a form of center "use" *precisely because they are not going to receive a "service."* Moving laterally from such community meetings to regular community social gatherings would, I believe, quickly foster a sense of community spirit. It would also enhance the likelihood that the center's activities will become more self-sustaining, with greater democratic involvement of a larger proportion of colonia residents of both genders and all ages. Otherwise, there is the very real danger that the center will never truly become a community center. Rather, it will be a center for downward-flowing resources, located within a settlement.

Six

Conclusion: Texas Colonias and the Next Policy Wave

Policy-making and Public Intervention: A Job Only Half Completed

It was ten years ago that Texas government got its wakeup call to the colonia "problem," and to the existence of some fourteen-hundred-plus settlements and 340,000 people living in what were quickly deemed to be "Third World" housing conditions. Throughout Texas and especially in the border region of the United States and Mexico, colonias appeared as a form of urbanization by stealth visited upon counties by land developers who, alone it seemed, recognized that there was a rising demand for low-cost housing that neither the public nor the private sector was capable of or interested in providing. Unlike most of their Third World counterparts, however, these developers had the perspicacity to develop colonias legally, usually through Contract for Deed. This legal form of land development contract was highly advantageous to the developers since it offered the ready option of foreclosure and recovery if purchasers failed to make payments, and because it required minimal site investment and outlay on services. Profits were high, and developers were able to duck the issue of when to install basic infrastructure, and who would do it.

The fact that they were able to get away with such naked exploitation of worker groups was in large part explained by the relative "invisibility" of colonias located, as they invariably were, well beyond the boundaries of cities, and even their ETJs. This placed them under the jurisdiction of county government, which accentuated their invisibility, given the relative weakness of that level of government to respond to colonia needs. Sometimes, too, developers were in cahoots with county officials who turned a blind eye to the promotion of colonias. Moreover, the location of these settlements at a considerable distance from the city meant that they were not considered to be urban at all, but rather rural. To the extent that any level of government was responsible for colonias, it was the Farmers' Home Administration (FmHA) and the Rural Development Administration (now merged as the RECDA). The possibility that many lots in these settlements were being purchased by undocumented Mexican workers further added to their invisibility. Urbanization by stealth was following a "recipe" that was perfected by developers such as Cecil McDonald in Webb County (see epigraph).

The wakeup call, when it came in 1987 or thereabouts, was prompted by a small number of increasingly powerful voices within NGOs such as Valley Interfaith and EPISO, which had themselves emerged from the Texas Industrial Areas Foundation a few years earlier. Slowly, too, politicians came to realize colonias were a double-edged sword: insofar as they were inhabited by U.S. citizens, voter registration drives might offer access to voters, but colonia poverty and neglect were also a major political embarrassment and potential liability. At this time, too, Texas was beginning to turn its attention south toward Mexico as an increasingly important trading partner, particularly now that Mexico was emerging from the heavy tariff protectionist era, having entered GATT in 1986. No longer was the border just an area of potential *maquila* assembly activity and twin cities; it began to be an area of economic osmosis between the two countries. Eyes far beyond Texas were beginning to focus upon the border region as well, and upon the opportunities in Texas and beyond.

So the Texas Legislature sought to respond to the colonias problem by seeking to leverage funds from the federal government, having learned that the state would be ineligible for support until steps were taken to prevent further colonia expansion and creation. Responding rapidly in 1989, the legislature passed a series of measures to prevent the proliferation of unserviced colonias (the Model Subdivision Rules), and to create an Economically Distressed Areas Program (EDAP) that would bring financial assistance, in colonias whose development had been "grandfathered" prior to the MSR legislation, to certain designated counties in the border region.

This spate of activity, including what is often referred to as the Colonias Water Bill, was expanded in the 1991 legislative session, and had a significant positive impact upon many Texas border colonias, especially once service installation began in earnest from 1995 onward. Nevertheless, many problems of implementation and underfunding remain, and even in this arena of (water) infrastructure provision, there is little cause for the state government to rest upon its laurels (LBJ 1997, vol. 2).

Enforcement of the MSRs remained a problem, and in 1993 a Colonias Strike Force, established under Texas Attorney General Dan Morales, began to prosecute some developers under the Deceptive Trade Practices Act and the Health and Safety Code. The aim was to put a stop to further colonia development, as well as to create a pretext for the sequestration of colonias, stripping them away from the land developers. This led to a further spate of legislation during the 1995 session. Senate Bill 336 sought to level the playing field for purchasers acquiring lots through the Contract for Deed mechanism, and provided far greater information and protection for purchasers, virtually turning these contracts into the functional equivalent of mortgages, at least in EDAP-designated counties and those within two hundred miles of the border. Furthermore, House Bill 1001, passed in 1995, sought to close the loopholes for continued development and sale of plots carried over from the 1989 legislation. Developers in specified counties must now get county approval for plat development, and must also provide water, sewage, and drainage services from the outset. This prevents new colonia development once and for all. It also applies to unsold lots in existing colonias (even "grandfathered" ones), and to lots that have been repossessed under Contract for Deed. Today, one of the principal problems remaining is the way in which many of these provisions apply differentially in different parts of Texas. Outside of designated counties and those beyond the two-hundred-mile limit, Contract for Deed and the potential for further colonia development appear to be alive and well.

While much has been achieved during the last ten years, particularly in arenas such as water provision, the curtailment of colonia development, and residential contract law, the task is still less than half completed. How so? First, as I have demonstrated in this study, many colonias that are eligible for water and basic services have yet to receive them. According to the TWDB, funding authorized under the Colonias Water Bill was only 60 percent of the total required. Inadvertently, too, House Bill 1001 has created difficulties by requiring that homes cannot be provided with new gas or electricity services unless there are adequate water and sewer services installed. Prior to this bill it was fairly easy to get electricity hookups; now even long-term residents will have to wait until the more costly "second stream" (lumpy) services are on line. Second, in many colonias between one-third and one-half of lots are not yet settled. Some lots remain unsold, others have been repossessed, others are held by absentee owners, many of whom are not readily traceable. Thus, there is a continuing and urgent need (and opportunity) to *settle* new families in colonias, if only to raise the threshold of population that will make further public- and private-sector improvements financially viable, and to enhance cost recovery that will help to retire existing bonds and finance new ones. As mentioned above, current legislation inhibits the sale of un-sold lots, particularly in those colonias which are not fully serviced, thereby making densification in such cases even less likely. To the ex-tent that plot occupancy and electricity installation may be inhibited, it seems that good faith efforts like HB 1001 may exacerbate the prob-lem rather than relieve it.

A third area of future concern and policy-making is in social de-velopment. Thus far, the focus has been almost exclusively upon physical infrastructure. Yet this is only one side of the coin. Social infrastructure has been neglected or underemphasized, both in terms of the availability and range of coverage of social services, and com-munity outreach efforts that will foster informal social infrastructure within the colonias themselves, and thereby enhance their ability to promote self-help and mutual aid. The aim should be one of support-ing efforts that will shift colonias away from a dependency relationship with government toward one of greater autonomy and self-reliance. But as things stand in Texas colonias, such local organization rarely happens spontaneously: rather, it needs to be cultivated. Finally, major weaknesses exist in the capacity of political entities to exercise author-ity over matters pertaining to colonia development, as well as in the triangle of intergovernmental relations—state, cities, and counties. Institutionally speaking, colonias have often been relegated to a sort of no man's land, falling through jurisdictional cracks at the slightest excuse or opportunity. Lack of incentives, turf wars, administrative in-capacity and inability, sometimes even incompetence and corruption, have often conspired to do that which comes easiest in such circum-stances—nothing.

I realize that some legislators and public officials will find these comments unwelcome. Nor will they leap to embrace my argument that the task and challenge of public policy for colonias in Texas are still far from complete. However, before they take umbrage I would like to reiterate two points: first, many positive advances have been achieved since 1989, and state and local governments are to be congratulated on the progress made in policy-making and implementation. My second point is that the opportunity to deal definitively with the problem of colonia housing and development is *within grasp*. Moreover, resolution of the colonia problem is not primarily a question of finding additional resources and appropriations. Rather, it requires the following low-cost (economically) commitments and change: (1) greater political will by legislators and officials; (2) a shift in thinking and paradigms about colonia development; (3) the exercise of greater imagination and willingness to move toward lower-tech solutions, minimum norms, and sometimes, even, the adoption of temporary dual standards that apply only within colonias; and (4) concerted efforts to cut through bureaucracy and empower agencies and officials to get the job done without fear of reprisal or personal and institutional liability. In some respects, of course, these requirements are considerably more difficult to achieve than finding additional resources, particularly in the weak-executive system of state government that we have in Texas. For that reason alone, I suggest that political commitment is the first step in the process, just as it was ten years ago when senior officials such as Bill Hobby, Ann Richards, and Bob Bullock stepped forward to exercise the leadership necessary to begin to address the colonia problem. Now new leadership is required to intensify and to achieve the follow-through.

Future Policy Imperatives for Texas Colonias

This study began with the premise that by comparing colonias on both sides of the border we might better understand how to analyze their true nature, meaning, and process. In addition, it was hoped that we in Texas might learn from Mexico's much wider and longer experience in handling colonia development, and from specific public policies that had been tried and tested in that country. And so it has proven: by using Mexican colonias and policies as a mirror to our own, we have been able to look more intently and more critically at the sociological and political processes that colonias embody in Texas. By comparing the important differences in colonia formation on both sides of the border we have come to appreciate how colonia improvement and upgrading can be enhanced in Texas through more sensitive and appropriate public policies. In all previous chapters I have systematically compared and contrasted the nature of colonia development in the paired border cities. The reader will have observed important variations in colonia development on either side of the border: in the modes of land acquisition; in the self-help house building process itself and in dwelling styles; in colonia size and population density; in community organization and in the propensity for social mobilization and mutual aid; in colonia integration within the wider political process of citizenship, and the legitimacy that colonias are thus accorded; and in the levels of institutional efficacy of different political jurisdictions in responding to low-income housing needs.

Although these differences are of intrinsic interest for an academic study, taken by themselves they have little significance. For my purpose the true significance of this comparative study is in the *insights* that these differences offer about alternative policy approaches, and about the prioritization of actions that will lead to substantive improvements in the life chances of Texas colonia residents in the new millennium. Provided, of course, that we are prepared to listen, to learn, and to adapt. Thus far, each chapter has identified the policy implications and possibilities that arise on both sides of the border, and especially here in Texas. My intention in this final chapter is not to repeat all of these recommendations in detail, since they are better evaluated and understood in the context of the specific discussion in each chapter. Instead, I propose to draw attention to what may be regarded as the broad policy imperatives. In so doing, I hope that this study will offer some guidelines to Texas leaders about the next steps required if a solution is to be achieved.

Imperative I: A New Paradigm for Thinking about Colonias

The way in which a society "constructs" reality will determine the way in which one tends to go about analyzing segments of it, and the way in which one seeks to order progress and development through law and through public policy formulation. Social constructions in the United States and in Texas are different in many important ways from those that obtain in Mexico. In Texas, as in the rest of the United States, there is a much stronger emphasis upon the individual and upon individual freedom and rights. In terms of government, this translates into a decentralized structure of weak states and "strong" local governments (at least in terms of their relative autonomy and powers). Moreover, in Texas, this individual freedom translates firmly into land policy which has traditionally privileged the rights and interests of individual developers over the broader community. Partly for this reason, of course, land-use planning and zoning laws in Texas are either lacking (as in counties and even some cities) or are relatively weak. Where cities seek to exercise greater communitarian control, they are likely to be resisted by developer coalitions, either head-on at the city council level, or by recourse to the state legislature.[1]

Although the Homestead Law grew out of a populist movement designed to protect small property owners from bank seizure at the turn of the century and during the Depression, the principle of individual land and home ownership was sacrosanct in Texas. It was repealed only in 1997, allowing the use of one's dwelling as equity on loans. Although the law had long since become an anachronism and an impediment to consumerism and to multiple property ownership, its retention in Texas demonstrated the intrinsic value accorded to private property and an individual's primary home. However, even though revisions in the Homestead Law demonstrate that major changes are always possible, generally speaking, the underlying constructs of society tend to be very slow to change. The following proposals and recommendations, therefore, are *not* predicated upon changing those underlying values and principles, but instead require rather more superficial (but nevertheless important) modifications in the ways we order and shape our thinking about colonias in Texas.

In housing and community development research, one also finds a close link between the paradigm or framework used to analyze housing and land development processes, and the sort of policy prescriptions that are proposed (Jones and Ward 1994). This linkage is clearly apparent in the many comparisons made throughout this book between the ways in which colonias are perceived and socially "constructed" on either side of the border. In Mexico, although colonias are often illegal in origin, they are seen as legitimate working-class communities. Colonia residents are citizens with full political rights, to whom public institutions are responsible. Colonias form part of an integrated public and private housing production process, and settlement problems and infrastructure deficits are considered within a paradigm of general economic development. This is not to argue that policy-making and public intervention in Mexico have been adequate or always appropriate to overcome the enormous social costs suffered by the millions of Mexican citizens who live in colonias, but simply to point out that the approach adopted has been radically different.

In Texas, colonias are seen as dysfunctional outcomes of economic development: they are marginal to development processes, not integral to them. There is a tendency to see colonias as transitional settlements in which people live while trying to get a foothold in the American dream. Sometimes, too, they are seen as sojourner (migrant) areas, whose residents are not accorded equal rights of citizenship, either because they are viewed (incorrectly) as aliens (legal or not), or because they are in transit to other parts of the United States. While it is much more widely recognized today that colonias are neither transitional nor populated by undocumented aliens, it remains relatively rare for colonias to be viewed as legitimate working-class settlements whose occupants comprise the working poor, and whose economic opportunities and wage levels make them ineligible for formal housing acquisition through the regular marketplace. Instead, they continue to be seen as unfortunates in need of public assistance, thereby intensifying the dependency paradigm and the sense that they must be "helped." Although these are "self-help" settlements, the ability of colonia populations to help themselves is not appreciated, and rarely is it enunciated in public policy. While no longer likely to be "criminalized," all too often colonias are seen as providing refuge for illegals, for gangs, and for adolescents and others who are engaged in petty crime. Certainly they are viewed as "pathological": as areas of low education, with serious problems of poor health and disease, where the lack of basic services leads to a vicious circle of ill health and contamination. My argument is not that these pathologies do not exist, but that the way in which they are *explained* is incorrect. Instead of seeing them as an inevitable and predictable outcome of regional economic development processes, and as neglect by the state of its worker population, the blame is cast upon the nature of the settlements and upon the populations themselves. The proliferation of colonias along the Texas border with Mexico must be seen as part of a regional economic logic of industrial and commercial development predicated upon the sharply differentiated wage rates of two border societies: one which is relatively rich, and the other poor.

As I have already stated, a major problem with any social "construction" is that it invokes a particular policy paradigm: diagnosis and treatment will depend heavily upon how one conceptualizes the problems that the patient presents. And so it is in Texas, since the rather limited diagnosis and understanding of colonias invokes the familiar but superficial approaches: task forces and strike forces to tackle specific problems; laws to prevent colonia proliferation; some physical infrastructure to improve health conditions and reduce contamination. All are top-down, "emergency" and dependency-cultivating measures that derive from an embedded social construction of these communities as social and cultural aberrations which require external intervention and assistance in order to bring them up to par with accepted standards. An alternative approach would take a more holistic and integrated view of colonias as outcomes of the development process— as is adopted in Mexico. Realistically, if one works from the assumption that substantial structural changes in wage rates and in the ways the economy is organized are unlikely, then an integrated approach would seek to develop a more multifaceted strategy aimed at empowering and enhancing colonias' ability to help themselves. Rather than wait upon top-down directives, initiatives, and resources, the aim would be to encourage opportunities for collaboration with local political jurisdictions, as well as with public- and private-sector institutions and organizations, in order to facilitate colonia development from the bottom up.

The following specific policy imperatives flow from such a paradigm shift, since it seems essential that the current rather paternalistic policy framework be replaced by one that is derived from a more nuanced and good faith understanding of the nature of the colonia development process, and one which empowers and demands collaboration between colonia populations and with governmental and nongovernmental agencies.

IMPERATIVE II: NEW INSTITUTIONAL PRACTICES AND INTERGOVERNMENTAL RELATIONS FOR COLONIA DEVELOPMENT

The largely negative and top-down view of Texas colonias has been compounded by local government structures and by poor intergovernmental coordination. Throughout this study we have seen how colonias have been caught within an institutional no man's land. Cities have been reluctant to incorporate colonias—located as they are beyond the urban edge—even when they have the authority to do so (i.e., when colonias fall within their ETJs). Understandably, the problem is primarily a lack of incentive to embrace colonias, which will accentuate the fiscal imbalance of cities, since colonias cost a lot to integrate physically and generate no tax revenues to speak of. Therefore, colonias are administered by county jurisdictions which are even less well geared to respond adequately. Counties are badly underresourced, and they lack the administrative capacity (breadth and depth) to integrate and upgrade colonias. Moreover, county commissioners and their offices often display little interest in working with colonia populations, who, traditionally, are more likely to have better and closer relations with the developers. At best, counties will contract certain social services such as fire fighting and policing from cities; at worst, they will ignore them. Nor have counties found it easy to exercise the controls and monitoring demanded of them under post-1989 legislation.

Thus, to the extent that any level of government has sought to offer concerted leadership, it has come largely from the state level. First, from the legislature through the enactment of new legislation; second, from the coordinating and funding role provided through the Texas Water Development Board; third, through the attorney general's office and the legal outreach that it has offered to counties; and fourth, through the Texas Department of Housing and Community Affairs (TDHCA). But even this four-pronged approach should alert us to part of the problem, namely, the *lack* of an integrated housing strategy. Instead of providing an integrated response, legislation has created several tiers of county jurisdiction: (1) EDAP-designated counties; (2) counties within two hundred miles of the border, and (3) other counties. The three principal actor institutions (TWDP, the AG's office, and the TDHCA) have different goals and foci. And compounding the complexity are city and county jurisdictions, often with their own public and other utility boards, which are often skittish about embracing colonias. Finally, there are two federal agencies which have responsibility for water and drainage infrastructure programs for colonias—the FmHA and the U.S. Rural Development Administration, recently merged into a single entity (the Rural Economic and Community Development Agency [RECDA]). All of this adds up to an institutional minefield that colonias find especially difficult to navigate, given their weak local leadership and organizational capacity, and the poorly defined channels of vertical linkage to supralocal institutions.

Probably because it has been better resourced since the Colonias Water Bill was passed, the TWDB has generally had greater success in bringing the various actors together, but as I have argued in this study, it has tended to accentuate the top-down, external, expert-intervention mentality on the one hand, and minimize any possible emergence of grassroots community development programs on the other. And although TDHCA officials may be well intentioned, the TDHCA has not been effective in offering an integrated housing and community development strategy, nor in promoting effective co-ordination and leadership among the various agencies and political jurisdictions.

In the future, the primary goal must be to achieve greater coordination and more effective empowerment of responsible institutions and levels of government. Empowerment as I am using it here means several things: a clarification of responsibilities and the creation of the capacity to fulfill them; a reduction of bureaucratic and institutional overlaps; the creation of incentives (and/or removal of disincentives) to intervene in colonias; and offering an integrated approach which seeks to enhance local capacity and sustainability *within* the communities themselves. Specifically, the following priorities should be considered:

At the State Level

- As part of a more generalized low-income housing strategy, widen legislation to remove or reduce the differential programs that may be applied in colonias in different parts of the state.
- Substantially extend the time frame of EDAP-type designations of counties to between six and ten years in order to facilitate longer-range integrated planning.
- Rescind the "grandfathering" of all previously platted subdivisions and open up such land and contracts to development controls approved subsequently.
- Remove the anomalies in HB 1001 (regarding densification and sequence of service provision) that inadvertently inhibit colonia development.
- Develop legislation that will encourage lot occupancy and consolidation in colonias (see "Densification Policies" below).
- Relax construction codes and subdivision standards that apply in designated colonias (see below) and move toward a minimum-norms framework and low-tech housing and infrastructure, thereby reducing development costs, enhancing public participation op-

portunities, and relieving cities and counties of possible liability associated with dual norms.

- Develop legislation that will provide for the creation of Social Interest Development Zones (SIDZs), which will allow for temporary below-code colonia housing development (see Chapter 2).
- Require planning and zoning in counties such that county commissioners and other officials are responsible and accountable for the long-term development of the county. (Alternatively, merge city and county roles in regulating land and housing development.)
- Strengthen the role and institutional capacity of a *single* agency statewide with a responsibility and mandate to develop an integrated housing and colonia development strategy and to coordinate effective integration of other bodies. Such an agency would be primus entre pares and would also be expected to develop other initiatives such as sites-and-services, a state credit underwriting standard, outreach, etc.

At the County Level

- To strengthen the administrative capacity of land-use monitoring to ensure compliance with the MSRs.
- In conjunction with cities, to develop long-term land-use plans for the county, ideally, augmented with zoning regulations and controls.
- Wherever possible, to contract with city providers for the extension to colonias of formal social services such as fire fighting.
- To strengthen ongoing liaison with and public participation of colonia populations through community centers, and to encourage the use of these facilities for social and recreational functions that will enhance colonia interaction and community (horizontal integration).

At the City Level

- To strengthen local (city) institutional capacity and responsibility for (existing) colonia integration, as well as for new forms of housing production such as state-aided self-help housing developments (sites-and-services, etc.).
- To develop and leverage incentives that will enhance the cities' willingness to annex colonias within their ETJs.

- In liaison with counties, to develop long-term land-use plans for the city that are congruent with anticipated economic and population growth in the ETJ and county. Such planning should be enforced through zoning regulations and controls.
- To promote the extension of city (social and other) contract services for colonias to counties.
- To strengthen vertical channels of liaison and public participation between city institutions and colonia populations, and to do so in ways that are sensitive and expeditious (i.e., outreach to neighborhoods, and *ventanilla única*–type schemes to minimize bureaucratic runaround).
- To review liability laws in order to adopt lower and achievable construction codes and subdivision planning standards for application in designated colonias (see below) and move toward a minimum-norms framework and low-tech housing and infrastructure, thereby reducing development costs and enhancing public participation opportunities.
- To incorporate colonias into the property tax assessment process so that improvement costs may be captured over time (see "Densification" below).

Imperative III: Policies to Promote Intracolonia Population Densification

One of the most marked differences observed in this study in colonias on either side of the border is the much lower population densities that obtain in Texas. This derives from the greater security of the process of land capture or acquisition; from the larger lots (usually more than double the modal lot size in Mexico); and from the high proportion of absentee ownership and nonoccupancy in Texas colonias. I sense that these low densities are generally viewed *positively* by Texas policymakers and public officials, since it means that there are fewer people actually living in the poor conditions of colonia environments, and because it lessens the level of likely contamination from poorly functioning or absent cesspools and septic tanks. In fact, these low densities make the colonia problem even more intractable. In fact, *colonias in Texas need to house many more people at much higher densities.*

When one thinks about why this should be the case, the reasons are obvious. Low densities mean far higher unitary costs of installing services and infrastructure, particularly if there is no way of passing on these costs directly or indirectly to absentee lot holders. If only those "beneficiary" households actually living in the colonia are expected to pay, or be liable for, the costs of hookups, then there is little incentive for providers to promote the service on the one hand, and the costs will be high for resident households on the other. High costs will tend to encourage "opting out" (further raising the costs for those who opt in). For those who pay these high costs, the money available to make ongoing dwelling improvements through self-help will be severely reduced. Low densities also inhibit what has come to be seen as "urban productivity," namely, the creation of added value and the generation of income-earning opportunities.[2] In the case of the colonias, this would primarily include microenterprises such as local stores, which are abundant in Mexico yet almost entirely absent in Texas. Other microenterprises include itinerant salesmanship, private transportation services, construction materials yards, etc.

Therefore, policies are urgently required to enhance lot occupancy in order to increase the demand for services and goods in colonias, and to improve their fiscal viability as far as cities are concerned, encouraging formal annexation. As things now stand, low density is a major inhibitor of development, and this is one area where Texas has a considerable advantage over Mexico, with the opportunity to make dramatic progress toward colonia development and integration. Carrot-and-stick policies are required (i.e., a mixture of incentives and penalties). The aim should be to facilitate the working of the marketplace, and to unlock the supply of lots to would-be colonia residents. Among the policies that need to be fostered are those which:

- Facilitate the identification of *all* lot ownership within individual colonias, and the requirement that lot ownership be registered in city or county property registers (even where full title has not yet been transferred to the purchaser).
- Provide for lot forfeiture (adequately compensated) after *n* (perhaps five?) years of unidentified ownership, or *n* (perhaps two?) years nonoccupancy or nondevelopment of one's lot.[3]
- Provide for an extension of property taxation to colonia lots. Taxation scales would reflect property values, but the land component would be weighted so as to be progressive for land occupancy and regressive where land lay undeveloped (i.e., penalize absentee land holders).

- Sponsor "land adjustment" policies which, where feasible, would swap unoccupied lots in order to create land parcels suitable to building shared tank and septic fields for single (or adjoining) blocks. Once established, they would be landscaped in a modest way.[4]
- Rescind those aspects of current legislation that inhibit lot sale and turnover (e.g., provisions of HB 1001 which prevent the sale of unsold or repossessed lots until services are provided).
- Provide tax "holiday" incentives for desired uses (ownership over rental, for example), levels of dwelling improvement achieved, participation in "land adjustments" (above), etc.

Thus, through this combination of imaginative policies, empowered by appropriate legislation and/or normative bylaws, it should be possible to kick-start the land market in ways that will enhance the feasibility of public and private cooperation for colonia infrastructure development, create new owner and renter housing opportunities, and enhance upgrading and development. In this way, the exercise of effective policy will achieve improvements through the marketplace; major external public resources are not necessary.

IMPERATIVE IV: THE REVIEW OF STANDARDS AND CODES AND THE ADOPTION OF MINIMUM NORMS

This is yet another policy imperative that comes without any significant additional costs. Once again, the costs are political: namely, a pragmatic acceptance that temporary (medium-term) dual standards are necessary and desirable in order to *expedite colonia development and improvement*. The aim is to lower the bar on standards in areas designated as colonias, or even more broadly, on certain submarkets of housing production statewide. In so doing, one significantly reduces the costs and raises the possibilities for self-help, for mutual aid, and for low-tech approaches to housing and community development. Were cities and counties empowered to move toward more modest but realistic minimum standards and codes, rather than having to aim at such high standards, then the burden of authorizations and permissions could be reduced, and upgrading and house consolidation would proceed apace. Nor should it be difficult to find ways to free jurisdictions from any liability that might arise from the application of a minimum-standards policy.

The key issue is, how low should those minimum norms be? Clearly, the idea is not to advocate a reduction such that housing and land conditions are dangerous or harmful. Rather than thinking about maximum protection, which drives up standards, we need to think about what is the minimum level of protection that we should demand. Colonia populations themselves need to be consulted and to participate in the setting of these standards. Public safety standards are often set very high, and a two-tier (dual) approach may not be unreasonable for designated areas or housing submarkets (such as the proposed SIDZs, or Social Interest Development Zones). Specifically, for example, there is no need for all streets to be paved: "austere" (*austero*) paving with caliche or bare dirt roads may work, at least until densities make paving economically feasible. And less costly concrete roads (as in Juárez) work better than tar macadam. Low-density public lighting (every third or fourth pole) will significantly enhance public safety, particularly for pedestrians, who need the street lighting the most.[5] Similarly, integrated piped networks to remove sewage are extremely high in cost and are invariably unnecessary. Modest low-tech on-lot septic tanks, properly designed and installed, are often perfectly adequate for a household's needs. Alternatively, shared tanks and septic fields built to the minimum size specifications acceptable could be created alongside the land adjustment proposals outlined in the previous section. Where there is concern that the field is too small, then access to the tanks should provide for periodic emptying. Broad recommendations here are:

- The adoption of a minimum-standards framework for infrastructure and utilities in colonias and other designated low-income housing areas.
- Make planning and construction permissions contingent upon the adoption of minimum standards for dwelling construction (thereby encouraging registration of plans and user compliance).
- Relaxation of regulations that inhibit either the sequencing of utilities or individual dwelling improvements.
- Encourage research, adoption, and marketing of alternative low-tech construction and utility options.
- Support opportunities for cost-reducing community participation in utility and service installation.
- Authorize public and private utilities to offer colonias "austere" options of service provision.

- Provide technical outreach that will promote use and adoption of low-tech and minimal codes, and train engineers and officials in their application and implementation.

IMPERATIVE V: THE ENHANCEMENT OF SOCIAL INFRASTRUCTURE AND PUBLIC PARTICIPATION

In Chapters 4 and 5 I argued that colonias in Texas are poorly integrated socially, measured in terms of their density of horizontal integration, and in terms of vertical linkages with local authorities. So much so, compared with their Mexican counterparts, that they may be characterized as "settlements" rather than "communities," and that they usually require some level of external trigger if they are to mobilize and hustle local authorities for utilities and infrastructure improvements. I also observed that social services such as health care, education, social supports, fire services, and the like have been underprioritized in Texas, at least relative to "hard" infrastructure like water, power, drainage, and so on. Moreover, to the extent that social services exist, providers tend to emphasize the end product, rather than taking an approach which would improve the means and the self-sustaining capacity of colonia populations to help themselves. Even colonia "centers" constructed by NGOs and funded by the counties appear to function as centers for the downward flow of resources and social services, rather than as catalysts for horizontal social organization and community empowerment.

This absence of informal social infrastructure on the one hand, and the rather superficial top-down approach on the other, are problematic because they sustain the dependency relationship of colonias with the local and state governments, and because they fail to take advantage of the considerable human capital and resources that colonias can offer through mutual aid, public participation, and organization. Albeit in good faith, public officials and organizations have grossly underutilized these colonia-based resources in the past.

Several of the aforementioned imperatives will go a long way toward improving the capacity of colonias to foster greater social density and work collaboratively with external actors and organizations. Specifically, higher population densities will improve neighboring and mobilization to achieve common goals. A more positive appraisal of colonias will accord greater legitimacy and self-worth to their populations. Greater sensitivity of officials and better channels of communication will also do much to foster community action. In Table 16 I offered a number of proposals for redistributing local power in order to achieve more effective horizontal and vertical integration. Below I outline just the broad brush strokes.

- Improve social services coordination and programs, perhaps by affiliating them loosely within independent school district administrative structures, allowing the broader gamut of social services to "piggyback" on the existing school system and infrastructure.
- Through organizations such as TDHCA, foster the formation of "community" through programs that enhance community participation (mutual aid projects, "focus" groups, colonia fiestas and sports tournaments, etc.).
- Through advertising, outreach, and purpose-built community centers, improve the information flow about colonia programs, and encourage greater public participation in that exchange.
- Raise the effectiveness of community centers and the sense of "local" ownership and governance of activities. Specifically, by expanding the services and activities on offer, promoting a wider range of participation opportunities (especially for men and children), and making opening hours more conducive to wider usage.
- Promote the creation of viable and representative participatory colonia residents' associations, and empower such associations by ensuring that public officials work collaboratively with them.
- Maximize public participation in the decision making process related to the prioritization of projects and their implementation and scheduling, as well as opportunities for residents to lower costs by putting up some of the labor. Also, promote popular participation on issues such as land adjustment, use of septic field amenity spaces, and monitoring of lot occupancy and usage (see Imperatives II and IV above).

Colonias: A Last Word

As I concluded in an earlier chapter, there is no single solution or silver bullet to resolve the colonia problem in Texas. There is a danger, however, that we falsely believe that the problem is primarily one of physical infrastructure. It is not. Colonias are a structural problem compounded by developers' greed, official neglect, ignorance, poor policy-making and weak administrative capacity, inadequate laws, and enfeebled social organization and local leadership. The structural conditions which lead to poverty and low incomes in the border region are unlikely to change significantly. But it is possible to change or recast pretty much everything else.

When I embarked upon this study I was skeptical of the direction in which public policy responses toward colonias were headed, particularly the Band-Aid solution that was being adopted: namely, finding ways of increasing physical infrastructure provision, the creation of task forces, and the general failure, for reasons of shame or arrogance, to look to countries such as Mexico for insight about possible approaches that had been tried and tested. Nor was I especially encouraged by the findings that my students reported for the Texas side when they returned from fieldwork early in 1995. It was apparent that the 1989 and 1991 legislation had not yet had a strong impact, and that while considerable resources had been generated for water provision, implementation had scarcely begun. Furthermore, the conference we organized in May 1995, designed to bring Texas and Mexican officials and representatives together in what we hoped would be a dialogue, was a disappointment. For the most part, academics "heard" what was being said; Mexican officials were sympathetic and solicitous in offering advice; but Texas officials appeared to be hesitant and uncertain, and were overly concerned about institutional rivalries and turf. They were defensive about their policies and quick to apportion blame to jurisdictions other than their own. One notable exception (the chief planner for Laredo) spoke out boldly, but insisted that her department was hidebound by health and safety codes and that she was not willing to buck them.

For these reasons, I allowed my skepticism to inform the "voice" of the Introduction to this book, even though in recent months I have become rather more optimistic about the very real improvements that have been achieved since 1995, and about the prospects for the future. Revisits to the Texas-side study colonias late in 1997 revealed the considerable progress that has been achieved, so much so that I ditched my earlier photographs in favor of the more recent (and representative) ones included here. On the Mexican side, however, it was obvious that much of the former dynamism of colonia physical development had slowed down considerably; building exteriors were showing the signs of wear and attrition, and community services and communal areas appeared to be under pressure and stressed. Notwithstanding the positive approaches taken by local, state, and federal authorities to legalize "clouded" land titles and install basic services, the long-term impact of a decade of austerity and the recent post–December 1994 economic crisis was clear to be seen. Inevitably, rates of consolidation had slowed, frontages and dwellings lacked the *pride* of paint that they would have had in yesteryear, and high densities and overcrowding were making internal plot organization more complex and almost certainly less healthy.

Somewhat paradoxically, observing this downturn in Mexican colonias made me more optimistic about the future for their Texas counterparts. It has strengthened my belief that a solution for Texas colonias is within reach. Texas colonia households, while poor and often below the poverty line, are considerably better off than their Mexican counterparts in real terms (living costs are not significantly lower in Mexico). Major progress is being experienced (finally) in bringing in water services. Population densities, while they need to be raised dramatically (see above), could with judicious planning be kept lower than in Mexico, where their effect threatens to become counterproductive. All that is lacking are the relatively low-budget policy imperatives identified in this chapter.

I hope that this recent optimism will not be misplaced. Of course, there can be no guarantees that things will change significantly in the directions that I have charted. Indeed, as I noted earlier in this chapter, despite their relatively low or even negligible economic cost, many of these changes, dealing as they often do with politics and institutional dynamics and resistances, may prove considerably more difficult to implement than it ever was to secure high-budget appropriations for infrastructure. But I do guarantee that if the next two legislative sessions (1999 and 2001) do not undertake significant policy shifts along the lines that I have proposed, then the colonia "problem" will never be satisfactorily or substantively resolved. Given that resolution is within Texas policymakers' grasp, colonias should be viewed not as a problem but as an opportunity. And the opportunity cost of doing too little, or of abdicating the responsibility to act, is just too high.

Notes

Introduction

1. Hereafter in this book, the term "colonia" will not be italicized.

2. The reproduction of labor power refers to the ways in which society seeks to maintain its work force, both "biologically," in terms of population growth, and "socially," in terms of housing its working population. References to "cheapening the costs of labor reproduction" refer to the ways in which a society seeks to reduce the costs associated with maintaining its working population in an active state—by ensuring low-cost housing alternatives, for example—which helps, also, to reduce the pressure for higher wage levels from these workers.

3. Published as a *Memoria*/Synthesis of the conference "Housing Production and Infrastructure in the Colonias of Texas and Mexico: A Cross-Border Dialogue," organized by the Mexican Center at UT-Austin, May 5–6, 1995. Copies of the *Memoria* may be obtained from the Mexican Center. Postal applications: The Mexican Center, Sid W. Richardson Hall 1. 310, Austin, Texas 78712-1167. It is also available for consultation electronically through UT-LANIC, on the Mexican Center Home Page, http://lanic.utexas.edu/ilas/mexcenter/.

4. Dr. Earle was then assistant director. In 1996–1998 he was director of the Center for Inter-American and Borderland Studies at the University of Texas at El Paso.

5. See acknowledgments at the beginning of this book for a listing of those students who participated.

1. Introduction to the Border Region and to the Case Study Cities

1. Generally speaking, the data in Texas show a marked step-down in socioeconomic indicators from the state to the county to the colonia lands (OAG 1993). This step-down is much less marked in Mexico.

2. This percentage of completion of the ninth grade rises to almost 50 percent in colonias (see OAG 1993, 8).

3. While some of these data are rather dated, the proportions and differentials, United

States to Mexico, still remain. Nor has the North American Free Trade Agreement (NAFTA) led to significant convergence in wage levels.

4. This latter figure for Webb County comes from Davies (1995, 47), since later data provided by the TWDB (reported in LBJ 1997) give the county total as 8,313 (see also Table 1). The discrepancy may have arisen from the removal from the reckoning of two of the largest colonias (Río Bravo and El Cenizo) after these received services.

5. The sections on the individual cities provide supplementary information to that already presented. Some of the figures in the individual city sections may differ slightly from earlier tables due to estimates by different sources. However, the differences are not substantial and do not affect the general trends already presented.

6. For all the Texas cities, statistics for 1990 are found in the 1990 U.S. Census data unless otherwise indicated.

7. These colonias are: Deerfield Park, Desert Glen, Homestead Homes, Homestead Meadows, Homestead Meadows South, Las Casitas, Las Quintas, and Southwest Estates.

8. According to one source the total number of residents is over 3,000 (LBJ 1997, 2:65).

9. Information for the Mexican cities for 1990 and 1980 are taken from the *X Censo General de Población* and the *XI Censo General de Población* unless otherwise cited.

10. In Mexico until the mid-1980s, the modal wage for workers was the statutory minimum. However, from that time onward inflation on the one hand, and statutory work policy on the other, reduced the value of the minimum wage dramatically—by around 60 percent between 1982 and 1988, according to some sources (Barry 1992; Ward et al. 1993). In response, however, the private sector raised average rates somewhat, so that the actual erosion of earnings was not quite as dramatic (Ward et al. 1993).

11. This is quite an impressive record relatively, since Mexico nationally was only meeting around one-fifth of the total demand through the formal sector (Ward 1990).

12. The only ambiguity that occurs in Mexico is where a city spreads in any substantial way into two or more municipalities, thereby effectively dividing responsibility for the city's administration into several parts. This is quite common in several large metropolitan areas, but fortunately does not apply in Ciudad Juárez. Indeed, split jurisdictions do not occur in any of the three Mexican border cities we analyzed.

13. Includes D5 Acres, Larga Vista, Los Altos, Old Milwaukee, Pueblo Nuevo, Ranchitos 359 East, San Carlos and San Enrique, Tanquecitos S Acres I and II.

14. It may relate, in part, to possible overinflation of population in the 1980 census (see Ward 1998b).

15. Although one county commissioner, Republican James Matts, has always been openly hostile, wanting them bulldozed.

2. Land and Housing Production in the Colonias of Texas and Mexico

1. Because the *campesino* sector (CNC) was so influential within the governing party (PRI), it was able to resist any concerted attempt by planners and other sectors to systematically head off these illegal land sales. Formally, this protection was articulated through the Agrarian Reform Ministry (SRA), and it was not until the late 1980s that the SRA's power

and informal but effective impunity from regulations governing urban development began to be withdrawn (Jones and Ward 1998).

2. At the time of fieldwork (1994), US$1 = approximately 3.5 new pesos. At the time of writing (1997), US$1 = approximately 7.5 pesos.

3. In 1996–1997 these counties were: Bee, Brooks, Cameron, Dimmit, Duval, El Paso, Frio, Hidalgo, Jim Hogg, Jim Wells, La Salle, Maverick, Presidio, Reeves, San Patricio, Starr, Uvalde, Val Verde, Webb, Willacy, Zapata, and Zavala (Texas Department of Housing and Community Affairs, Notice of Determination of Certain Counties, 21 Tex. Reg. 4181 [1996]).

4. As defined in Texas Senate Bill 2 from 1989.

5. In Texas, as in Mexico, most residents are very satisfied with their land capture and home consolidation achievements. In one study (Rogers et al. 1993, 34), more than two-thirds of those interviewed felt that life was better in the colonia than where they lived before. Many, too, felt that the environment was "safer, quieter or better" (ibid.). In Mexico, similar experiences are common, as is the often-quoted opportunity to "vivir más tranquilo" (Varley 1985).

6. Communication with Mr. Vic Hines, April 10, 1998.

7. In 1997 discussions were underway seeking to give counties greater planning and zoning powers (Swearingen 1997).

8. For example, El Paso Water Utility was given countywide water planning powers by the state legislature in 1995, and the role of water planning statewide has now been empowered.

9. The director of a Lower Rio Grande Valley FmHA told our researchers that she encourages contractors to hire locally but cannot require it. Even Brownsville Community Development Corporation director Don Curry said his microenterprise and housing rehabilitation project—to be funded by a HUD Community Development Block Grant—would rely primarily on professional bonded labor for liability and efficiency reasons, despite the fact that the grant application promised a "job training" deliverable outcome.

10. Although it must be noted that we know next to nothing about the citizen and socioeconomic profile of nonresident lot purchasers. These might well have a higher proportion of noncitizens who have moved to the interior of the country in order to remain "invisible." A systematic review of nonoccupant lot holders is an urgent priority.

11. The ETJ is one-half mile beyond the city limits in cities of less than 5,000 population, and increases to a limit of five miles for population centers with more than 100,000 inhabitants.

12. Indeed, it was in part a recognition of colonia citizens as voters and the drive to register them in the early 1990s that led to a quickening of political concern for colonia populations.

3. Servicing No Man's Land

1. With the exception of the rescinding of the Texas Homestead Law, there was no significant enabling legislation on behalf of colonias in the 1997 legislative session, after the big pushes in the 1989, 1991, and 1995 sessions.

2. This was the case until 1991, when the size for compulsory compliance with MSRs was raised from one to five acres.

3. In its consideration of other wastewater treatment systems the TWDB (1992) focused solely upon septic fields and evapotranspiration systems, which it thought might be appropriate in small colonias or in rural areas. However, even these alternatives are not really "low-tech" alternatives.

4. Settlements or Communities?

1. As outlined in Chapter 1, estimates suggest that 20–30 percent of colonia adults are not U.S. citizens, although almost all are documented aliens. However, it is not known what proportion of "absentee" owners falls into those two categories.

2. Governments support public participation because it reduces costs and acts to integrate low-income populations; liberals support it because it fosters a spirit of democracy, a sense of responsibility for undertaking self-help and seeking "bootstraps" approaches; the radical left approves because it sees it as a means to inculcate collective consciousness, organization, and empowerment; while multilateral agencies also see it as cost-effective (like governments), but also as a means to engage local populations in the decision making process in order to achieve better development projects more in tune with people's needs, and more sustainable in terms of cost recovery and ongoing maintenance. See also Skinner (1983, 126–127) for a full development of these latter points.

3. This is important, since my earlier work in Mexico City colonias revealed relatively low levels of owner-occupier involvement (rarely a majority of households) in community action programs, politicking for services, etc. But most residents were well aware of what was going on, who the local leaders were, and so on, which also may be construed as "participatory," especially in the often very large colonias with which we were dealing (Gilbert and Ward 1984).

4. In Mexico the long-term separation of Church and state, and the highly circumscribed extent to which religious leaders may intervene in secular affairs and organization, make Church-sponsored leadership in colonia-state negotiations almost nonexistent, although priests often exercise important moral leadership, as well as discreet organizational guidance to community residents. The exception, of course, is Chiapas since 1994, where priests have achieved prominence as interlocutors for indigenous and peasant communities.

5. These *carpas*, as they were called, were adopted in Mexico during the late 1970s–early 1980s, as well as in Mexico City during the 1990s. However, they have had limited impact precisely because they are superficial, ephemeral, and superimposed upon *existing* communities. They will work best in situations where there is a minimal sense of community spirit. Indeed, that is their rationale—to foster social interaction.

5. Social Services to Colonias

1. Measured in terms of total spending, private health care occupies 43 percent of total expenditures (Cruz et al. 1994).

2. At the time of writing there are eleven community centers in operation. In addition to the five listed, these are: Quad City Area (Laredo), Sebastian (Raymondville), Río Bravo (Laredo), Socorro (El Paso), Sierra Blanca (Laredo), and Monte Alto (Edinburgh). For further information see the Community Centers Web Page, http://chud.tamu.edu.

3. The TDHCA is also currently developing "Initiative Self-Help Centers," which will include health care, education, employment training, and counseling services.

4. Offered in Cameron Park only.

5. Co-prima is a primary health care program for those ineligible for Medicaid. Participants pay a nominal amount for receipt of medical services.

6. Community center officials believe the population is much higher.

7. All figures are rounded.

8. Throughout this analysis "center user" and "service recipient" will be used interchangeably, as will "center nonuser" and "service nonrecipient."

9. It should be noted that household use is synonymous with female head of household use, since she most often acquires services on behalf of her children.

10. Child utilization is counted as such if the child uses the community center independently of the mother.

11. Such a disparity is a derivative of the teams' failure to define "use" or "utilization." In Cameron Park, interviewers tended to classify male heads of household as nonusers if they had only used the community center once. In El Cenizo, it appears that one-time visits were counted as utilization.

12. At least this appears to have been the case until Río Bravo got its own center.

13. Not surprisingly, all fifteen of the service providers who responded *were* aware of Texas A&M's involvement.

6. Conclusion

1. Such was the case in Austin with the Save our Springs (SOS) Council legislation, which sought to rein in development. Although passed by the city, the SOS referendum threatened to founder on the rocks of developer resistance and opposition (Swearingen 1997).

2. The concept of urban productivity has emerged strongly in World Bank thinking in recent years and seeks to encourage the opportunities for local or household "rent-seeking" behavior. In less-developed societies these activities are often "informal" (i.e., they may be unregulated and unsupervised—street traders are a good example), but instead of harassing them out of existence, as in the past, the philosophy now is to remove restrictions and encourage the expansion of such income-earning opportunities, fueling market transactions, etc. See de Soto 1989; Doebele 1994; Jones and Ward 1994.

3. Under this arrangement, proof of ownership and of occupancy should rest with the lot holder rather than with local officials. Forfeited lots would be transferred to a public trust and sold to would-be colonia residents at the market rate, providing the basis for modest compensation for those who come forward with a claim after forfeit. Similarly, proof of lot occupancy would rest with users, not local officials. Definitions of what constitutes lot "development" would be decided locally, but these should allow for: (1) low-tech, minimum-

norms standards; (2) plot occupancy by households of either owners or renters (i.e., it should allow for subletting).

4. Such a policy would not only simplify and improve the adequacy of sewage provision systems in colonias, but would also guarantee the maintenance of some open space. This would also lessen the problem of densities potentially becoming too high, as is arguably the case today in many Mexican colonias.

5. After all, the purpose of street lighting is public (primarily pedestrian) safety, and not to provide lighted corridors for car circulation—cars carry headlights, and with poorly paved or unpaved roads are more likely to circulate circumspectly anyway.

References

Abrams, Charles. 1966. *Squatter Settlements, the Problem and the Opportunity.* Washington D.C.: Department of Housing and Urban Development.

Adams, John. 1987. *Housing America in the 1980s.* New York: Russell Sage.

Alarcón Cantú, Eduardo. 1993. "Nuevo Laredo, Tamaulipas: Cincuenta años de crecimiento urbano (1940–1990)." *Río Bravo* 2 (Spring): 1–23.

Angel, Solly, Ray Archer, and Emile Wegelin, eds. 1983. *Land for Housing the Poor.* Singapore: Select Books.

Arreola, Daniel D., and James R. Curtis. 1993. *The Mexican Border Cities: Landscape Autonomy and Place Personality.* Tucson: University of Arizona Press.

Assies, Willem. 1994. "Reconstructing the Meaning of Urban Land in Brazil." In Gareth Jones and Peter Ward (eds.), *Methodology for Land and Housing Market Analysis*, pp. 102–117. London: University College London Press.

Austin. 1994. "The Austin Memorandum on the Reform of Article 27, and Its Impact upon the Urbanization of the Ejido in Mexico." *Bulletin of Latin American Research* 13 (3): 327–355.

Ayuntamiento de Ciudad Juárez. 1994. *A mitad del camino.* Ciudad Juárez.

Baross, Paul, and Jan van der Linden, eds. 1990. *The Transformation of Land Supply Systems in Third World Cities.* Aldershot, UK: Avebury.

Barrera Bassols, Dalia. 1996. "Ser Panista: Mujeres en las colonias populares de Cd. Juárez, Chihuahua." Ph.D. dissertation, UNAM, Facultad de Ciencias Políticas y Sociales.

Barry, Tom, ed. 1992. *Mexico: A Country Guide.* Albuquerque, N.Mex.: Inter-Hemispheric Education Resource Center.

Bath, Richard, Janet Tanski, and Roberto Villarreal. 1994. "The Politics of Water Allocation in El Paso County: A Case Study of the Colonias." *Journal of Borderlands Studies* 9 (1): 15–38.

Bennett, Vivienne. 1995. *The Politics of Water: Urban Protest, Gender, and Power in Monterrey.* Pittsburgh: Pittsburgh University Press.

Betts, Dianne C., and Daniel J. Slottje. 1994. *Crisis on the Rio Grande: Poverty, Unemployment, and Economic Development on the Texas-Mexico Border.* Boulder, Colo.: Westview Press.

Bloom, Erik. 1994. *Health and Health Care in Mexico.* Documento de Trabajo del CIDE, Número 49. Mexico City: CIDE (Centro de Investigación y Docencia Económica).

Briggs, Charles. 1986. *Learning How to Ask.* Cambridge, UK: Cambridge University Press.

Briody, Elizabeth Kathleen. 1986. *Household Labor Patterns among Mexican Americans in South Texas: Buscando Trabajo Seguro.* New York: AMS Press.

Brough, Michael B. 1985. *A Unified Development Ordinance*. Washington, D.C.: Planners Press, American Planning Association.

Brown, Jane C. 1972. *Patterns of Intra-urban Settlement in Mexico City: An Examination of the Turner Theory*. Dissertation Series 40. Ithaca, N.Y.: Cornell University Latin American Studies Program.

Burgess, Rod. 1982. "Self-help Housing Advocacy: A Curious Form of Radicalism." In Peter M. Ward (ed.), *Self-help Housing: A Critique*, pp. 55–97. London: Mansell Press.

———. 1985a. "The Limits to State Self-help Housing Programmes." *Development and Change* 16: 271–312.

———. 1985b. "Problems in the Classification of Low-income Neighborhoods in Latin America." *Third World Planning Review* 7 (4): 287–306.

———. 1992. "Helping the Poor to Help Themselves: Third World Housing Policies and Development Strategies." In Kosta Mathéy (ed.), *Beyond Self-help Housing*, pp. 75–91. London: Mansell Press.

Bustamante, Jorge. 1992. "Interdependence, Undocumented Migration, and National Security." In Jorge Bustamante, Clark Reynolds, and Raúl Hinojosa (eds.), *U.S.-Mexico Relations: Labor Market Interdependence*, pp. 21–41. Stanford, Calif.: Stanford University Press.

Butterworth, Douglas, and John Chance. 1981. *Latin American Urbanization*. Cambridge, UK: Cambridge University Press.

Cabrero Mendoza, E. 1995. *La nueva gestión municipal en México: Análisis de experiencias innovadoras en gobiernos locales*. Mexico City: Miguel Angel Porrúa.

———, ed. 1996. *Los dilemas de la modernización municipal: Estudios sobre la gestión hacendaria en municipios urbanos de México*. Mexico City: Miguel Angel Porrúa.

Castells, Manuel. 1983. *The City and the Grassroots*. Berkeley: University of California Press.

Chant, Sylvia. 1984. "Las olvidadas: A Study of Women, Housing and Family Structure in Querétaro, Mexico." Ph.D. dissertation, University of London.

———. 1996. *Gender, Urban Development and Housing*. New York: United Nations Urban Development Programme (UNDP), Publications Series for Habitat II, Volume 2.

———, and P. Ward. 1987. "Family Structure and Low-income Housing Policy." *Third World Planning Review* 9 (1): 5–19.

Cole, Albert. 1979. "Federal Housing Programs, 1950–1960." In Gertrude Fish (ed.), *The Story of Housing*, pp. 277–334. New York: Macmillan.

Colonia Profile and Statistical Information for the U.S.-Mexico Border. 1994. El Paso, Tex.: El Paso Community Foundation.

Connolly, Priscilla. 1982. "Uncontrolled Settlements and Self-build: What Kind of Solution?" In Peter M. Ward (ed.), *Self-help Housing: A Critique*, pp. 141–174. London: Mansell Press.

Contreras, Oscar F., and Vivienne Bennett. 1994. "National Solidarity in the Northern Borderlands: Social Participation and Community Leadership." In Wayne Cornelius et. al. (eds.), *Transforming State-Society Relations in Mexico: The National Solidarity Strategy*, 281–305. San Diego: Center for U.S.-Mexican Studies, University of California, San Diego.

Cornelius, W. 1973. "Contemporary Mexico: A Structural Analysis of Urban Caciquismo." In R. Kern (ed.), *The Caciques: Oligarchical Politics and the System of Caciquismo*, pp. 135–191. Albuquerque: University of New Mexico Press.

———. 1975. *Politics and the Migrant Poor in Mexico City*. Stanford, Calif.: Stanford University Press.

———. 1992. "From Sojourners to Settlers: The Changing Profile of Mexican Immigration to the United States." In Jorge Bustamante, Clark Reynolds, and Raúl Hinojosa (eds.), *U.S.-Mexico Relations: Labor Market Interdependence*, pp. 155–195. Stanford, Calif.: Stanford University Press.

Craske, Nikki. 1996. "Dismantling or Retrenchment? Salinas and Corporatism." In Rob Aitkin, Nikki Craske, Gareth Jones, and David Stansfield (eds.), *Dismantling the Mexican State?* pp. 78–91. London: Macmillan.

Cruz, C., F. Alvarez, J. Frenk, C. Knaul, C. Valdés, and R. Ramírez. 1994. *Las Cuentas Nacionales de Salud, y el financiamiento de los servicios.* Mexico City: FUNSALUD.

Cymet, David. 1992. *From Ejido to Metropolis: Another Path.* New York: Peter Lang.

Davies, Christopher S. 1995. "Colonia Settlements: Working-class Refuge Stations along the Texas-Mexico Border." *Planning Forum* (Journal of the Community and Regional Planning Program, UT-Austin) 1: 33–53.

———, and Robert Holz. 1992. "Settlement Evolution of the 'Colonias' along the US-Mexico Border: The Case of the Lower Rio Grande Valley of Texas." *Habitat International* 16 (4): 119–142.

Dawson, Andrew. 1984. *The Land Problem in the Developed Economy.* Totowa, N.J.: Barnes & Noble.

de Soto, Hernán. 1989. *The Other Path: The Invisible Revolution in the Third World.* London: Tauris.

Doebele, William. 1987. "The Evolution of Concepts of Land Tenure in Developing Countries." *Habitat International* 11 (1): 7–22.

———. 1994. "Urban Land and Macroeconomic Development: Moving from 'Access for the Poor' to Urban Productivity." In Gareth Jones and Peter Ward (eds.), *Methodology for Land and Housing Market Analysis*, pp. 44–54. London: University College London Press.

Dresser, Denise. 1991. *Neopopulist Solutions to Neoliberal Problems: Mexico's National Solidarity Program.* San Diego: Center for U.S.-Mexican Studies.

Durand Lasserve, Alain, and R. Pajoni. 1992. *The Regularization of Irregular Settlements in Cities in the Developing Countries: Techniques, Procedures and Policies; Synthesis of Main Findings.* Paris: CNRS.

Earle, Duncan. 1995. "Defining *Colonias*: Perspectives and Solutions on the 'Problem' in Texas." In Peter Ward et al., *Memoria of the Bi-national Conference: Housing Production and Infrastructure in the Colonias of Texas and Mexico.* Austin: The Mexican Center of ILAS, University of Texas.

Eckstein, Susan. 1988. *The Poverty of Revolution: The State and the Urban Poor in Mexico*, rev. ed. Princeton, N.J.: Princeton University Press.

———. 1990. "Poor People versus the State and Capital: Anatomy of a Successful Community Mobilization for Housing in Mexico City." *International Journal for Urban and Regional Research* 14 (2): 274–296.

Fischel, William A. 1990. *Do Growth Controls Matter? A Review of Empirical Evidence on the Effectiveness and Efficiency of Local Government Land Use Regulation.* Cambridge, Mass.: Lincoln Institute of Land Policy.

Fox, Jonathan, and Josefina Aranda. 1996. *Decentralization and Rural Development in Mexico: Community Participation in Oaxaca's Municipal Funds Program.* La Jolla, Calif.: UCSD, Center for U.S.-Mexican Studies, Monograph Series no. 42.

Friedman, Joseph, et al. 1988. "The Demand for Tenure Security in Developing Countries." *Journal of Development Economics* 29: 185–198.

Friedmann, John. 1992. *Empowerment: The Politics of Alternative Development*. Cambridge, Mass.: Blackwell Publishers.

Gabriel, Tom. 1991. *The Human Factor in Rural Development*. London: Belhaven Press.

García, James E. 1995a. "Bills Would Improve Standards on Colonias." *Austin American-Statesman*, March 4, p. B5.

———. 1995b. "State Takes Over Colonia Bid to Help Residents." *Austin American-Statesman*, March 4, p. B5.

Garrocho, Carlos. 1995. *Análisis sociospacial de los servicios de salud: Accessibilidad, utilización y calidad*. Mexico City: El Colegio Mexiquense, A.C.

Gilbert, Alan. 1994. *The Latin American City*. New York: Monthly Review Press.

Gilbert, Alan, and Ann Varley. 1991. *Landlord and Tenant: Housing the Poor in Urban Mexico*. London: Routledge.

Gilbert, Alan, and Peter Ward. 1982. "Residential Movement among the Urban Poor: The Constraints on Housing Choice in Latin American Cities." *Transactions of the Institute of British Geographers*, New Series, 7: 129–149.

———. 1984. "Community Action by the Urban Poor: Democratic Involvement, Community Self-help or a Means of Social Control?" *World Development* 12 (8): 769–782.

———. 1985. *Housing, the State, and the Poor: Policy and Practice in Three Latin American Cities*. New York: Cambridge University Press.

Gobierno del Estado de Tamaulipas. 1991. *Programa Estatal de Población 1991*. Victoria, Tam., Mexico.

Gómez de León, José. 1995. *The Demand for Health in Mexico*. Mexico City: Consejo Nacional de Población.

González Aréchiga, Bernardo. 1992. "Undocumented Mexicans on the Mexican Northern Border: Their Identity and Role in Regional Development." In Jorge Bustamante, Clark Reynolds, and Raúl Hinojosa (eds.), *U.S.-Mexico Relations: Labor Market Interdependence*, pp. 319–352. Stanford, Calif.: Stanford University Press.

González-Ayala, Salvador. 1995. "A Summary of the Preliminary Approach in Developing a Comprehensive Urban Transportation System for Ciudad Juárez, Mexico." Unpublished.

González Block, M. A. 1991. "Economic Crisis and the Decentralization of Health Services in Mexico: Self-help Housing during Recession: The Mexican experience." In M. González de la Rocha and A. Escobar (eds.), *Social Responses to Mexico's Economic Crisis of the 1980s*, pp. 67–90. La Jolla, Calif.: Center for U.S.-Mexican Studies, UCSD, Contemporary Perspectives Series 1.

———, R. Leyva, O. Zapata, R. Loewe, and J. Alagón. 1989. "Health Services Decentralization in Mexico: Formulation, Implementation and Results of Policy." *Health Policy and Planning* 4 (4): 301–315.

González Rubi, R. 1984. "La vivienda: Un desafío atroz." *Comercio Exterior* 34 (May, July, and August): pp. 390–396, 592–598, 728–734.

Guillén López, Tonatiuh. 1993. *Baja California: Balance de la transición democrática*. Tijuana: El Colegio de la Fontera.

Haber, P. 1994. "Political Change in Durango: The Role of National Solidarity." In Wayne Cornelius et. al. (eds.), *Transforming State-Society Relations in Mexico: The National Soli-*

darity Strategy, pp. 255–280. San Diego: Center for U.S.-Mexican Studies, University of California, San Diego.

Ham-Chande, Roberto, and John R. Weeks, eds. 1992. *Demographic Dynamics of the U.S.-Mexico Border*. El Paso: Texas Western Press.

Handelman, Howard. 1975. "The Political Mobilization of Urban Squatter Settlements: Santiago's Recent Experience and the Implications for Urban Research." *Latin American Research Review* 10: 35-72.

Hatcher, Jeanette, et al. 1995. *The Border Health Authority: Issues and Design*. U.S.-Mexican Policy Studies Program, Occasional Paper no. 6. Austin: LBJ School, University of Texas.

Herzog, Laurence A. 1990. *Where North Meets South: Cities, Space and Politics on the U.S.-Mexico Border*. Austin: Center for Mexican American Studies, University of Texas.

Holguín, Angélica. 1994. "Data Analysis Using SPSSX or SPSS/PC+: A Survey about Housing." Unpublished study.

Hughes, Sally. 1994. "You Can't Eat Basketball Courts." *El Financiero Internacional*, January 24-30, p. 15.

INEGI. 1980 and 1990. *Censo General de Población y Vivienda, Tamaulipas: Resultados, Tomo II*. Mexico: INEGI.

Jensen, Jeryl Ann. 1996. "Regulation of Residential Contracts for Deed in Texas: Senate Bill 336 and Beyond." M.A. Professional Report, LBJ School of Public Affairs, UT-Austin.

Jones, Gareth, and Peter Ward. 1993. "The Land Market under Salinas: A Real Estate Boom Revisited?" *Environment and Planning A* 25: 627–651.

———, eds. 1994. *Methodology for Land and Housing Market Analysis*. London: University College London Press.

———. 1995. "The World Bank's New Urban Management Program: Paradigm Shift or Policy Continuity?" *Habitat International* 18 (3): 33–51.

———. 1998. "Privatizing the Commons: Reforming the Ejido and Urban Development in Mexico." *International Journal of Urban and Regional Development* 22 (1): 76–93.

Lamporte, Richard B. 1992. "The Environmental Protection Agency's Integrated Environmental Plan for the U.S. Border: An Ex-Ante Assessment of Implementation Feasibility in El Paso Colonias." Major Paper submitted to the Virginia Polytechnic Institute and State University in partial fulfillment of M.A. requirements. Blacksburg, Va.

Langewiesche, William. 1993. *Cutting for Sign*. New York: Pantheon.

Larson, Jane. 1995. "Free Markets in the Heart of Texas," *Georgetown Law Journal* 84: 179–260.

Lau, Rubén. 1989. "Ciudad Juárez: Grupos de presión y fuerzas políticas." In Rubén Lau (ed.), *Sistema político y democracia en Chihuahua*. Juárez: Universidad Autónoma de Ciudad Juárez, Instituto de Investigaciones Sociales.

LBJ (Lyndon Baines Johnson School of Public Affairs). 1997. *Colonia Housing and Infrastructure*, vol. 1, *Current Characteristics and Future Needs;* vol. 2, *Water and Wastewater*. Policy Research Report No. 124. Austin: University of Texas; vol. 3, *Regulatory Issues and Policy Analysis*.

Linn, Johannes. 1983. *Cities in the Developing World: Policies for Their Equitable and Efficient Growth*. New York: Oxford University Press.

Lloyd, Peter. 1979. *Slums of Hope*. Harmondsworth, UK: Penguin.

Lomnitz, Larissa. 1977. *Networks and Marginality*. New York: Academic Press.

Lorey, David E. 1990. *United States–Mexico Border Statistics since 1900.* Los Angeles: UCLA Latin American Center Publications.

Mabogunje, Akin, Jorge Hardoy, and R. P. Misra. 1978. *Shelter Provision in Developing Countries,* Scope II. New York: John Wiley.

Mangin, William. 1967. "Latin American Squatter Settlements: A Problem and a Solution." *Latin American Research Review* 11 (3): 65–98.

Marcuse, Peter. 1990. "United States of America." In Willem van Vliet (ed.), *International Handbook of Housing Policies and Practices,* pp. 327–376. Westport, Conn.: Greenwood Press.

Martin, Christopher. 1994. *Schooling in Mexico: Staying in or Dropping Out.* Aldershot, UK: Avebury.

Martínez, Oscar J. 1994. *Border People: Life and Society in the U.S.-Mexico Borderlands.* Tucson: University of Arizona Press.

Mathéy, K., ed. 1992. *Beyond Self-help Housing.* London: Mansell Press.

Merla Rodríguez, Gerardo. 1987. *La region noreste de México: Consideraciones generales, cuadros geostadísticas.* Colección Folletos de Historia del Noveste no. 1. Monterrey.

Mettling, Stephen. 1982. *The Contract for Deed.* Chicago: Real Estate Education Company.

Montaño, Jorge. 1976. *Los pobres de la ciudad de México en los asentamientos espontáneos.* Mexico City: Siglo XXI.

Moser, Caroline. 1989. "Community Participation in Urban Projects." *Progress in Planning* 29: 74–133.

———. 1996. *Confronting Crisis: A Comparative Study of Household Responses to Poverty and Vulnerability in Four Poor Urban Communities.* Environmentally Sustainable Development Studies and Monographs Series No. 8. Washington, D.C.: World Bank

Myerson, Allen R. 1995. "This Is the House that Greed Built." *New York Times,* April 2, Section 3, pp. F1, F14.

Nolasco Armas, Margarita, and María Luisa Acevedo Conde. 1989. *Los municipios de las fronteras de México.* Mexico City: Centro de Ecodesarrollo.

Nord, Bruce. 1994. *Mexican Social Policy: Affordability, Conflict and Progress.* Lanham, Md.: University Press of America.

OAG (Office of the Attorney General, Texas). 1993. "Socioeconomic Characteristics of Colonia Areas." White Paper. Austin, Tex.: OAG.

———. 1996. *Forgotten Americans: Life in Texas Colonias.* Austin, Tex.: OAG.

Pan-American Health Organization. 1991. *U.S.-Mexico Border Health Statistics.* El Paso, Tex.

Pardo, María del Carmen. 1996. "El proceso mexicano de federalización educativa en marcha: Apuntes para un análisis." In Victoria Rodríguez and Peter Ward et al., *New Federalism, State and Local Government in Mexico. Memoria*/Synthesis of the Bi-National Conference Held at the University of Texas at Austin, October 25–26, 1996. Austin: The Mexican Center of ILAS, University of Texas.

———, ed. 1998. *Aprendizajes y dilemas de la federalización educativa.* Mexico City: El Colegio de México.

Patrick, J. Michael, and Armando Alonso. 1993. "Improving Living Conditions in Colonias in the Rio Grande Valley of South Texas." *Rio Bravo* 2 (Spring): 85–103.

Peña, Devon G. 1997. *The Terror of the Machine: Technology, Work, Gender, and Ecology on the U.S.-Mexico Border.* Austin: Center for Mexican-American Studies, University of Texas.

Perlman, Janice. 1976. *The Myth of Marginality: Urban Poverty and Politics in Rio de Janeiro.* Berkeley: University of California Press.

Pezzoli, Keith. 1987. "The Urban Land Problem and Popular Sector Housing Development in Mexico City." *Environment and Behavior* 19 (3): 371–397.

Prieto, Francisco. 1995. "Production of Housing and Infrastructure in the Cities of the U.S.-Mexican Border." In Peter Ward et al., *Memoria of the Bi-national Conference: Housing Production and Infrastructure in the Colonias of Texas and Mexico.* Austin: The Mexican Center of ILAS, University of Texas.

Pugh, Cedric. 1997. "The Changing Roles of Self-help in Housing and Urban Policies, 1950–1996: Experience in Developing Countries." *Third World Planning Review* 19 (1): 91–110.

Rainwater, Lee. 1966. "Fear and the House as Haven in the Lower Class." *American Institute of Planners Journal* 32: 23–31.

Ramírez Saíz, Juan Manuel. 1986. *El movimiento urbano popular en México.* Mexico City: Siglo XXI Editores.

Reed, Cyrus B. H. 1994. "The Ties That Bind: Community Organization and Water Infrastructure in the Colonias of Hidalgo County." Professional report (unpublished), University of Texas at Austin.

Regalado, Jorge. 1995. *Lucha por la vivienda en Guadalajara.* Guadalajara: Universidad de Guadalajara.

Roberts, Bryan. 1978. *Cities of Peasants: The Political Economy of Urbanization.* London: Edward Arnold.

———. 1994. *The Making of Citizens: Cities of Peasants Revisited.* London: Edward Arnold.

Rodríguez, Victoria. 1995. "Municipal Autonomy and the Politics of Intergovernmental Finance: Is It Different for the Opposition?" In Victoria Rodríguez and Peter Ward (eds.), *Opposition Government in Mexico,* pp. 153–172. Albuquerque: University of New Mexico Press.

———. 1997. *Decentralization in Mexico: From Reforma Municipal to Solidaridad to Nuevo Federalismo.* Boulder, Colo.: Westview.

———, and Peter Ward. 1992. *Policymaking, Politics and Urban Governance in Chihuahua: The Experience of Recent Panista Governments.* Austin: Lyndon B. Johnson School of Public Affairs, University of Texas.

———,———. 1994. *Political Change in Baja California: Democracy in the Making?* Monograph Series 40. La Jolla: Center for U.S.-Mexican Studies, University of California, San Diego.

———,———, eds. 1995. *Opposition Government in Mexico.* Albuquerque: University of New Mexico Press.

———,———. 1996. "The New PRI: Recasting Its Identity." In Rob Aitkin, Nikki Craske, Gareth Jones, and David Stansfield (eds.), *Dismantling the Mexican State?* pp. 92–112. London: Macmillan.

Rogers, George O., et al. 1993. "Cinco Colonia Areas: Baseline Conditions in the Lower Rio Grande Valley." Unpublished paper. College Station: Texas A&M University, Center for Housing and Urban Development.

Rossi, Peter H. 1955. *Why Families Move.* Glencoe, Ill.: The Free Press. (2d ed., 1980, Beverly Hills, Calif.: Sage.)

Ruf, Kevin. 1995. "Low-Income Housing in Cd. Juárez: Neo-Liberal Responses to Urban Crises." Mimeo.

Russell, Y., et al. 1988. *Third Symposium on Health and Human Services in the United States and Mexico, April 10–12, 1988, Brownsville, Tex.* Galveston: University of Texas Medical Branch.

Schiffman, Irving. 1989. *Alternative Techniques for Managing Growth.* Berkeley: Institute of Governmental Studies, University of California.

Schteingart, Martha. 1989. *Los productores del espacio habitable: Estado, empresa y sociedad en la Ciudad de México.* Mexico City: El Colegio de México.

———. 1991. "Producción habitacional en la Zona Metropolitana de la Ciudad de México (1960–1987)." In Martha Schteingart (ed.), *Espacio y vivienda en la Ciudad de México,* pp. 225–250. Mexico City: El Colegio de México.

Secretaría de Desarrollo Social (SEDESOL). 1994. *Solidaridad: Seis Años de Trabajo.* Mexico City: SEDESOL.

———. 1996. *Programa nacional de desarrollo urbano, 1995–2000.* Mexico City: SEDESOL.

Secretaría de Gobernación y Gobierno del Estado de Tamaulipas. 1988. *Los Municipios de Tamaulipas.* Victoria, Tam., Mexico.

Shoup, Donald. 1994. "Is Under-investment in Public Infrastructure an Anomaly?" In Gareth Jones and Peter Ward (eds.), *Methodology for Land and Housing Market Analysis,* pp. 236–250. London: University College London Press.

Shultz, Michael M., and Jeffery B. Groy. 1986. *The Premature Subdivision of Land in Colorado: A Survey with Commentary.* Monograph 86-10. Cambridge, Mass.: Lincoln Institute of Land Policy.

Siembieda, William. 1995. "Mexican Suburbs American Style: Reforming Border Spatial Theory." In Peter Ward et al., *Memoria of the Bi-national Conference: Housing Production and Infrastructure in the Colonias of Texas and Mexico.* Austin: Mexican Center of ILAS, University of Texas.

Skinner, R. 1983. "Community Participation: Its Scope and Potential." In R. Skinner and M. Rodell (eds.), *People, Poverty and Shelter: Problems of Self-Help Housing in the Third World.* London: Methuen.

Sklair, Leslie. 1993. *Assembling for Development: The Maquila Industry in Mexico and the United States.* La Jolla: University of California at San Diego, Center for U.S.-Mexican Studies.

Staudt, Kathleen. 1998. *Free Trade? Informal Economies at the U.S.-Mexico Border.* Philadelphia: Temple University Press.

Stickel, George W. 1990. "The Land as a Social Being: Ethical Implications from Societal Expectations." *Agriculture and Human Values* 7 (1): 33–38.

Suárez y Toriello, Enrique, and Octavio Chávez. 1996. *Perfil de la frontera México–Estados Unidos / Profile of the United States–Mexico Border.* Ciudad Juárez: FEMAP. (Volume is in English and Spanish.)

Swearingen, Scott. 1997. "Environmental City? The Historical Emergence of Austin's Environmental Meaning." Ph.D. dissertation, University of Texas at Austin.

Texas Department of Commerce. 1989a. *The Border Region MSA Report.* Austin: Texas Department of Commerce.

———. 1989b. *The El Paso MSA Report.* Austin: Texas Department of Commerce.

Texas Department of Human Services. 1988. *The Colonias Factbook.* Austin: Texas Department of Human Services.

Texas Governor's Office Border Report. 1993. Austin: Office of the Governor.

Texas Health and Human Services Commission. 1995. Request for Legislative Appropriations for Years 1996–97. Austin, Tex.: DHSS.

Texas Water Development Board (TWDB). 1992. *Water and Wastewater Needs for Colonias in Texas.* Austin: Texas Water Development Board.

——. 1995. *Water and Wastewater Needs of Texas Colonias: 1995 Update.* Austin: Texas Water Development Board.

Tipple, A. G., and K. G. Willis, eds. 1991. *Housing the Poor in the Developing World: Methods of Analysis, Case Studies and Policy.* London: Routledge.

Turner, John F. C. 1968. "Housing Priorities, Settlement Patterns and Urban Development in Modernizing Countries." *Journal of the American Institute of Planners* 34: 354–363.

——. 1976. *Housing by People: Towards Autonomy in Building Environments.* London: Marion Boyars.

——. 1982. "Issues in Self-Help and Self-Managed Housing." In Peter Ward (ed.), *Self-Help Housing: A Critique,* pp. 99–114. London: Mansell Press.

Turner, John F. C., and Bob Fichter. 1972. *Freedom to Build: Dweller Control of the Housing Process.* New York: Macmillan.

Ugalde, Antonio, Leslie Olson, David Schers, and Miguel von Hoegen. 1974. *The Urbanization of a Poor Mexican Neighborhood.* Special Publication of the Institute of Latin American Studies, University of Texas at Austin.

UNCHS (United Nations Center for Human Settlements). 1996. *An Urbanizing World: Global Report on Human Settlements, 1996.* Oxford: Oxford University Press.

United States Census: 1990, STF3C. 1990. Washington, D.C.: Bureau of the Census.

United States–Mexico Border Statistics since 1900: Supplement. 1993. Los Angeles: UCLA Latin American Center Publications.

van Lindert, Paul, and O. Verkoren. 1986. "The Housing of the Poor in Latin America: Competition for Space in La Paz, Cd. Juárez and Chihuahua." In J. Kleinpenning (ed.), "Competition for Rural and Urban Space in Latin America: Its Consequences for Low-Income Groups," *Netherlands Geographical Studies* 25: 93–110.

Varley, Ann. 1985. "Ya somos dueños: Ejido Land Regularization and Development in Mexico City." Ph.D. dissertation, University of London.

——. 1987. "The Relationship between Tenure Legalization and Housing Improvements: Evidence from Mexico City." *Development and Change* 18 (3): 463–481.

——. 1989. "Settlement, Illegality, and Legalization: The Need for Reassessment." In Peter Ward (ed.), *Corruption, Development and Inequality: Soft Touch or Hard Graft?,* 156–174. New York: Routledge.

——. 1994. "Housing the Household, Holding the House." In Gareth Jones and Peter Ward (eds.), *Methodology for Land and Housing Market Analysis,* pp. 120–134. London: University College London Press.

Villarreal, Diana, and Victor Castañeda. 1986. *Urbanización y autoconstrucción de vivienda en Monterrey.* Centro de Ecodesarrollo, D.F.: Editorial Claves Latinoaméricas.

Vogel, Ronald. 1995. "Crossing the Border for Health Care: An Exploratory Analysis for Consumer Choice." *Journal of Borderlands Studies,* 10: 19–44.

Ward, Peter M. 1976. "Intra-city Migration to Squatter Settlements in Mexico City." *Geoforum* 7 (6): 369–381.

——. 1978. "Social Interaction Patterns in Squatter Settlements in Mexico City." *Geoforum* 9 (4/5): 235–243.

——. 1982a. "Introduction and Purpose." In Peter Ward (ed.), *Self-Help Housing: A Critique,* pp. 1–13. London: Mansell Press.

———. 1982b. "The Practice and Potential of Self-help Housing in Mexico City." In Peter Ward (ed.), *Self-Help Housing: A Critique*, pp. 175–208. London: Mansell Press.

———. 1984. "Mexico City: Beyond Sites and Services." In G. Payne (ed.), *Low-income Housing in the Developing World: The Role of Sites and Services and Squatter Upgrading*, pp. 149–158. New York: Wiley.

———. 1986. *Welfare Politics in Mexico: Papering Over the Cracks*. Boston: Allen and Unwin.

———. 1989a. "Land Values and Valorization Processes in Latin American Cities: A Research Agenda." *Bulletin of Latin American Research* 8 (1): 47–66.

———. 1989b. "Local Leadership and the Distributional Benefits Wrought by Illegality in Third World Community Development." In Peter Ward (ed.), *Corruption, Development, and Inequality: Soft Touch or Hard Graft?* New York: Routledge.

———. 1990. "Mexico." In Willem van Vliet (ed.), *International Handbook of Housing Policies and Practices*, pp. 407–436. Westport, Conn.: Greenwood Press.

———. 1993. "Social Policy and Political Opening in Mexico." *Journal of Latin American Research* 25: 613–628.

———. 1995. "Policy Making and Policy Implementation among Non-PRI Governments: The PAN in Cd. Juárez and Chihuahua." In Victoria Rodríguez and Peter Ward (eds.), *Opposition Government in Mexico*, pp. 135–154. Albuquerque: University of New Mexico Press.

———. 1998a. "From Machine Politics to the Politics of Technocracy: Charting the Decline of Partisanship in the Mexican Municipality." In *Bulletin of Latin American Research* forthcoming.

———. 1998b. *Mexico City*, 2d ed. London: John Wiley and Son.

———, and Sylvia Chant. 1987. "Local Leadership and Self-help Housing." *Progress in Planning* 27: 69–136.

———, E. Jiménez, and G. A. Jones. 1993. "Residential Land Price Changes in Mexican Cities and the Affordability of Land for Low-income Groups." *Urban Studies* 30 (10): 1521–1542.

———, and Chris G. Macoloo. 1992. "Articulation Theory and Self-help Housing Practice in the 1990s." *International Journal for Urban and Regional Research* 6 (1): 60–80.

Wilson, Robert, and Peter Menzies. 1997. "The Colonias Water Bill: Communities Demanding Change." In Robert Wilson (ed.), *Public Policy and Community: Activism and Governance in Texas*, pp. 229–274. Austin: University of Texas Press.

World Bank. 1972. *Urbanization*. World Bank Sector Working Paper. Washington, D.C.: World Bank.

———. 1983. *Urban Land Policies: Issues and Opportunities*. Washington, D.C.: World Bank.

———. 1991. *Urban Policy and Economic Development: An Agenda for the 1990s*. Washington, D.C.: World Bank.

World Health Organization (WHO). 1988. *A Community-based Survey Methodology for the Analysis of Environmental Health in Low-Income Settlements*. WHO Offset Publication no. 100. Geneva.

Index